LEAVEN

The Hidden Power of Culture in the Church

This challenging and uplifting book uses the biblical metaphor of leaven to explore positive and negative aspects of the church's life-style that seriously affect the credibility of its witness.

David Brown believes that 'the church needs critical friends.' Here he demonstrates his penetrating critique of the church's systems and customs as well as his own deep loyalty to the gospel. These reflections are well informed, clearly structured, tightly argued, and illustrated with telling examples from many walks of life. His controversial and stimulating observations are supported by a rich seam of biblical exposition. His vision of radical Christian living, true to the values of God's kingdom, is of wide ecumenical relevance – not least for those in positions of leadership.

Bishop David Tustin

David Brown sets out a compelling argument for an urgent need on the part the church to make some long term fundamental changes by facing its inherited culture. He believes that this is essential if the church is to be both healthy and relevant in its mission to communicate and model the good news of Jesus Christ, and to see people respond by becoming his disciples. He challenges much of the current culture within the church and pleads for a radical change in leadership, training, thinking, and structure. He longs to see a lively healthy church at the heart of every community. His book is timely with the Church of England currently engaged on a Reform and Renewal programme.

Philip Johanson OBE,
Chief Secretary of Church Army 1990 to 2006

for Tom with best wishes November 2020

LEAVEN

The Hidden Power of Culture in the Church

David Brown

David Brown

RoperPenberthy Publishing

RoperPenberthy Publishing Limited
19 Egerton Place
Weybridge
KT13 0PF
United Kingdom

ISBN 978 1 903905 93 7

All Scripture quotations are from the New Revised Standard Version
(HarperCollins) unless otherwise stated.

Typeset by Avocet Typeset, Somerton, Somerset TA11 6RT

Printed in the United Kingdom

CONTENTS

Thanks and Acknowledgements

Thanks are due to many people, for I never set out to be a writer. This book is born of long reflection since retiring from a Bishop's side in 2004, poised to enjoy retirement's broad meadows. A pattern of uninvited thoughts began to redirect my life before I had taken two steps in any meadow. This continued. Then in 2008 the Foundation for Church Leadership published my booklet 'Releasing Bishops for Relationship'.

From this point Malcolm Grundy, its then Director, has been my chief mentor, helping and advising on countless occasions. This book is the outcome, and I am grateful now for his Foreword. Without him, this book would not have been written. My gratitude is enormous.

My understanding of church dynamics underwent a gradual conversion after 2008. My earlier booklet suggested ameliorative measures for fruitful leadership within the existing system. I marvel at the way so many bishops and clergy achieve obvious fruitfulness despite our Church's inherent complications and obstacles. Yet I've come to believe that we, the Church, have tended to look in the wrong direction in our efforts to make it a better Gospel instrument.

I now see inherited culture as the greatest influence on Church life patterns. Yet our reforming effort is usually directed at the detail, at individual components: patronage, episcopacy, synodical governance, finance, liturgy, theological training, mission – and so on. The list is endless; all elements largely shaped by inherited culture. This is what deserves primary attention. It begs the question; how does it fit in with the culture Jesus revealed?

Thanks and Acknowledgements

Many friends have helped me along this thought-journey. I am especially grateful to my sister-in-law Annabel Brown, to John Broadley, Jeremy Clare, Janet Goodall, Martin Hines, Humphrey Norrington and Regina Stierlen. In different ways they have encouraged me, challenged my arguments, and helped improve the book's flow and shape. And especial thanks to the Revd Mike Starkey for deploying his editorial skills to great advantage, and to Robin Greenwood, David Tustin and Philip Johanson for their encouraging commendations.

Above all, my debt of appreciation to Katie, my wife, is beyond words. She has stood by me all the while and kept me going despite my absences from her life, in person – or mind!

LEAVEN

'And again [Jesus] said: "to what shall I compare the kingdom of God? It is like leaven a woman took and hid in three measures of flour, until it was all leavened".'

Luke 13.20,21 (also Matt 13.33) (ESV)

'[Jesus said] … "Beware of the leaven of the Pharisees, which is hypocrisy. Nothing is covered up that will not be revealed, or hidden that will not be made known. …'

Luke 12.1 (ESV)

'Jesus said to [the disciples]: "Watch and beware of the leaven of the Pharisees and Sadducees." … Then they understood that he did not tell them to beware of the leaven of bread, but of the teaching of the Pharisees and Sadducees.'

Matt 16.8,12 (ESV)

'And [Jesus] cautioned [the disciples], saying, "Watch out, beware of the leaven of the Pharisees and the leaven of Herod."'

Mark 8.15 (ESV)

Paul wrote: *'Your boasting is not good. Do you not know that a little leaven leavens the whole lump? Cleanse out the old leaven that you may be a new lump …'*

1 Cor 5.6,7 (ESV)

And again: *'You were running well. Who hindered you from obeying the truth? This persuasion is not from him who calls you. A little leaven leavens the whole lump.'*

Gal. 5.7-9 (ESV)

Foreword

There are many ways in which strong feelings can be communicated. Some methods will draw in followers and gain support while others will antagonise and alienate. An approach which uses metaphor and illustration based on experience has everything to commend it. In this compelling book David Brown has chosen the metaphor of leaven as it influences and changes the culture of organisations. He develops this to full advantage since he believes that cultures are open to many competing influences. It is an attractive idea since he defines leaven as against yeast. Leaven forms from the natural stimuli of the atmosphere while yeast is an ingredient which is added to existing materials. Applying this in relation to the presence and contribution of Christianity in the world provides a challenging and stimulating argument.

A servant of the Church as well as a Christian layperson with years of service in the Royal Navy, David Brown addresses the 'culture' of the church as he experiences it, seen primarily the Church of England. He observes with some sadness the effect of high office and of hierarchy on the culture and structures of his church. With informed observation he can write tellingly, 'It looks as if the church does not know what the laity is for.' I think of another cartoon caption, 'What kind of an army are we if we only train our musicians and our chaplains?' David Brown begins with an all-encompassing vision, that the love of God is for everyone and consequently in the church divisions between laity and clergy are less than helpful. His basis is in the unswerving conviction that it is the love of God shown in the life and person of Jesus Christ which is the leaven which transforms without preference. He writes as someone who knows this in a personal way which has been worked through in a life which has seen its own challenges, frustrations and consolations.

Metaphors can be limiting as well as liberating. With some knowledge of structures and authority he enters the sensitive territory of examining whether the Church is an organism or an organization. His metaphor of leaven can only lead in one direction. Growth and development are organic and draw breath only in the atmosphere and culture of the challenging questions which face our world. Yet he is well aware of the need for structure and the means by which the message of faith can be transmitted. In a nuanced but critical way he says that rigid hierarchy 'is for solo flyers.'

Leaven is not just an image which is developed to ameliorate the impersonal culture of large organisations. It is one drawn from his reading of the scriptures which give content to the metaphor. He argues that it is the Christian concept of love which acts in the leavening process. Christian love changes and transforms organisations and has the power to reveal more of the nature and characteristics of God's Kingdom in the world.

To develop the metaphor of leaven and its influence on any culture a bridge is proposed. 'Time invested in relationships is seldom wasted,' says Brown the experienced leader who has also sat alongside many senior church leaders. His statement is much more than distilled management wisdom since the heart of this book is an exploration of God's purpose for Creation revealed in the scriptures and in the person of Jesus Christ.

In a wonderful way David Brown begins the development of his argument not with exhortation but by asking the question what would life be like without the dimension of faith worked out as leaven in an often uncaring and frequently a suffering world. His answer is that ours would be a loveless world and his adoption and development of the concept of 'lovelessness' is an appropriate starting-point. It takes us precisely to the right series of explorations. He brings this to bear significantly in the debate about the Church as an organism or an organisation. He laments with an illustrated passion the dilemma he sees in church and state both perpetuating a culture of 'lovelessness in an institutionalised world.' There is much more for others to explore here.

I have seen this book through it's many drafts and forms. I have accompanied the author as he has consulted many local people, as he has asked advice from other writers and as he has approached publishers, and taken to heart the advice which they have offered. With a humility characterised in his writing and a bravery with which he has taken and responded to criticism and advice, David Brown lives out the gospel which he commends.

There is a devotional evangelical fire in this book which will impress and challenge readers. For David Brown, a life spent meditating on the person of Jesus Christ forms a bedrock for his life as well as for his arguments. In each chapter and section of the book he returns again and again to the central theme of the places where God in Jesus Christ touches the most sensitive areas of human need. He laments the instances when the churches and their leaders do not live up to their calling and where lovelessness persists.

The argument for Christian love as leaven is one which is incontrovertible and which offers a basis in hope for the gradual transformation of church and world. The leaven for which David Brown argues speaks of a love which God has for all creation. It is a leaven which nurtures the qualities of God's Kingdom in the life and structures of the church so that a 'loveless' world searching for something else might see something of that Godly love in who we are and in what we try to build.

Canon Dr Malcolm Grundy
Visiting Fellow, York St John University

Introduction:
Four reasons why Church culture *really* matters

Culture is an extraordinary thing. It is much discussed in secular and religious circles as 'something out there.' Yet it is seldom discussed, so it seems, as 'something in here.' Culture partly explains why we are tempted to notice cultural malaise in others, yet less ready to ponder what culture might be doing to us – individually or corporately. This is surprising if we profess to follow Jesus; for his whole ministry was rooted in exposing bad culture, and offering instead a culture that brought health, well-being and coherence. Over and again he warned his hearers of 1st century Palestine's dominating culture: the life-draining culture of Herod, the Sadducees, scribes and the Pharisees. He warned them in straight teaching, in parable, and in confronting its advocates. The gospels are full of it.

The Kingdom of Heaven meant that, under the Lordship of Christ, all patterns of living and relating would be transformed into a new and beautiful culture. All worldly culture would be exposed and supplanted.

Life is full of decisions; decisions to think, speak or act. Whether others decide something, or we do (or we avoid a decision), each occasion may affect the course of an hour or a lifetime. Equally each may change the lives of individuals or communities. Less obviously, they help shape cultures – of families, communities and their organisations, and nations – investing a hidden commodity, like a seed, but with unknowable consequences. For when repeated they form habits, then form customs, then traditions and thence embed into culture.

Culture is part of life. It is in the air we breathe – hard to discern, or define with precision. We might neither see it nor size it up. And human nature may make us unreflective of its characteristics – benign or destructive – and of the way it works. It beguiles and can take us captive.

Culture comes from communities that are in the main inherited; unchosen by us. We were first inducted into our family's culture, then school's and friends'; then into other communities as our circle enlarged. At some point family, work-place, neighbourhood, regional and national cultures mixed a cocktail unique to each of us, shaping our understanding and life patterns.

Culture's core characteristic is power, whether of God or the world. It establishes norms, then tends to press compliance. We can see the power of our world's cultural norms in the emergence of 'political correctness'. As memory of the Judaean/Christian revelation of God's culture – how to live and how to relate – fades, worldly culture chooses to fill the vacuum with something more congenial, but spiritually toxic. Political correctness is the new yardstick, a new norm of spurious ethics and morality.

Worldly norms have always been around and caused much harm. For centuries people went along with slavery, or with the denigration and subjugation of women, or with smoking. For half a century many have gone along with convenience-abortion. And quite recently, bankers have gone along with inordinate bonuses, and parliamentarians with inappropriate expenses. They simply did not 'get it', and went on not 'getting it.' Such is the grip of worldly culture and its norms, to which all are vulnerable.

Neither did Herod, the scribes and Pharisees 'get it' (1 Cor 2.8). Their governing culture's norms locked them in a vice-like grip. Then at God's strategic moment they trashed Jesus in a public and merciless execution, despite God's glory resting on him. This cosmic denouement of worldly culture is at the core of our message.

Yet our Church, as an institution, is not immune to culture's hidden dangers. For although our Church culture focuses on individuals, our sins and need of repentance, and on the sins and culture gripping the 'world out there', we seem to give little thought to that inherited Church culture we put on display to the world God loves. The culture that dominates our Church – our customs, traditions, the way we relate and the way we are organised – seems exempt from scrutiny. Sadly, that is how worldly culture works. It does not look in the mirror.

This book attempts to look clear-eyed at any cultural infiltration in the corporate lifestyle of our Church that is not of God, yet seems accepted without much demur; maybe even venerated.

Jesus condemned the culture of his time vehemently, yet did not go round judging people. He commanded us to follow his pattern. His non-judgmentalism intrigued people. It seemed pathetically weak. How could someone preaching God's righteousness be so indifferent to the strange company he kept? Did he not mind any past harm inflicted by some of his associates on people and communities? Nicodemus may have been surprised to hear he had not come to judge the world. Jesus was not fixated by how people were in the present. It rather seems his imagining showed him how they might yet be. It's clear, anyhow, that we cannot pass judgment reliably on anyone. For we can measure neither culture's power nor its reach; how it has helped, or skewed, a person's lifestyle and deeds. If someone lies or cheats, who can say it was considered and wilful, or whether it was the contaminating power of cultural norms at work; inherited unconsciously, but never chosen?

As we navigate through our received culture, as individuals, we tend to focus on daily life's individual elements. Christians and their Churches are prone to follow this 'moral' approach. Sins are defined and good deeds affirmed. But what of our institution's culture? As I shall show, a good number of senior clergy recognise that not all is well in our institutional life. Regardless of the quality of individual leaders, many clergy and laity seem to struggle with institutional loyalty. Too many of its processes seem not to foster as much trust nor confidence as they might. So, typically, fresh commissions get set up, major reports get written and initiatives taken. Whilst there may be gains, some dismay – even division – may ensue. Any underlying cultural malaise may remain unnoticed.

Here lies a major challenge for today's Church, as institution. We seem not to 'get it'. If some Japanese innovation in factory or production-line effectiveness arouses the interest of British industrial leaders, they will fly to Japan to investigate. The Church sometimes reaches into the secular world to locate and import 'good practice'. But which secular body has ever knocked at Church House, Westminster's door to find out how *we* achieve community wellbeing and unity?

And if no-one ever has, why so? Is this not to be our treasure, our identifying characteristic?

Whether we like it or not, we are all intimately engaged in culture-shaping and equally in culture dynamics. Our words and actions as individuals contribute to culture, in building customs and traditions; and we shape culture, either by accepting its norms unquestioningly, or by challenging them. Worldly cultural norms have the power to spoil lives, and the power to spawn organisational systems and practices that work against unity, and against well-being. But that is not all: institutions, as well as individuals, are players in the culture 'game'.

I think there are four big reasons why the Church must take its culture seriously, for there are four identifiable strands in the air that, if allowed, can distort and disable Kingdom culture. They penetrate Church life if we let them:

- a worldly use of controlling power,
- a worldly enchantment with historic customs,
- a worldly individualism, and
- a worldly dogmatism.

Kingdom culture offers us a better way.

Jesus was neither a moraliser nor a 'single issue' pedant. With his crucifixion imminent, he said to the twelve, *'In this world the kings and great men Lord it over their people, yet they are called 'friends of the people.'* **But among you it will be different.** *Those who are the greatest among you should take the lowest rank, and the leader should be like a servant.' Lk 22.25,26 (NLT).*

He had ministered for three years into his disciples' cultural awareness and that of the crowds – and indeed, the nation. Now he reiterated his consistent message for the last time; defining their inherited culture's harsh reality, and reiterating the good news of his Kingdom's supplanting culture. God's future entailed regime change and a new culture. He reached right behind wrong culture's manifestations, to its roots.

Desmond Tutu has said, *'There comes a point where we need to stop just pulling people out of the river. We need to go upstream and find why they are falling in.'* This perfectly explains Jesus's ministry. He was engaged in the battle of cultures; his words and deeds promoting one, and exposing the fraudulence of the other. He went 'upstream' to deal with the cause of 'people falling in.' He saw how one culture had power to empty a community of life and lead to death: its power being lovelessness. He gave his life to unveil and launch a greater culture, with power to destroy death and bring fullness of life: its power was and is unquenchable love. His ministry invested profoundly in culture, addressing it more persistently and consistently than we readily recognise. We must follow his pattern, holistically, and not exempt ourselves from culture's challenge – and opportunity.

Jesus called it Leaven. Following the approach of Jesus, I use the terms 'culture' and 'leaven' interchangeably.

* * * * *

Leaven is this book's governing metaphor. Some New Testament translations use the term 'yeast' rather than 'leaven'. This may be unhelpful since yeast was not developed as an *additive* for bread-making until more recent times. It did not exist in biblical times. Lumps of dough, formed of flour and water, were left standing for some days. Fungal spores in the air would penetrate the lump, initiate fermentation – leavening – that caused the dough to rise, ready for baking. Today's sourdough bread is made like this. It is usual to keep back a small lump in order to leaven subsequent batches. In biological terms, fungal strains form a *culture* within the dough: in scripture, leaven forms a culture within a community. In each case, it is a silent, somewhat hidden process that releases power and changes outcomes without human intervention. It propagates and reproduces.

* * * * *

Worldly culture was the backdrop to Jesus's life and ministry. We, the Church, have inherited today's variant; unique in history yet purveying the same four destructive strands. These run deep, damaging relational sinews and thence community life.

We see community distress wherever we look. We see it globally too, in the sinews of international alliances, in the European Union, and in responses to severe human need. In the UK we see it in a creeping indifference to the value of nationhood. We see a decline of allegiance: in membership of political parties and unions, in willingness to engage in community politics, and in life-long loyalty to an employer when staff coming and going after only a few years has become normal. Regardless of benefits this may accrue, organisational loyalty – enthusiasm for 'belonging' – would seem to be a significant loss.

We may see it in the slow migration from a modest-pay/high-professionalism ethos of former years to one where cultural norms sanction 'professionals' putting financial gain as their highest aim, regardless of consequences.

We may also see community distress in those great public sector enterprises, set up to provide community well-being: our health service, our educational system, our legal and policing systems, and in systems of local government. We catch glimpses of too many people not enjoying being where they are, of too much bureaucracy, and of attempts to improve things by 'targets' rather than investment in human relationships. We see it in community fear of the stranger.

Lastly we see the distress in family life: in unacknowledged and unsustainable levels of personal debt, in children's behavioural problems, in the failure of too many old people's and children's homes in providing effective care, in the divorce rate, the number of young people needing to live on the streets, and in the need for street pastors and food-banks. We see the massive cost of social provision where the sinews of family life have weakened.

The point is this. God has set us in the world for 'such a time as this'. The leaven of the Kingdom is his perfectly crafted solution, powerful beyond measure and imagining. Our Church's privilege is to purvey this Leaven the random way leaven works. It is our role and God-given purpose. But we must first search out and destroy any *old leaven* that has silently attached to his Body and evades attention. For our ever-present temptation, as Church, is to ignore culture and blame people. Jesus seemed to do the reverse. Astonishingly – as mentioned – he did not judge people. He loved, drew, encouraged and supported them; sometimes with tough love. Yet at the same time he excoriated his day's dominant culture, exposed it and began supplanting it with Kingdom culture.

Culture change is a long haul. It involves many people, much thought and prayer, deep longings and the exercise of faith. God can do it; yet we can hinder him.

Here are no quick fixes.

So this book focuses primarily on leaven. It touches on a wide spectrum of Church life: relationships, the way it organises itself, the nature of ministry, mission, leadership and the use of power, learning and training, God's power, the Church's vocation, and most importantly Jesus's aspiration for today's Church. Hundreds of books have been written on such topics. This focuses instead on leaven. For only leaven has the power to influence, then shape, each of these important areas in God's way. Fresh Kingdom-style patterns of relationship, organisation, ministry, mission, leadership, use of power, and learning and training will emerge when uncontaminated Kingdom leaven comes to dominate the Church. It would recharge our culture. We could dare to expect increasing signs of God's power, God's fruitfulness. Our vocation may be reclaimed and Jesus's prayer answered.

Whilst I have written this book mainly from, and for, a Church of England perspective, I am convinced the points I make will have relevance across denominational boundaries. This book is for those who wrestle with the challenges of Church structure, organisation and custom; not just for those in higher responsibility levels, but for all clergy and laity who long for a greater convergence towards New Testament patterns – who wish to find a deeper connection with Christ, reaching through the frustrations of prevailing Church culture.

It is impossible to offer the possibilities of refreshed faith and restored relationships without facing, in the first several chapters, facing the serious and complex issues of an inherited culture that cannot endure.

Part 1: Cultural Realities

Culture only exists in community – precisely that place where God works with his passion for relationship. It is shaped by two opposing powers: two leavens. Their mutual enmity and incompatibility is commonly acknowledged. Yet their respective strength, range and characteristics too easily evade scrutiny. We prefer to focus on consequences more than culture itself. Here we identify four dominant leaven – fungal – strains, each capable of supersession by the greater strains of Kingdom leaven. Two particularly infect corporate life: the fixation with controlling power, and the 'aspic–fixation' with historic formularies. And two mainly infect personal lifestyles: unhealthy individualism, and undue dogmatism. I call them the Big Four. Such cultural strains seem to reinforce each other, mutating into a toxic culture of lovelessness that works precisely against God's purposes. We, the Church, need to reflect on such realities.

Today: Culture and the Church

'A culture is made up not simply of works of art, or literary discourses, but of unwritten codes, signs and symbols, rituals and gestures, and common attitudes that fix the public meaning of these works and organise the inner life of a society.'

Orlando Figes[1]

I approach a cathedral, honey-hued and fine textured. Palms to each side and blue sky above provide a frame. Its large stones were once embedded in the earth, without clear purpose. Rough and seemingly unsuitable for anything, they were selected by master masons. These craftsmen saw their potential, then shaped them for a specific niche. They now fit together, holding firm through wind and storm: across centuries. Yet, for all this, it is the building – not the stones – that commands attention. It lingers in the mind. The Mediterranean light that enthralled some of Europe's finest artists bathes these stones, granting them a glow not of themselves. The glory belongs to the sun.

The interior delights the senses; cool space dignified by masterpieces of long dead craftsmen. The marble floor gleams. Baroque ornamentation in walnut, ironwork and stone surrounds the visitor, yet is subservient to the altar's brilliance. Five or six encircling chapels are barricaded and hard to comprehend. These too have costly ornamentation, statues and religious paintings; mostly dark, some teetering on the macabre. Its adjoining museum offers more dark paintings, lavish arrays of gilt and silver utensils and ornaments, and costly episcopal robes.

My visit unsettled me. Were there audible whispers of divine love, of Good News for the poor, the broken-hearted and oppressed? Were there hints of the glowing life of one Jesus of Nazareth? Perhaps not. There was no explanatory literature in any language; no interpreter at hand. The stories of the building and its treasures were largely untold, and certainly their whole purpose – the larger story – withheld.

I wondered what unschooled visitors might make of it. Would they notice its unintended symbolism? Back in the sixteenth century, they built this fortress of a cathedral to keep raiding Berber pirates out. Today, an embedded bias of unwelcome endures. I only discovered the unsigned entrance on turning the corner to its fourth side. Admission cost €5. The ticket told me my mandatory charge was a donation: its reverse conveyed four prohibitions and an exhortation.

An old friend, a cradle-Catholic but now agnostic, once challenged me. How can the Church with its beautiful buildings, exquisite music, pomp and grandeur explain how these connect with ordinary people in their struggles with life in a Cowley council estate?'

This conversation, and that cathedral visit, point to culture's mysterious power; how it can mis-shape and conceal, element by element, silently and over time. Cultures come to present themselves as 'the norm', thus worthy of respect. If born within this culture, I doubt I would have questioned much. Coming from outside I saw differently.

A degree of blindness to surrounding culture afflicts everyone. It is unavoidable. Visitors to my home or to my country may see how we live with a greater clarity than we ourselves see.

So how did this cathedral's cultural incrustation come about? Should not bishops and clergy have done something?

But, more importantly, what of the Church of England and our unheeded institutional culture? For something is not working. We bicker and fragment. We slide towards crisis, apparently unfazed by declining stipendiary clergy numbers,[2] diminishing income and our unaffordable portfolio of church buildings[3] – and without sign of a joined-up, coherent response.[4] We cannot shrug it all off as mere human frailty; human, understandable and forgivable. For our *institutional* problems are derided too often; despite our many fine church leaders and much fine parish ministry. We do not notice we have little of *institutional* example to offer the world, nor that clerical and lay confidence in the *institution* can seem worryingly thin: sure signs of institutional distress.[5]

Voices outside the Church deserve a hearing. The writer Ben Okri once issued a sharp challenge, perhaps responding to bishops voting against each other in House of Lords' ethical debates:

> 'To whom do we turn for guidance in our modern world? ... The Church speaks with a broken voice.'[6]

Church voices, not least of some senior clergy, are increasingly audible. They have spoken of our divisions, our credibility, our rank-system and bureaucracy, institutional incoherence and structural fragmentation. Their words command attention. They call for a fresh realism and a new approach. They see a church that is not working well, as organisation. Archbishop Justin Welby has warned of the divisions in the wider Anglican Communion:

> 'It is a dangerous place, a narrow path we walk as Anglicans at present. On one side is the steep fall into an absence of any core beliefs, a chasm where we lose touch with God, and thus we rely only on ourselves and our own message. On the other side there is a vast fall into a ravine of intolerance and cruel exclusion. It is for those who claim all truth, and exclude any who question.'[7]

Bishop Nigel McCullogh said it was not that people do not believe in God, but that they do not find the churches credible.[8]

Lord Hope – archbishop, then with refreshed insight as parish priest – has highlighted the Church's rank-system and bureaucracy. He sees:

> 'how the church today needs urgently to shake off the disabling shackles of hierarchy and bureaucracy so that it can be free to travel light, to embrace an altogether new asceticism ... to live the gospel light so that the light and life of Jesus may be the more manifest to all.'[9]

Canon Robin Greenwood presses for a new approach in a book review:

> '... the only way up for the Churches is down. Churches with complex histories, ailing structures, and shrinking membership, suggests the

author, should seriously consider stopping pushing against the odds. … Churches now … need to dig down to a deeper option.'[10]

Then, Bishop Steven Croft shows similar realism:

'We find ourselves living in a period of significant social, economic, technological and cultural change such that the inherited way of being church is no longer working well.'[11]

Two diocesan bishops provide further diagnoses. One commented on the child protection scandals investigated in 2013 in the Chichester diocese,

'The significant point about the Chichester report is the recognition that the safeguarding failures are largely *the result of institutional incoherence, a failure of leadership and structural fragmentation.*'[12]

And in 2012 the concerns of his diocese's working prompted the recently-installed Bishop of Lincoln, Christopher Lowson, to initiate an independent Central Services Review.

Our sister Roman Catholic Church hears similar voices. The late Cardinal Martini offered his Church a final 'testament':

'The Church is tired in affluent Europe and in America. Our culture has grown old, our Churches are big, our religious houses are empty, the bureaucracy of our Churches is growing out of proportion, our liturgies and our vestments are pompous…. The Church is 200 years behind the times. How come it doesn't rouse itself? Are we afraid? Fearful instead of courageous?'

The Tablet described him as speaking truth to power, as having the authenticity of an Old Testament prophet and castigating the mighty in the name of the Lord. 'The Church should be grateful for it.'[13]

With such voices, we must ask if we – the Church as a whole – see ourselves as others see us. Or, more importantly, do we see ourselves as we are? If our Church is either creaking badly or has dysfunctional characteristics, we are hindered in showing Christ's love to the loveless, that they might lovely be.

Jesus's Kingdom model in the gospels portrays fruitfulness in the face of opposition. So, if voices within and outside the Church see things are wrong, there may be a substantial message to heed. Maybe we proclaim love too readily, whilst institutionally portraying something else. We have some fine clergy, not least in our inner-cities, and some fine leaders. But if the edifice of the Church's organisation and structures, and its underlying culture, neither attracts much interest or respect of those outside – nor engenders confidence amongst too many of its members – its mission is undermined. As with a ship, a church always reflects its master. A local church's mood and demeanour is similarly palpable within minutes of visiting it. The question we need to face, recurrently, is: who is the God we are commending through our corporate mood and demeanour?

We seem in denial or paralysed by this challenge of institutional distress. Though we have much to be grateful for, we cling to customs and accept an institutional lifestyle not heading obviously towards that profound coherence and supernatural relationship anticipated by Jesus.

We certainly have not lacked gospel initiative: the Church Urban Fund, the ordination of women, Decade of Evangelism and Fresh Expressions being examples. Local developments such as Alpha and the new monasticism are having a considerable reach. Numerous commissions, debates and books have addressed Church issues and components of its organisation and ministry. We have expended great effort, *and* tried fixing the complex machinery, yet without a greater coherence emerging.

It is time to delve deeper, beneath the scope of such initiatives and beneath analyses of structures and methods. There is little point in adjusting my car's clutch whilst ignoring its corroded chassis. The time for ecclesiastical spanner-work has passed. Deeper and larger issues need exploring.

We must face that large theme of culture; recognising its mysterious *spiritual* influence, suffusing communities and institutions, affecting silently the understanding and shape of everyone's life. We get it the wrong way round. We root our sense of identity in a particular culture, then unthinkingly use religion to reinforce it. In contrast, Christ invested his gospel culture with power to supplant the corrupt endemic culture.

Scripture lends us the fascinating metaphor of leaven – an 'insignificant' fungal process with silent power – infiltrating, permeating, replicating and influencing. Unsurprisingly it is known biologically as a culture. A culture's power rests in its reproductive ability, spreading laterally and generationally for good or ill.

Building a robust tradition or culture is critically important. Back in 1941, Admiral Sir Andrew Cunningham commanded the British Mediterranean fleet. In the heat of battle of Crete, General Wavell challenged him about risking terrible naval losses in evacuating the army from Crete. His reply was profound:

'You have said that it will take three years to build a new fleet. I will tell you that it will take three hundred years to build a new tradition'.

This book examines Jesus's and the apostles' lifestyles and relational patterns; wondering how they learned, and then acted and reacted the way they did. It explores how they lived in – and conveyed – this new Kingdom culture. It offers a particular way of looking at the apostolic heritage, and suggests an entry–point for change.

We must look clear-eyed at how enveloping culture has discoloured our Church and impacted our mission. We must not to fall into 'the 'ecclesiocentric trap', the myopic approach to mission that starts with church: doing it better, doing it differently', of which Paul Bradbury, a pioneer minister, warns. He has asserted that:

'Church will shape its mission more authentically when it dies to the Church that it has become, or to the one it wants to be, and it stops long enough to listen to the gospel, to the community around it, and to the Spirit of God.'[14]

This book emphasises the Church's urgent need to express by example how a relational body can work, as *organism* to *organisations* in the secular world. It therefore explores how relationship may be developed at individual and institutional levels inside the Church, how the Church may be transformed to model a love-centred institutional life, and how it may better purvey God's love to the loveless; and display God's glory and wisdom.

To this end, it suggests ways *it may die to the Church that it has become, or even to the one it wants to be,* to become more like the Church for which Jesus prayed. He prayed for us, the Church, to manifest his glory in the world and declare his wisdom in its rich variety to the rulers and authorities in the heavenly places.[15] Some vocation.

Jesus had much to endure from his Judaean culture, with the Roman occupier's added pressures. Yet he never blamed individuals. He warned against *blame,* against judgmentalism: he knew how culture worked.

Certainly no-one can gauge the balance of volition and enculturation behind anyone's actions or character. Blaming individuals is inappropriate anyhow, for cultural creep depends on substantial complicity across a constituency. We come to love the adjusted culture as it inches along; it is *normal* and therefore right. And we feel safe in being no different from thousands of others. We do not gauge the scale of its consequences, perhaps not seeing them at all. We all share responsibility for colluding with our culture's dark sides, however unthinkingly.

Culture distorts our bearings. We can now see how the creep of Nazi culture in 20th century Germany subverted the proud – even moral – Prussian culture of the Wehrmacht. It drew high-calibre, thinking German Generals into complicity with Nazi values. Their culture prompted them to value loyalty and obedience to an irrational degree. The emergence of a criminal as national leader was outside their frame, so some found themselves participants in large-scale atrocity. They had missed their earlier chance to oppose, and were trapped. Hitler exploited their cultural blindness ruthlessly.

Walter Wink's books alert us to the reality of Principalities and Powers. Ecclesiastical culture, like its secular sibling, has its power systems. Historic convulsions – notably those of Constantine and Luther – have shaped it, as have lesser jolts over time. Some outcomes may have been good, but others – where secular culture has slipped through unnoticed – questionable. Yet all can spawn unintended consequences, some emerging long afterwards. Thus, culture creeps largely unnoticed, through decades, centuries and even millennia. It acquires a patina, gaining respect and affection along the way.

The momentum of unhelpful elements may be too much for any one person to address, regardless of their position. It is a spiritual problem and we have to see it as such. A particular reason is that its location, its amorphous and confused shape, and its dimensions are beyond our power to define. Elements of church culture may be capable of leaking into the surrounding secular culture, but the church is certainly prone to infection from the latter.

Whilst we cannot blame anyone for our enwrapping culture, including that of our Church, we have no mandate to do *nothing*. How then may we challenge culture, and contribute to its reshaping? Human wisdom cannot develop membranes to limit cultural reach. We need a greater wisdom.

Jesus faced aspects of his culture head-on, and so should we, his Body.

Much of our teaching has focused on the personal aspects of life. Yet, culture matters. We need to note, and absorb, the gospel way of *facing* culture.

Sometimes we are criticised unjustly for our stand in matters of faith or ethics; yet sometimes, deservedly and unsurprisingly for our human frailty, and because we fail to command respect as a coherent and professional body.

Does our Church's professional reputation matter? Is it not just a sign of inevitable human frailty?

It matters very much, for diligent churches and ministers are thereby undermined. If low in institutional credibility, some of those seeking answers in life will simply look elsewhere. Weak institutional reputation also affects bishops' standing, and their ability to communicate at a regional or national level. It affects members' appetites to give it wholehearted support. It affects morale of both clergy and laity who look for something better; and clergy in particular. By entrusting the whole of their working lives to the church, with many sacrifices of spouse and children, they need to find the church trustworthy. They have reason to expect the Church's quality of pastoral care, its handling of critical issues of appointment, ministerial development, nurture and encouragement – and of conflict resolution – to surpass that in the outside world. Sorrowfully, for many, it does not.

Jesus's world-view embraced evil's reality and seriousness. He was a marked man from his ministry's outset, being watched covertly and not-so-covertly, and reported upon to the Jerusalem authorities. He was the target of undermining, of theological and political ambush, of menace and attempts on his life. There were coercive pressures on his followers. His words were laced with reference to the powers of darkness. Yet his disciples, like us perhaps, preferred a superficial, triumphalist view that persistently rejected the Calvary path he unveiled. Unsurprisingly, his Final Discourse alerted them, and alerts us still, to the significance and presence of evil power. Jesus demands a necessary and healthy fear.

Of course, this dark force exposed its depravity utterly on Calvary (Luke 22.1-4), in its seemingly final destruction of the source of Love; before the greater power of resurrection overturned it in full view of the cosmos. In the words of Tom Wright:

> 'The result [of his exegesis of Jn 8.31,32] is a fresh analysis of the threat that these same Judaeans have posed to Jesus because of their rejection of his message. 'Now you seek to kill me,' declares Jesus, 'someone who has told you the truth I heard from God.' By contrast, the evil power that has spread its corruption throughout the world, and even within God's chosen people, is a liar and the father of lies, and is thus the archetypal murderer.'[16]

What then are this dark force's dynamics, and what are the instruments for dealing with it? For while the Church concentrates on Jesus's teaching on individual faith responses and discipleship, we give less emphasis on how he tackled it in a wider sense, by addressing and supplanting cultural evil.

In the Judaeo-Christian tradition, the law of love is defined through its demarcations: what belongs to God, others and ourselves. It was seen in the Old Testament emphasis on land boundaries. If backs are turned on this Judaeo-Christian reliance on boundaries, all boundaries are ultimately rejected, with unknowable consequences. This seems to be happening before our eyes.

Which human government has the ability – the spiritual authority and power – to move such boundaries or devise new norms with any prospect of permanence or indeed, acceptance? Pragmatic law-making and regulation, without reference to external norms, is intrinsically temporary; gaining primacy and attention only until superseded by something else. And unlike their Judaeo-Christian predecessors, new *norms* will be impelled by political expediency; by a government's desire to stay in control, succeed, gain popularity with one vested-interest-group or another, or to bring economic gain. Such a stance increasingly relies more on threat than a shared conviction: it weakens sinews of societal trust and damages community life. The law – framed in love – is based on what *we owe to others*. Culture has subverted it to a law protecting what *others owe to me*. Impregnated with self-interest, it divides and may foster hatred. This is the inevitable trajectory when legislation is driven by nothing more than retention or extension of power.

The historian Michael Burleigh writes tellingly of the impact on culture of totalitarian rule.

> 'It is important to grasp the grubby reality of both the Nazi and the Communist systems, because they claimed to have instituted reigns of public virtue through such slogans as "healthy popular instinct."[17] Both dictatorships abandoned traditional moral norms based on transcendental authority or natural law to institute the regimes of hate rather than love that Churchill spoke of…'[18]

Once targets, statistics and economic indicators come to dominate the processes of governance, considerations of individual wellbeing recede into the mist. Mechanical techniques turn people into objects – to serve statistical objectives, however worthy – rather than subjects whose intrinsic worth means that governance's prime purpose is to serve *them*.

Thus we may glimpse culture's power, unless checked: power to subvert law, to remove healthy frameworks, and draw us into a trackless desert without landmarks and without that which supports life. We end up in a place where no human effort, law or formula has power: in bondage. It is the terrible outcome of godless culture and there is only one way out. Such thoughts may illuminate something of the *world view* behind Jesus's ministry, seen in his concern for *the lost*.

The political context of Jesus's life resonates with periods of our own history and of parts of today's world; yet such volatility and danger seems far removed from what we in the West have come to view as our rightful norm. As we shall consider, Jesus was surprisingly non-judgmental of both sin and social need when dealing with individuals and the crowds. Instead, he saw them as lost, as missing out – not knowing which way to turn, or how to handle life's difficult questions.

People needed a shepherd or a rescuer, not a judge or critic.

Jesus gave the authorities of his day no obvious priority of time or attention. He saw through the mirage of their questionable authority in the nation; saw their blindness to spiritual reality. Corruption was rife and ordinary people suffered. When dealing with the religious leaders individually, his responses were courteous yet appropriate to the attitude they showed. He responded non-judgmentally and redemptively whether it was Nicodemus or the rich young ruler. Throughout the manipulation and injustices of his trial, he responded with silence or quiet restraint. Over against this, we need to weigh why he inveighed against Herod, the scribes and Pharisees, forcefully and publicly.

Today, reports of decay in many important British institutions seem commonplace. How are we to view them?

Some may put their finger on *morality* – more emphasis or teaching needed here; on *accountability and oversight* – more attention needed; on *greed* – to be named and faced, and so on. A Christian should see such things as symptoms more than causes; the underlying reason being a lack of understanding of how life works under a creator God, of the utter centrality of relationship and of how things fit together. If so, today's predicament may be described as a profound lostness; with people neither seeing boundaries as instruments of blessing or, in Jesus's words, 'not knowing what makes for peace.'

Such thoughts emphasise culture's role. For without received bearings and boundaries, people will be influenced by the fickle currents of self-serving, directionless culture, and act accordingly. They will be comforted by spurious 'norms': bad cultures' deceptive fruit.

How then should we, the Church, respond to the challenge mounted by today's culture? We know the culture of Jesus is the complete answer, but how is this to be conveyed? The Church's implicit answer is that it happens through one person at a time; each believer carrying Christ's light into the work-place and the world. Such of course is the baptismal vocation of each Christian, but is it the full answer? Maybe not, for Jesus and the apostles define another vocation that receives far less attention: the vocation of the Church as Christ's body. Much of the New Testament is addressed not just to individuals, but to the Church, to be pursued in parallel. Its vocation was expressed by Jesus in his Great High Priestly prayer in John 17, and through Paul (eg in Eph 3.10) who saw the Church as 'pivotal in the struggle against the powers of evil',[19] and obliged as a body to 'take no part in the unfruitful works of darkness, but instead expose them'.[20]

A priest and former civil servant Douglas Hollis said as much in a newspaper article. '*Church* and people … are to make the love of Jesus explicit in the world of everyday.' This resonates with Jesus's aspiration in his High Priestly prayer – to evince God's reality through a people in coherent, fitting relationship with him and each other, displaying godly love in community regardless of circumstances. Such a culture, unachievable naturally, would arrest attention and challenge all other cultures.

Where else can we head?

Two Leavens

Much of life is unchosen. Some are born in Calcutta slums and others in palaces. We did not choose our parents, our race, our received religion, our country or time of birth, nor the complex culture these elements combine to form. Culture's power rests in its provision of norms, some good and some not. It therefore follows that we shall make many life choices according to the way we understand and respond to our received culture. Robin Greenwood and Hugh Burgess make this point,

> 'The identity of a particular person is not to be found somewhere deep inside him or her: he has no self, centre or soul, or other form of private existence before being exposed to the *world of relationship*.'[21]

The newly demonstrated Way – seen in the lifestyles of Jesus and the apostles – contrasted with their inherited culture. They warned of the hostility that this variance would provoke. It was in *enmity* with the world. Their package of example and teaching showed their followers how to respond, following two themes. They *proclaimed* and lived out the Kingdom of God's love, and they defined and *declaimed against* 'the kingdom of this world.'

Jesus spoke of two types of leaven. He compared the kingdom of God with the leavening of bread[22] – a culture empowered by the inside-force of divine love. But he twice warned his disciples against another leaven – a culture – of Herod, the scribes and Pharisees.[23] As shall be argued, their culture is well summarised as lovelessness, that fermenting influence directly opposing God's love. It is the 'default' power of worldly, secular rule.

The significance of unleavened bread in God's rescue of the Jews, and in the Passover feast, is well known. Less known, less emphasised, is the associated searching-out of old leaven. Throwing out those fermenting lumps of dough in kitchen corners formed a ritual within the Jewish Feast of Unleavened Bread.

The leavened bread used at the time of the Exodus was like today's sourdough bread. Interestingly, it originated in ancient Egypt. Unlike other breads, no yeast is added. Over a few days, spore in the air penetrate the lump of dough, starting a fermentation that makes the dough rise.

Not only was this sourdough recipe rooted in Egyptian daily life – a life from which God was delivering the Jews – this leaven's spore came from the Egyptian air they breathed. Culturally, it represented the Egypt that held them in bondage. God instructed his chosen people to comply with this ritualistic discipline of cleaning out, and destroying old leaven – corporately and individually. It continues within Judaism after three and a half millennia. In every sense, they had to leave Egypt behind. By the time of the incarnation, the leaven of Herod, the scribes and Pharisees had come to engulf God's people – superseding that of Egypt, and more recently of Assyria.

The Church has given dominant place to the annual disciplines of Lent observance, and the regular disciplines implicit in the eucharist – each emphasising the importance of repentance and re-commitment. For centuries, the Church has tended to view such cleaning-out in personal more than in corporate terms. Cranmer's collect for purity, 'cleanse the thoughts of our hearts by the inspiration of thy Holy Spirit' is an example. So is the collect for Low Sunday, 'Grant us so to put away the leaven of malice and wickedness that we may always serve you in pureness of living and truth.' But any need for a parallel discipline – a ritual searching-out of old leaven lying in corners of the *Church's institution and communities* – seems to have escaped attention.

We ought to examine our complex, inherited Church culture and search out old leaven with prayerful rigour. Paul, after all, saw the need to press the *whole church* in Corinth to 'get rid of the old leaven and then you will be a new batch of unleavened dough.'[24]

Martin Luther's Easter hymn, *"Christ lag in Todesbanden für unsre Sünd gegeben"*, well known in the German Church, follows this theme:

'Christ lay in death's bondage, given for our sins. Invited to unleavened bread, we eat and live well.
The old leaven dough shall not coexist with the gospel's grace; Christ wants to be the only one we feed on, and solely feed the soul; faith does not want to be fed by any other. Hallelujah'[25]

The Challenge

These rituals mount a question for today's church. It is not a matter for blame or judgmentalism, for we have all eaten wrong-leavened 'bread'. Every church member has colluded in varying degrees. We have inevitably ingested our culture's – spores – fungal strains from the air we breathe, and 'it is notoriously difficult to gain insights into one's own familiar culture.'[26] A trivial example is the way the Church of England has exported gothic windows across the Anglican Communion as a desirable feature of church buildings, perhaps with stained glass – even in the tropical jungle!

We need clear-eyed realism, and a motivation to unmask the wrong culture. We need to own our collusion, and work out how God's culture might specifically displace it. We need a leaven-check if we are to take our Church vocation seriously. How else may the power of divine love – the Kingdom's leaven be manifested though us? What might this mean, what do we look for and how do we handle it?

We need to see that immense spiritual power is involved. Leaven is not merely a desirable additive – its power transforms and shapes the whole lump. Our whole world is shaped by cultures – and cultures are more than the sum of human deeds. Spiritually empowered, their spores spread laterally through families and communities, and vertically, passing down through generations. We are confident the Kingdom's leaven packs much more power than the other sort, dangerous though that is. God indicated as much when giving Moses the Law, with parental lovelessness harming children through to the *third and the fourth* generation, but steadfast love reaching through 'to the *thousandth* generation of those who love me and keep my commandments.'[27]

John's prologue similarly asserts God's dominant power:

> 'What came into existence was Life, and the Life was Light to live by. The Life-Light blazed out of the darkness; the darkness couldn't put it out.'[28]

We now consider these two leavens further.

1. The Leaven of Herod, the scribes and Pharisees

How weighty were Jesus's warnings and what did he mean by them?

A leader needs to identity any confronting problem before defining an aim and then responding. For God, the problem was the culture fostered by Herod and the religious leaders – anti-God and anti-life. The Trinity's aim was to supplant it – thus Jesus launched the infinitely more powerful Kingdom culture. Love was to supplant the resident power of lovelessness.

Living by the law of love, Jesus did not attack individuals. His targets were never personal. Herod, individual Pharisees, teachers of the law and the Sadducees were not, in themselves, the problem. Neither did Jesus engage philosophically in the politics of the day, secular or politico-religious. It is significant that the Pharisees' purpose was, in its way, redemptive – at first glance not too different from the purpose of God's Son. Bishop Tom Wright writes that 'their goals were the honour of Israel's god, the following of his covenant charter, and the pursuit of the full promised redemption of Israel.'[29]

Jesus saw deeper. He made no attempt to get alongside hierarchies and try to influence either the religious leaders nor Herod and his court, although interestingly his influence was present in both locations.[30] His enmity was toward the underlying powers. He targeted the spiritual forces that energised these people's misunderstandings – shaping their attitudes and lifestyles. These cultural powers were the problem – the great spoilers. They were fighting the Kingdom culture he was bringing to birth, with its drawing force of love.

Jesus defined their leaven on different occasions as hypocrisy (Lk 12.1), as corrupt or deceitful teaching, and as oblivious to the 'signs' (Mt 16.12), unbelieving of physical evidence (Mk 8.14-21). He painted a picture of their invasive culture in his teaching. When

Jesus ministered, the secular and religious leaders seemingly planted observers in the crowds, to report back.[31] When they intervened with criticisms and loaded questions, his responses laid bare their governing culture's nature. His parables often carried sharp criticisms of it, and then there were the 'woes'. Individual scribes and Pharisees would have had little doubt as to where the 'battle lines' were drawn.

The New Testament consistently uncovers murder as this culture's destination. Herod the Great showed his hand at Jesus's birth. The Magi's arrival in town triggered a display of insecurity and fear – then of deceit, with his declared intention to go and worship the baby.

He accepted the authenticity of prophecy for locating the Messiah – then rejected its authority for defining a Messiah who deserved submission and worship. Thus, he disclosed his incoherent mind. Fuelled by insecurity and fear, his resolve turned to infanticide.[32] In Joseph's mind, his son, Herod Archelaus, had a similar reputation.[33]

This culture drove another son, Herod Antipas, to murder John the Baptist – and subsequently connive in Jesus's murder. Luke's account of Herod meeting Jesus, within his Jerusalem 'trial', portrays a man paralysed by spiritual blindness. He trivialises a power that heals and delivers. He opts for the spectator role because of his inability to interpret and engage with reality. Devoid of shame, he demands entertainment of the one who created everything.[34]

This culture was profoundly anti-God and anti-life. The New Testament, and later on, Josephus and Eusebius, describe its trajectory.

It pressed forcefully toward Calvary from the awakening of Jesus's ministry. He was warned that Herod Antipas wanted to kill him.[35] As his ministry continued, so the purposes of Herod and the religious leaders merged.

A fear of Roman over-reaction to 'unrest' lay behind it all.[36] Fear looms large in the New Testament narrative. The urge to dominate, at all costs, began to rage. They reached for the 'power tools' of threat, lies, deceit, propaganda and physical force.

The gospels emphasise the seriousness of Jesus' warnings – his 'bewares'. As the time of the Passion approached, the rage of opposing culture mounted. John captured its reaction to the healing of the blind man and the much-witnessed resurrected life of Lazarus – fear-fuelled and irrational.[37] The pressure was on. 'The Festival of Unleavened Bread, which is also called Passover, was approaching.' That 'the leading priests and teachers of religious law were *plotting* how to kill Jesus'[38] says it all – teachers of the law that forbade murder, now plotted to kill.

The mention of unleavened bread intensifies the drama. Here were two parties preparing to celebrate the same festival – the religious leaders, and Jesus and his followers. The former denied – or were oblivious of – its meaning. They concentrated on the externals. Meanwhile, God-in-Christ was working through the depths of meaning, preparing a cosmic re-enaction of God's great deliverance from slavery to freedom and new life. The forces of lovelessness impelled the former – governed by fear and bent on murder. The religious leaders were heedless of the implications of running counter to the whole law of which they were teachers. In contrast, Jesus was impelled by the greater force of love, governed by humble trust in his Father – albeit stretched to near breaking-point – in order to release God's powers of life and love of which he was custodian. We may be sure Jesus quietly prayed for Herod, Caiaphas and Pilate during the course of his trial.[39] Yet the cross, with all its other benefits, was the denouement of the leaven of the scribes, Pharisees and of Herod – a final unravelling and exposure of its inner reality.

The religious leaders gave prominence to the Festival, unheeding its meaning – for what old leaven did they seek out within their ritual? In contrast, Jesus re-enacted and applied prophetically for all time that inner meaning for the sake of the world he loved so much.

Whilst we may not judge those who conspired to murder Jesus, any more than he judged them, for he saw they knew not what they were doing – or any more than Peter judged them.[40] Yet we do need, like him, to heed their culture's devilish power, pressing them to this outcome.

Jesus prayed, 'My Father! If this cup cannot be taken away unless I drink it, your will be done',[41] and 'Father, forgive them, for they do not know what they are doing.'[42] In vivid contrast, the purported leaders of the religion of the living God met 'at the residence of Caiaphas, the high priest, plotting how to capture Jesus secretly and kill him. But not during the Passover celebration', they agreed, 'or the people may riot.'[43]

It seems the religious hierarchy were 'on the case' from the outset of Jesus's three-year ministry.[44] Their surveillance provided the backcloth to his unfolding of the Kingdom. Luke mentions three times their presence to watch and entrap, and there are some fourteen occasions recorded in the gospels of Herod or the religious leaders plotting to arrest or kill him.

Jesus's ministry of warning formed part of his ministry of love, hope and healing. He was speaking and preaching against the leaven – the culture of the scribes, Pharisees and Herod – in parallel to proclaiming Kingdom leaven. In the latter days, he told a startlingly direct, prophetic parable about tenants killing the property owner's son, to no obvious effect – and further laid at *their* door the killing instinct of their predecessors in killing the prophets. He regularly laced his teaching with warnings of a choice to be made between broad and narrow ways, between darkness and light, and between death and life. He regularly told his hearers to reject the hypocritical patterns of their religious leaders.

His publicly stated 'woes' named the corrupt culture that had to be faced. Jesus reinforced his early 'beware' challenge to his followers with specific examples of that bad leaven's product. Yet at the same time, from his platform of love, he was offering the religious leaders the chance to waken to the leaven's hold on them – to recognise its corruption and repent. Prior to his death, some of the Jewish leaders became closet believers. Maybe Nicodemus, Gamaliel, Joseph of Arimathea and other Council members were helped by such warnings.[45]

How do we, the Church, replicate Jesus's pattern of warnings? When and how are we to expose and denounce, in his name, any culture of religiosity and religious power- mongering, today? We eagerly proclaim the positive, but are averse to the negative – unwittingly implying there is some neutral ground people may occupy until they choose to follow Jesus. It does not exist. The leaven – against which we are warned – stealthily draws people away from God and life, in the direction of killing and death.

This deadly culture lived on beyond the crucifixion – its trajectory unchecked – as Peter and the apostles found after Pentecost. Irrational killing continued. Perhaps one year after Pentecost, Herod had John's brother James killed by the sword (Acts 12.2). Luke reports the jealousy aroused by the apostles' popularity (5.17). Murder is the authority's response to the seeming threat – as a first resort (5.33). Later on, the religious authorities grabbed Paul in the Temple. They would have killed him, had not a Roman military commander intervened (21.31-33). Then a Judaean group plotted to kill Paul after his appearance before the High Council (23.12-15). Eusebius and Josephus tell of the Jewish authorities murdering Jesus's brother, James, in the Temple precincts in about AD62. He was thrown from a temple parapet; his broken body then stoned and clubbed.

The nation and key elements of Judaism were destroyed in AD70. The temple, the priesthood and sacrificial practices were finished. Herod and the religious leaders had learned nothing – the culture they unconsciously inhabited had done its work. But its depraved underlying power was alive and well.

All worldly power, unless checked, heads in the same direction as the leaven of Herod, the scribes and Pharisees. Jesus warned that 'the hour is coming when whoever kills you will think he is offering service to God.'[46] He chose us to come out of the world's grasp – he recognised its inherent God-hatred.[47]

It is implicit in Paul's warning, 'Don't let anyone capture you with empty philosophies and high-sounding nonsense that come from human thinking and from the spiritual powers of this world, rather than from Christ.'[48] He warned against returning to our previous godless understandings, 'When we were children, we were in slavery under the basic principles of the world. ... how can you turn back again to the weak and beggarly elemental spirits? How can you want to be enslaved to them again?'[49]

As the Church gained experience in the apostolic era, and with the faith spreading beyond Judea, descriptions expanded to reflect the dark cultures of the wider world. Paul in particular warned of the behaviour and customs of this world,[50] against forms of godliness that lacked its power, and the profound theme of principalities and powers. NT Wright makes this assessment,

'(Paul) will have identified Rome as the leading edge of opposition to the suddenly inbreaking Kingdom of God.'[51]

The leaven's momentum and reach increased, with its power to harden hearts and minds, and its characteristics of judgmentalism, blindness to reality, and visceral opposition to God. This leaven is active today – seen vividly in political systems that are avowedly secular, atheistic or anti-Christian. The influence of bad leaven is increasingly visible in the so-called Christian West – where nations have the privilege of inherited legal systems and historic institutions framed or informed by Christian belief. Hitherto 'Christian' cultures are being subverted.

'The principalities, the powers, the politicians,
The ones who pose in the spotlight
Centre-stage, and magnetise us as they stalk
Towards bankruptcy, murder, betrayal, suicide,
And other traditional exits…..'[52]

2. The Leaven of the Kingdom

From the start, Jesus's person and lifestyle displayed a different world – an order of life that was 'not of this world.' He described it in parable and teaching. He was different. He showed no petty dislikes, he related with all, he was humble yet had mysterious authority. He was on the side of the wretched, the mixed-up and the derelict. In particular, he lived in an aura of deep peace and contentment. He walked sure-footedly, unfazed by crises, threat and danger. His words were important, but unlike others who tried to change the world – his persona and lifestyle marked him out decisively.

We know that Jesus's High Priestly Prayer (Jn 17) defined *relational* unity as the means of showing God's glory – revealed in the burning bush and at the Old Temple's consecration. Glory was shown in Jesus, and purposed as a primary endowment upon his New Temple. He referred enticingly to future Church, picturing church life as it should be. He showed how love may win, and lovelessness be supplanted.

It was fitting that, in the Pentecost festival, the Jews presented two baked *leavened* loaves at the Temple altar – a prophetic sign that, after seeking out and destroying the old leaven, God imbued his Church at its birth with the Pentecost power of love to energise its culture.

The leaven in the individual
The New Testament offers significant glimpses into the inner lives of just two people: Saul-who-became-Paul, the total victim of one culture, and Jesus, the complete beneficiary and benefactor of the other.

Paul and Luke give valuable insights into Saul's bondage to the leaven of Herod, the scribes and Pharisees. So tight was this bondage, it took extraordinary divine intervention to break it; without Saul's permission! We shall examine these scriptural insights of Paul's cultural entrapment in Chapter 7. We see today signs of the same leaven that trapped him – in all the genocides, daily cruelties and turmoil of today.

In contrast, we turn to explore Jesus's 'interior life' in the Gospel narrative.

First, the eyewitness accounts point to an important truth: Jesus, although God's Son and we now see, a member of the Trinity, did not say his words and do his deeds because he was God. He said and did them because he became fully human – a human captivated by, and filled with the fullness of the Godhead – following perfectly the will of his Father. As Paul explained:

'he gave up his divine privileges; he took the humble position of a slave and was born a human being. When he appeared in human form, he humbled himself in obedience to God and died a criminal's death on the cross.'[53]

Paul urged the same attitude upon us. Thus Jesus, whilst being God in his core identity, lived his incarnated life solely as a man. Indeed, his example would be pointless and discouraging if he were not like us. It wouldn't touch us. The power he manifested was the power implanted in his human body by the Holy Spirit at his baptism; the power of the Kingdom. He had no ministry before this event. From now on, he had the Spirit's power.[54]

On this basis we can glimpse something of his interior life. The life chosen to launch and manifest the leaven of the Kingdom was self-evidently, by choice, inherently powerless. Jesus had eschewed personal power and lowered himself to be a conduit of the highest power in the cosmos. So we may expect to glimpse within his interior life how this could happen.

According to Peter, Jesus, 'anointed with the Holy Spirit and with power, went about doing good and healing all who were oppressed by the devil, for God was with him.'[55] He used neither violence nor threatening behaviour. He scattered no-one, drawing large crowds to himself. He focused intense love on everyone who came to him. He revealed the law's love-basis, supplanting all legalism. And his sense of identity rested simply on two things – his specific knowledge of his Father's love and his Father's calling.

The picture emerges of a life that flowered from sustained intimacy with his Father, and his joyous yet inflexible obedience. That was all. John's gospel asserted Jesus's attentive, habitual obedience – some 30 to 40 times in 17 chapters. No other element of Jesus's lifestyle receives such emphasis. It demands attention. Jesus precisely followed the suffering servant's intimacy and close obedience which Isaiah described.[56] Obedience rested on his discipline of listening, recognising and hearing his Father's voice.

Yet there are gospel hints of an obedience that Jesus had to learn. This is glimpsed in John 7.1-9; then vs.10. It begs the question – since Jesus would not have lied, what must have happened in the gap between vs.9 and 10? This habit is seen in John 11.6,15,21,22: how was Jesus able to walk sure-footedly down this humanly incomprehensible track? And maybe seen in the gap between John 2.4 and 2.7-10; and in John 6.15 – how did he realise they were planning to snatch him? And also seen in Matthew 15.21-28, in his encounter with the Syro-Phoenician woman – his understood vocation to the Jewish nation had now to be adjusted to embrace anyone who crossed his path – anticipating its final expansion in Matthew 28.19. Then again in Matthew 26.39,42 – what caused Jesus's shift in understanding, then acceptance? Such hints make sense of the Hebrews' (5.8) reference to his needing to learn obedience, following a chapter emphasising the need to 'hear God's voice, and not harden one's heart.'

Jesus was establishing God's benchmark for us all. Cultural influences conspire to tell us we are inherently competent and our hands need to be on the tiller. Jesus's temptations in the wilderness had the same voice. His ministry could not begin until he had decisively rejected all of that.

Jesus has long been ranked as the epitome of good leadership. Yet scripture suggests this was a consequence of 'followership.' This evidence of followership challenges any notion that true leadership derives from charisma or the power of human personality. Jesus may have had both, yet his leadership derived from intimacy with Father. John 10.3,4 is interesting in this context. The gatekeeper opens the gate for the shepherd, and the sheep hear his voice. He calls his own sheep by name and leads them out. When he has brought out all his own, he goes ahead of them, and the sheep follow him *because they know his voice.* Followership therefore depends on voice recognition, listening and obedience.

Taking together the elements of intimacy, listening obedience and followership, we have the remarkable implication that Jesus was not just Son, but also disciple. In his thirty- three or so years prior to death – before and after empowerment with the Holy Spirit – we see Jesus's deliberate self-positioning 'at his Father's feet', as disciple.

Such are the hallmarks of the leaven of the Kingdom. They lie behind all that is good in the world.

Thus our world has only two basic powers on offer, two leavens – the cultural power of the Kingdom, of love, trading in fullness of life – and the cultural power of lovelessness, trading in death. All cultures that reject the Kingdom will thus be variants of the culture of lovelessness, always heading in the direction of death, however beguiling.

In scripture's symmetry, it describes three times the Kingdom leaven's supplanting that other leaven in one entrapped man, Saul of Tarsus. We read of the gentleness of Jesus loving an enemy, hell-bent for Damascus with unmitigated malice. We see Jesus doing good to one who hated him, blessing the one who cursed him.[57] Jesus saw Saul's need rather than any embedded evil. Over against this, it was the grip of toxic Pharisaic leaven that aroused Jesus's hostility.

We need to see culture – leaven – as a spiritual entity. Not contained by any discernible membrane, leaven's microscopic processes hide within the lump. Having endured the cruelties of totalitarian Soviet communism, Aleksandr Solzhenitsyn testified,

'Gradually it was disclosed to me that the line separating good and evil passes not through states, nor between classes, nor between political parties either – but right through every human heart – and through all human hearts. This line shifts. Inside us, it oscillates with the years. And even within hearts overwhelmed by evil, one small bridgehead of good is retained. And even in the best of all hearts, there remains ... an unuprooted small corner of evil.'[58]

Equally, wherever its contagion touches the Church, the line separating the powers of love and lovelessness passes not between denominations, nor between 'churchmanships', nor between lobby-groups either – but right through every Christian heart. As Paul asserted unambiguously,

> 'We are not fighting against flesh-and-blood enemies, but against evil rulers and authorities of the unseen world, against mighty powers in this dark world, and against evil spirits in the heavenly places.'[59]

Thus, the real problem Jesus endured was not Herod, the scribes or the Pharisees. It was that unseen power propelling them. We must therefore peer into the characteristics of these mighty powers, and God's mightier powers.

Opposing Powers:
Love and Lovelessness

3

Napoleon rampaged around Europe across some 20 years. He had superb military skill. Yet he slaughtered some six million people in his wars, whilst siphoning the treasure of nations into the Bourse. His nation's mood buttressed his tyranny. Culture made it acceptable.

Contemporary observations on 18th century Corsica – of Napoleon's formative culture – are telling:

'(Corsica's) valleys are fertile and the sides of those mountains produce a fine grape, and were the natives less savage than they are it might abound in corn and wine and oil. But they are a curiosity in Europe. Surrounded by civilised nations, there seems to have been no improvement in their manners, nor their arts, since the Christian era. They plough with a crooked billet and pound their corn in a mortar...'

They have no idea of restraint by laws, or making an appeal to them when injured, the blood of the offender can alone appease them; they are always armed, even when they go to church.

Every man of them travels in the country with a rifle, a gun and a dagger, with which he kills with admirable dexterity such game or Englishmen as he may chance to meet in his way ... and do it with the same composure that an old butcher kills a pig.'[60]

The absence of effective government and successive invasions – akin to Afghanistan's experience across recent centuries – made for a deep instability and restless population. Whilst yet in his mother's womb, Napoleon's parents were involved in the Corsican guerrilla movement, the Maquis, against the newly arrived French rulers. They had to leave home and live in a cave. Returning home, their large house was shared with uncles, aunts and cousins. It was not a haven of peace. His father became a secretary to Paoli, the resistance leader, dying when Napoleon was 16.[61]

Napoleon's contemporary Madame de Staël saw the consequences of his Corsican family culture in his character and world-view:

'Far from reassuring me, further acquaintance with Bonaparte made him seem even more frightening. I had the disturbing feeling that no emotion of the heart could ever reach him. He regards a human being like a fact or a thing, never as an equal person like himself. *He neither loves nor hates.*... The force of his will resides in the imperturbable calculations of his egotism. He is a chess-master whose opponents happen to be the rest of humanity... Neither pity nor attraction, nor religion nor attachment would ever divert him from his ends. I felt in his soul a cold steel, I felt in his mind a deep irony against which nothing great or good, even his own destiny, was proof; for he despised the nation which he intended to govern, and no spark of enthusiasm was mingled with his desire to astound the human race.'[62]

The historian, Paul Johnson, has written,

'No dictator of the tragic twentieth century – from Lenin, Stalin, and Mao Zedong to pygmy tyrants like Kim Il-sung, Castro, Peron, Mengistu, Saddam Hussein, Ceaucescu, and Gadhafi – was without distinctive echoes of the Napoleonic prototype.'

'.... We have to learn again the central lesson of history: that all forms of greatness, military and administrative, nation- and empire-building, are as nothing – indeed are perilous in the extreme – without a humble and a contrite heart.'[63]

This is how lovelessness works, how it breeds further lovelessness. Like leaven, it has innate power.

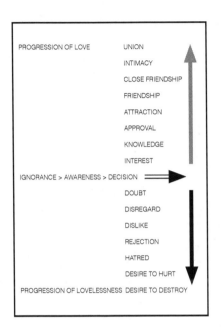

PROGRESSION OF LOVE   UNION

INTIMACY

CLOSE FRIENDSHIP

FRIENDSHIP

ATTRACTION

APPROVAL

KNOWLEDGE

INTEREST

IGNORANCE > AWARENESS > DECISION

DOUBT

DISREGARD

DISLIKE

REJECTION

HATRED

DESIRE TO HURT

PROGRESSION OF LOVELESSNESS DESIRE TO DESTROY

The Powers' Progression

People sometimes tattoo the words LOVE and HATE on their knuckles – a common view of opposites. Thesauruses have it wrong at this point – theologically, logically and maybe linguistically. They offer *hate*, or *hatred*, as love's primary antonym. One thesaurus lists 24 synonyms for the noun 'love', and the single antonym, 'hatred'. It then lists 14 synonyms for the verb with two antonyms, 'detest' and 'hate.'

Culture may suggest – even to Christians – that it is enough to shape our lives on a resolution to avoid hatred. I have lived much of my life on this premise – failing to notice my wider proclivity to lovelessness. Avoiding hatred is not enough.

Love is God's highest value and dominant characteristic – Jesus's summary of the law says it all. He aspires to draw all people into union with himself. It is where he is heading, relentlessly. His power is vested in the leaven of the Kingdom of God.

Love's diminution or its absence, lovelessness, must therefore be what God loathes above all. Lovelessness seems the only word for that spectrum of attitudes ranging from unintended neglect – through betrayal to violent murder. Its inherent power is the leaven of Herod, the scribes and Pharisees. It presses directly away from love. It supplants love by demeaning, manipulating and harming others. It surfaces in the neglect of the young, vulnerable and needy; in the failure to model love, especially in front of the young; in the treating of people as objects, in coercion, bullying and violence; in the destruction of others' reputations, in the use of fear and menace. These all demolish well-being – or worse. The cultures' characteristics and consequences, as indicated in the above table, are in utter contrast. We need to choose our lifestyle agenda from the top half, alone. Each leaven power opposes the other. These cosmic powers of God and of evil, in total opposition, are at the heart of our world's story and of everyday life.

Paul stressed this opposition,

'These two forces are constantly fighting each other, so you are not free to carry out your good intentions.'[64]

Each power moves to dominate culture. Each culture establishes 'norms' – then each 'norm' affects individuals' understandings, conduct and relationships. Unseen, they then press us hard to want to appear 'normal'. There are few pressures as strong as the desire to appear 'normal' within family, work-place and community, inevitably culture at work, for good or ill. The norms' influence extends by penetrating institutions, shaping structures, systems and habits of working. Aided by such realities, their power regenerates and spreads, for good or ill. They deserve careful attention.

Jesus illustrated in many ways the powers' mutual opposition, and love's greater force. A vivid example was his three-fold healing of a man who was demon-possessed, blind and unable to speak – and his following explanation found in Matthew 12.22-37.

Love always draws in the direction of coherence and fullness of life. Lovelessness presses towards fragmentation and incoherence – and ultimately, death. Seldom have these dark features been more visible than in the conflict between the totalitarian powers of Nazism and Stalinism. Any residual constraints of law or conscience were swept aside in the battles that raged in 1942 and 1943. Hitler had developed a Hunger Plan to kill 30 million Soviet citizens to cure the problem of overpopulation in 'the occupied territories.' Of three million Red Army prisoners captured by October 1941, thousands died on forced marches. In one year, more than 2 million died from starvation, disease and exposure.[65]

The pandemic of lovelessness

The lovelessness pandemic presses for a world where love – invariably of God[66] – fades to illegibility, its presence removed and memory wiped.

Its hiddenness deceives us easily. For although love's absence might not be hatred, it's not nothing and it's not neutral. A lack of intention towards lovelessness neither excuses nor prevents it. The great mass of human distress and disorder, physical, mental, relational or spiritual, stems from love's absence. Lovelessness has momentum. It regenerates laterally across communities and vertically through generations and inherited culture. Most harmfully, the absence of love's example shuts down the range of what the loveless may imagine or glimpse; it diminishes understanding of its significance to wellbeing, and of hope itself. Angela Tilby has observed:

'One of the spiritual tragedies of our time is the loss of personal relationship in daily life that has come through our increasingly automated world. We are in danger of becoming spiritually autistic, isolated and empty, aware of our own needs and incapable of recognising the reality of other people. Christ shows us that our neediness cannot be met by grasping at what we imagine will satisfy us. Ultimately, we need to recognise our emptiness and turn away from ourselves to the love that already embraces us.'[67]

If love is central to God's nature and purposes, then relationships are everything. Nothing is more important in the world, in a nation, in a business or industry, in a community, in the Church, in a family, or in an individual life. Love matters to God more than anything.

Yet Scripture suggests love is a means, not an end – an essential, wholly beneficial means directed towards a wholly beneficial end. 'God so loved the world *that* …..' was John's profound understanding.[68] God's desired end for the whole of creation is redemption through Christ – relationship gained – God-intended, coherent relationship.

Jesus did not divide the world he loved into secular and spiritual. The Church must follow suit. A hunger for real relationship that works is surely the deepest hunger of billions, even though they might neither recognise nor so describe it. For lovelessness afflicts us all, and all of creation. It deprives everyone, in differing degrees, of the ingredient that nourishes life in God's way; prompting us to short-change others of this vital commodity. It is the seat of all human need.

Even worse, lovelessness is the breeding ground for sin and social need, amplifying and energising all that is destructive. Then in turn, sin and social need collude to reproduce and promote lovelessness. It infects us unnoticed, without our consent. Its only antidote is love – and lovelessness is God's entry point for addressing our human condition.

Lovelessness can enter communities, organisations and institutions like rampant Japanese knotweed. Large institutions, hitherto person-centred and of good repute, can come to lose the custom of welcome and attentiveness; supplanted by a drivenness, or carelessness, indifference to individuals' well-being. Lovelessness once kept at arm's length is now in control. De-motivation is the evil fruit.

Thus both lovelessness and love have an inherent momentum, a power. Each is receivable and each conveyable: a childhood disfigured by lovelessness equips the young adult to pass on the same, or worse, except love intervenes in some way. Nevertheless, if love surrounds that childhood, the young adult has a reservoir of experience to enhance relationships with those they meet. This understanding of positive or negative flow, passing in varying degrees into the life of another, whether family or a wider community, colours this book's argument.

When Samuel Crossman wrote his hymn '*My song is love unknown*,'[69] he clearly used the term *loveless* poetically rather more than empirically. Everyone must have ingested at least a 'milligram' of love at some stage from someone. Each of us will have been short-changed in love, and have short-changed others. Yet even severe love- deprivation does not extinguish the capacity for love. Love-deficit conveys part of my desired meaning but not all, so I use 'lovelessness' to describe a general condition; as one might equally use such expressions as 'poverty', 'poor public health', dispirited communities' or 'moral bankruptcy'. Lovelessness, like love, has power. Love draws us towards the one who is love, and lovelessness drives away. Love frees a person, releasing a power to love others and become a whole, creative person. Lovelessness diminishes and imprisons, damaging a person's ability to form relationships. It releases a power to damage others.

George Orwell described the pathway of lovelessness 60 years ago in his novel '1984.' O'Brien spoke thus to Winston:

'Progress in our world will be progress towards more pain ....
Already we are breaking down the habits of thought which have
survived from before the Revolution. We have cut the links between
child and parent, and between man and man, and between man
and woman. No one dares trust a wife or child or friend any longer.
But in the future there will be no wives and no friends.'[70]

Lovelessness is insidious. It worms its way into the bloodstream of
individuals and organisations. Ceaucescu's policy was to increase the
Romanian population, which happened. The endemic poverty meant
poor families could no longer cope with the demands of parenting, so
he provided State orphanages. Ceaucescu might not have intended the
ensuing cruelty; it may well have stemmed from inadequate systems,
training and finance, and the lack of oversight and accountability.
The child abuse was then unhindered by any governmental culture or
system of accountability for human welfare. They placed the children
out of sight, where they remained. Romanian communist leaven
contained few strains of compassion.

The analyst Charles Murray saw bleak social consequences –
of neglect in relationship – in four primary institutions: family,
community, vocation and faith. Within these is found the 'stuff of
life: the elemental events surrounding birth, death, raising children,
fulfilling one's personal potential, dealing with adversity, and intimate
relations'. He goes on,

'Think of it this way: families are not vital because the tasks of
raising children and being a spouse are fun, but because the family
has responsibility for doing important things that won't get done
unless the family does them. Communities are not vital because
it is fun to respond to our neighbours' needs, but because the
community has the responsibility for doing important things that
won't get done unless the community does them.'

Referring to social need he had seen in the US, he continued,

'We have seen increasing numbers of children raised in unimaginably
awful circumstances, because of dysfunctional families and the
collapse of neighbourhoods.'[71]

Invidiously, the absence of example and experience diminishes the victim's imagining: their understanding of the loss, and the possibilities of hope. Matthew Fforde, a Christian academic, observed:

'Social decay also carries within it the very dangerous propensity to eliminate elements – feelings, sensibilities and forms of behaviour – from people's experience which, when lost, no longer provides alternative ways of being and living that could serve as signposts forward by which to escape malaise and error.'[72]

A newspaper correspondent emphasised:

'the importance of parental attitudes as an inhibitor or a spur to educational advancement. In my career I came across many young people in "sink estates" who passed the 11+ but never fulfilled their potential because their parents' poverty of knowledge, and the perceived lack of importance of that knowledge, was transmitted to their children. Breaking the vicious circle of intellectual poverty is one of the great educational challenges.'[73]

The 18th century father of economic theory, Adam Smith, made a parallel observation,

'The real tragedy of the poor is the poverty of their aspirations.'

A lack of intention towards lovelessness neither excuses nor prevents it. So it is that we all, even if otherwise good people, and good organisations, even the Church, are not immune to its unseen penetration. There will always be consequences.

Lovelessness: its hidden dimension
Hospital tragedies have recently hit the headlines. Scandalously, amongst them, old people were believed to have died or been harmed by an inadequate intake of daily fluids. Doctors in one hospital had to prescribe water to address this shortfall of care. Nonetheless, it is unlikely any hatred was involved. Neglect and a lack of compassion had to be the primary causes: an absence of proper thought, oversight and accountability.

Jesus's parable of the Pharisee and Tax Collector at prayer is instructive on the hidden dimensions of lovelessness.[74] The Pharisee, who I imagine represents most of us, is living at the level of morality. It's the Tax Collector who breaks down, having grasped his failure to live at the level of relationship. He leaves the temple justified. The Pharisee had shaped his life by avoiding the gross and visible sins, extortion, evil-doing and adultery; by comparing himself selectively and superficially with others; and by public displays of piety. Jesus gave us an insight into bad leaven's ability to foster self-deceit.

It is painful to recognise that the religious culture I absorbed in my earlier years was pitched more at avoiding gross and visible sins than at searching out all possible ways of channelling love. We can thus look at ourselves – perhaps in comparison to how we see and judge others – and feel comfortable, like the Pharisee. We may not notice that moral achievement does little to fulfil Jesus's summary of the law. Love needs to flow from us like oil, entering peoples' lives and communities wherever there is absorbent attitude, and the minutest nooks and crannies of opportunity.

The hidden dimension of lovelessness is greater than we realise naturally. I never thought of it as an issue – let alone in myself – until Samuel Crossman's hymn *'My song is love unknown'* hit me between the eyes. Its unintended neglect of opportunity-after-opportunity cuts a swathe of hurt and depression. Only the Holy Spirit can switch on our 'radars'. Jesus was the most sensitive person to have walked this earth. Earthly leaven desensitises us, shaping us to look at externals, and effects. In contrast, Kingdom leaven equips us to 'look inside', to see root causes. Jesus was utterly unfazed by the most grievous *effects* of wrong-leavened life. We are offered eyes, ears and minds to see, hear and understand what Jesus would see, hear and understand. We are equipped to see behind *effects*, and offered wisdom to understand *cause*.

Every contact we have with any other person is a God-given opportunity for grace to flow. Its vehicle might be an apology, a gentle question, a compliment, a kindness or an affirmation: grace's repertoire is endless. We have to look and listen, and ponder. No encounter is complete unless we have given something to that person. This is how Jesus lived. 'He went about doing good and healing all who were oppressed by the devil, for God was with him,' as Peter testified.[75] He intends this same life for us.

Lovelessness: destructive power

The gospel stories, and our own experience, show how many needs of individuals, families and communities arise from hurt in relationships; from relational failure or perversion where better had been expected. In 2010, Raoul Moat was a killer on the run in northern England. When cornered by the police in July, before turning his gun on himself, he lamented, 'I have no dad and nobody cares about me.' The press had reported his mother recently saying she felt her son would be 'better off dead.'[76] He was 37 years old.

Lovelessness works specifically against that life 'in all its fullness' Jesus brought. Just as love is the pivotal dimension of God's character, working always towards coherence, faith and hope, so lovelessness is the point of entry for havoc: spawning chaos, distrust and despair. It closes down understandings of what might be, of those mechanisms that make for peace. It degrades personhood, relationship and community. Nowhere does Jesus contrast light and darkness more vividly than when considering love and lovelessness.

We need to see our world's desperation for real love – the God-intended version – for real relationships that deliver. The causes of relational famine are many, but the absence of wholesome example seems particularly significant; having grave consequences in individual lives and the wider social fabric.

Yet this relational deficit, this lovelessness, does not simply reside somewhere out there. We may all contribute to it by neglecting the law of love. And there is a further hazard from within our trinitarian selves, of our relationship of mind, body and spirit becoming dysfunctional. The body's urges can press the mind and spirit to go against their judgement or normal inclination. The mind can work against the body when deciding to terminate a pregnancy; the body nourishing the foetus and the mind intent on rejecting it. And when, for whatever reason, the mind or spirit despises its bodily appearance or gender, the human trinity can suffer discordance.

A woman suffering from personality disorder described how her life did not unfold in some 'big picture' of reality. She lived in millions of little pictures, millions of pieces of reality and could not tell what was going on around her like other people. It made no sense. 'In one part of the picture, I care about you but in another part of the picture I remember out of context when you said this or that, and then I can't trust you any more, or until the next moment when two picture pieces fit briefly together. This is my experience.'[77]

Such incoherence, discordance or dislocation contrasts with the wholeness Jesus offered, whether of mind, body and spirit, of marriage and family, of community and between communities. Love's power deals specifically with human distress.

The opposing powers of love and lovelessness can be seen in some forms of malnutrition. In times of war and famine we are sometimes shown disturbing pictures of severely under-nourished (marasmic) children, with extremely thin bodies and stick-like limbs. Often, their bleak, staring eyes give a clue to an associated emotional deprivation, as when the mother has died. This was seen in Albanian and Romanian orphanages after communism collapsed. Hundreds of such infants were found in the very basic conditions of State institutions. Dr Janet Goodall,[78] who gave me this insight and analogy, helped in some of these orphanages. Many in these institutions were *social* orphans, not necessarily bereft by death. Poor parents could not afford to feed them and sent them away for physical care. But on its own, this was not enough. Deprived of personal input many little children suffered delayed development whilst others died, unloved. 'Proper food matters, but relationships matter too: a child's appetite for the former may well depend on the faithfulness and warmth of the latter.'

Such tragedies illustrate a profound truth. The love of God never ceases, but to reject or separate ourselves from it causes the human spirit to languish and to die. The meaning is plain. Love's power heals, whilst lovelessness has the power of death.

Extreme cruelties confronted the Revd Pat Robson in a Romanian orphanage after the collapse of communism. They were sufficient to give most people recurrent nightmares,

'Pat gently opened one of the doors to go in, but it was like entering a cage of wild animals. The children rushed to the door and jumped on her, clawing and clinging, so that she had to unclasp their fingers and hands and back out. She found this a very hard thing to do, emotionally as well as physically. It was obvious that the children were desperate for help and love… She saw evidence that the children had really been tied to their cots – apparently because there were only three women to look after more than one hundred

59

and sixty children and otherwise they could not have coped... She saw demonstrations of these habits [of children rocking backwards and forwards and regurgitating] at Remeti, where it happened quite frequently. Also, although the children were more free here, many were sitting up in their cots still unable to walk or even stand because they had never learnt how to do so. Many were scratching their faces and making animal noises... When she first met Dinu... he was only tiny, but he was twelve years old and had enough strength to hold the blanket tightly down over his head. *He could neither walk nor talk*; the only sounds he could make were those of the rats with whom he had shared the cellar.'[79]

There is more here than the horror of marasmus. We see how an absence of human presence denies the essential example of how-to-live. Whilst many influences may help a child learn to walk and talk, example is essential. Little Dinu was abandoned to follow the example of rats. Example is one of God's great tools in his transmission of love.

Universal truth
Jesus's impulse of love, as demonstrated by these orphanage accounts, illustrates a universal truth. For those entrusted with care for nations, lesser communities, families, individuals, God's animals and plants, and God's air, oceans and soil: *treat that which you oversee well, and it will flourish.* Our Western 'culture' strangely ignores it. Those whose highest aim is success, wealth or achievement of some target, give bare attention to such ideas. The former African slave Olaudah Equiano wrote, with the wisdom of experience and Christian faith, back in the 18th century,

'By changing your conduct, and treating your slaves as men, every cause of fear would be banished. They would be faithful, honest, intelligent, and vigorous; and peace, prosperity, and happiness would attend you.'[80]

The diagnosis of our world's condition is bleak. Unconstrained lovelessness leads to death.

How did Jesus see people?

What did Jesus apparently register when gazing on the crowds? Our church culture might expect his focus to have been on their sinfulness, hence need of repentance; or maybe on their sickness and social needs, requiring intervention.

In surprising contrast, the gospels give us several insights into what Jesus saw. His diagnosis was different.[81] He saw the people as harassed and helpless, like sheep without a shepherd. They could not recognize the things that made for peace. Whilst signs of the kingdom were in evidence – they had seen God's power – they were unwilling or unable to recognize them, and lacked faith. Some were ashamed of him and his words, and unwilling for protection within their anti-God, violent, adulterous and sinful culture. Wonderfully, he saw they were ready for harvesting.[82]

These glimpses may be summarised further as their being out of God-intended relationship. Lovelessness – in varying degree – made them lost and alone, spiritually blind, unmotivated and fearful, and ashamed. Yet these were people ripe for transformation to being fully human as God intended; by harvesting. This no-blame gaze of the master physician saw beyond the presenting symptoms and made a true diagnosis. These symptoms describe people made for wholesome relationship with God and each other. Unaware of their love-lack and unaware that God's love means relationship, they were unaware that God could bring both protection and direction into the loneliness of life's raw circumstances.

Those who are lost need finding. We need, as church, to be clear about a self-evident, non-judgmental truth: there is no middle ground. We cannot be slightly lost, or slightly found. No-one misunderstands this with regard to car-keys or straying dogs, or more seriously with abducted children. Yet the Church is always tempted to back away from black-and-white spiritual realities in a way that Jesus did not.

Such 'lostness' was thus, for Jesus, the inevitable outcome of love's absence; of lovelessness. This was not new. The Old Testament repeatedly describes how this condition touched God's heart; the Jonah story being but one example. Here God said,

'Should I not be concerned about Nineveh, that great city, in which there are more than a hundred and twenty thousand persons who do not know their right hand from their left, and also many animals?'[83]

People did not know intuitively how to live: with themselves, each other, the created order, or the living God. Jesus's love was the full solution. He was and is the ultimate exemplar.

Here, as elsewhere, the Gospels show us things our curiously selective eyes are prone to miss. Jesus saw beneath the surface and described the various manifestations of relational famine. He saw lives drifting inexorably towards waste, missing God's invitation to fullness of life. He saw their need to surmount the ravages of their sinful and adulterous culture. Nowhere did Jesus's disclose his perspective more vividly than at the cross. 'Father, forgive them, they know not what they do,'[84] was neither simplistic nor glib. He saw his persecutors as lost, without any moral compass in their understandings. They were enslaved by a corrupt culture they did not understand and which, unchecked, always pressed in the direction of death.

Lovelessness drains the human spirit of life. It promotes that weariness the suffering servant came to address: 'The Lord GOD has given me the tongue of a teacher, that I may know how to sustain the weary with a word.'[85]

If neither Church nor society acknowledges *the huge dimensions of lovelessness*, we can hardly challenge its awful progress. We will thence underestimate the need for robust relationships. Space and opportunity for wholesome example will inevitably be crowded out. In focusing upon lovelessness, matters of sin and personal accountability are not unimportant; yet God alone can weigh between victimhood and culpability in each person.

How, then, are we to move? Lovelessness is a human condition: it is endemic. If hunger is a community condition, aid agencies provide food. The condition is what has to be treated in the first instance. The causes of that hunger might stem from climate and weather, from chaotic or corrupt government, from war, inadequate soil and water, poor farming techniques, inherited poverty and so on. Such things equally need addressing but with different timings, entry points and means. In God's economy, love is his exceptional and precise instrument for addressing the lovelessness condition *and* for subverting all its causes. The point of entry for tackling those causes starts to emerge: it is through relationships that we learn about life itself and how to live.

The example and planting of love is God's way of defeating – then reversing – the corrosion of lovelessness. It's the only way.

The power of love

It is not possible to separate the pervasive power of God's love from the Holy Spirit's power: it is one power, of the one who is Love. We may track through the New Testament narratives and note how, whenever the Spirit moved to do God's purposes – through Jesus or the apostles – we see the focused application of God's love.

This power has several important characteristics. Since this world's powers appear stronger than love's 'soft' power, we need to be equipped with answers. God's love, like its opposite, works through culture and individuals with the 'fungal' energy of leaven. In his classic book *Mere Christianity*, CS Lewis describes it as a *good infection*,

'... the statement "God is love" ... is perhaps the most important difference between Christianity and all other religions: that in Christianity God is not a static thing – not even a person – but a dynamic, pulsating activity, a life, almost a kind of drama. Almost, if you will not think me irreverent, a kind of dance...

'... The whole dance, or drama, or pattern of this three-Personal life is played out in each one of us: or (putting it the other way round) each one of us has got to enter that pattern, take his place in that dance. There is no other way to the happiness for which we were made. Good things as well as bad, you know, are caught by a kind of infection...

'... [Christ] came to this world and became a man in order to spread to other (people) the kind of life He has – by what I call "good infection". Every Christian is to become a little Christ. The whole purpose of becoming a Christian is simply nothing else.[86]

Tom Wright uses the term 'infect' powerfully in his commentary of 1 Corinthians:

'As with Jesus' healings, in which he touched lepers and other unclean people and, instead of being infected with their diseases, infected them instead with God's new life, so Paul believed that holiness could be more powerful than uncleanness.'[87]

Whilst the purpose of lovelessness is to divide and destroy, love's *purpose* is always to draw into relationship; into a place where love's power will bring increasing benefit. Lovelessness has an abhorrent outcome, so will always adopt forms of disguise.

Nelson Mandela's death brought the power of love to the world's attention, yet again. 'He knew the importance of reconciliation, and had harnessed the power of forgiveness,' wrote one commentator. He became an instrument of love, overcoming apartheid's demons and saving his nation from a cauldron of bloodshed.

Love's glory is its openness and generosity. Being non-judgmental, undeserved, unearned, unconditional and non-manipulative, it has a unique appeal. It can penetrate the defences of the loveless; but it has to be on offer. Love reaches into the territory of lovelessness and pulls people out.

The complementarity of coherence

Love's great ally is coherence: the pieces that belong together fitting together. Indeed, it is love's conjoined twin.

In his great Christological summary, Paul wrote that in Christ 'all things hold together'. Eugene Petersen's paraphrase, The Message, puts Colossians 1.15-20 like this:

'And when it comes to the church, he organizes and holds it together, like a head does a body.

He was supreme in the beginning and – leading the resurrection parade – he is supreme in the end. From beginning to end he's there, towering far above everything, everyone. So spacious is he, so roomy, that everything of God finds its proper place in him without crowding. Not only that, but all the broken and dislocated pieces of the universe – people and things, animals and atoms – get properly fixed and fit together in vibrant harmonies, all because of his death, his blood that poured down from the Cross.'[88]

In describing Jesus's pre-eminence, Paul emphasises his agency in reconciliation – the drawing all things towards himself to be held together – through the blood of his cross. This agency vested in a person carries with it authority and power to attract – to pull – the whole of creation into relationship where everything fits together for pre-ordained purpose. Logically consistent, everything becomes united and holds together as parts of one mass.

Christ's redemptive power overwhelms the powers of fragmentation, and his love draws towards coherence in Christ, where things hold together. It is an ongoing activity: through Christ, God is reconciling to himself all things … and making peace. His ministry of coherence is emphasised.

The synonyms of *coherent* and its close cousin, *integrity,* taken together release a heady fragrance:

Coherent: lucid, understandable, congruous, connected, consistent

Integrity: goodness, incorruptibility, veracity, completeness, cohesion.[89]

Coherence speaks of the God we worship – the God who is love. It contrasts with the acrid stench of lovelessness: confusion, incomprehension, incongruity and disconnection, and of evil, corruption, deceit, fragmentation and incoherence.

Paul wrote that the fragrance that comes from knowing Christ spreads *through us* in every place. 'For we are the aroma of Christ to God among those who are being saved and among those who are perishing.' Paul then raises the bar for true Christian living: 'For we are not peddlers of God's word like so many; but in Christ we speak as persons of sincerity, as persons sent from God and standing in his presence.'[90] The fragrance is not to be discerned in our words so much as in our underlying integrity, our given authority and in the power of Christ's irradiation. His Spirit lives in us, whose first fruit is love. So, just as an expensive perfume lingers in the air, his love should so pervade our lives that our presence reminds others of him. Thus, are the spores of Egypt's culture – in the air we breathe – supplanted by holy spores of Kingdom leaven, of love.

The gospel of love-coherence needs to reach deeply, in invitation to join in God's coherence, aligning ourselves without condition to his coherent purposes.

The divine example of coherence

The Trinity is our primary example of coherence; rooted in love, in God's person. We may only understand it in a faint, incomplete way. Yet this is enough, for scripture testifies to the unity, coherence and interdependence of the Godhead; and to the outflow of wisdom, love and activity that continues the work of creating. Wm Paul Young's book, *The Shack*, describes the interaction of the persons of the Godhead with insight and delightful imagery. At one point Papa (the Father) is conversing with Mack, who as the bereaved father of a murdered child questions God's love:

> 'What's important is this: If I were simply One God and One Person, then you would find yourself in this Creation without something wonderful, without something essential even. And I would be utterly other than I am.'

> 'And we would be without …?' Mack didn't even know how to finish the question.

> 'Love and relationship. All love and relationship is possible for you *only* because it exists within Me, within God myself. Love is *not* the limitation; love is the flying. I *am* love.'[91]

Coherence and love are predominant in the Trinity's inter-relatedness, linked inextricably in Christ. From these, all God's other characteristics derive:

- wisdom, for wisdom expounds the reality of divine love-coherence
- truth, because love is not love except it trades in truth
- mercy, for this is love to the undeserving
- service, for love desires to serve the other
- justice, since love-coherence demands fair treatment
- patience, since this is love giving time to the other
- forgiveness, for love bears no grudge and desires restoration
- faithfulness, for love knows no end, and

- effective communication, for love-coherence demands openness and clarity.

The wonder of coherence in creation

God's creation, down to its sub-atomic detail – and Paul's adoption of the body analogy – point to the essentiality of system. The physical body only works because its atoms and molecules interact in unity, in specific ways within a system. Equally, Christ's Body can only work properly, as Christ intends, if its members interact in unity within a proper system. Body members that do not follow this pattern reflect either a deficient system or a disorder within themselves. In either case, healing is essential. System is of first order importance in Christ's body.

God does not intend us for isolated service; rather for unity within his Body, with service the outcome. This way we pursue his coherent purposes by coherent means. Without the ministry of coherence, *agape*-love barely stands. This ministry of coherence is too often undervalued. It will receive further emphasis in what follows.

The former Chief Rabbi Lord Sacks offered an interesting insight on coherence in an article about Darwin, '*Religion teaches us that we are part of the whole*':

'Without fully realising what he had done, Darwin was pointing us to the central drama of civilization. Biological evolution favours individuals, but cultural evolution favours groups. So, as Judaism and Christianity both knew, there is a war within each of us as to which will prevail: self-regard or concern for others, egoism or altruism. Selfishness is advantageous to individuals, but disastrous to groups, and it is only as members of a group that we can survive at all. As Darwin himself put it, "Selfish and contentious people will not cohere, and *without coherence nothing can be effected.*"'[92]

Since we were created in God's image, love and coherence must constitute a large part of what the human heart craves. Such cravings – or appetites for ultimate wholeness – may be undeveloped or suppressed, yet assuredly capable of springing to life on encountering the reality of God's love. They can impel people to the Son. They are palpable love; warmth that may be felt, then appropriated, because it signifies integrity and coherence. Love coming from integrity is like an open doorway to a warm spring garden, seen from a cold dark room. Through this door can be smelt, felt and glimpsed ultimate reality and ultimate wholeness; Son-shine pouring on the dark, cold spirit.

There are only two great powers in the world: the driving power of lovelessness heading towards fragmentation, isolation, chaos ... and death; and the drawing power of love, heading towards wholeness, harmony and coherence ... fullness of life. Each utterly opposes the other. As Graham Tomlin has written:

'Ultimately evil is overcome not by violence but by love – in fact that is the only force in the universe strong enough to defeat evil – it was true then (at the cross) and it is true now.'[93]

* * * * * *

Love is the strongest weapon
   known to mankind.
Other weapons blow people up.
Only Love puts them back together again.............

If you're beginning to understand
   then welcome to the real world.[94]

Dominant Leaven-Strains

4

Worrying viruses such as bird flu sometimes emerge in the animal kingdom, capable of mutating into forms that affect humans. Giving medical care to those infected is not enough, high priority is also given to preventive measures. In the parallel world of cultural influence, we too readily focus on outcomes more than causes and appetites; on human distress more than culture's unaccountable power.

So we now explore some dominant strains of worldly culture transmitted by spores that attach, then penetrate, then distort individual and corporate life with hidden power. We reflect later on the Church's, the Body's susceptibility to such uninvited influence.

FEEDERS OF LOVELESSNESS

The cultures surrounding our lives do not form rationally. A wide range of influences shapes them over time. They emerge, then metamorphose without human oversight. Rational control is impossible. They influence the instincts and responses of communities, and entire populations, in varying degrees. These readily absorb the 'spores in the air', forming leaven. The leaven of Herod, the scribes and Pharisees, powered by lovelessness, is alive and well in the 21st century, having morphed its way through societies afflicted by tyranny, materialism and secularism.

We live unavoidably with unchosen cultural powers trying to suborn our chosen loyalties. It is a battleground. 'Brush fires' may break out anywhere, in our Church as well as our wider society. In our fears, we scurry around to tackle them as if they constituted the whole, or even our main business. Yet these are but manifestations or consequences of underlying lovelessness; its deadly leaven fermenting within secular society and the Church whenever it gets the chance.

Walter Wink writes of the materialist world-view, with no heaven, no spiritual world, no God, no soul: nothing but what can be known through the five senses and reason. This view has penetrated deeply even into many religious persons, causing them to ignore the *spiritual dimensions of systems* or the spiritual resources of faith.

He goes on to argue that what people in the Bible experienced as and called 'principalities and powers' was in fact the actual spirituality at the centre of the political, economic, and cultural institutions of their day.

The Kingdom of this world – of the 'principalities and powers' – regenerates its lovelessness, often unnoticed. Four cultural strains seem to inflict particular harm. I call them the Big Four:

- a worldly use of controlling power,
- a worldly enchantment with historic customs,
- a worldly individualism, and
- a worldly dogmatism.

Superficially, there may not seem much wrong with these elements. Power has to be exercised if the world is to work; historic loyalty will carry good things forward in time; the individual always has a unique role to play, and some dogma is essential. Nonetheless, it's in the nature of worldly cultural strains to subvert something good and natural.

Common attitudes within a culture fix people's understanding and shape how life is organised. If love is dominant in that culture, then wholesome relational attitudes, and wholesome organisational structures and systems, develop. But if lovelessness dominates, societal cohesion and all types of organisational arrangement are disturbed. Dysfunctionality invariably results.

So, whilst recognising that some merit might be found in any culture, these four assailants convey lovelessness into all cultures as entry is gained. These spores infect communal life, and are commonly accepted as unexceptional and even inevitable. Leaven describes the process aptly.

It seems that each strain powered the leaven of Herod, the scribes and Pharisees; working unfailingly against community life, dividing and destroying. As with HIV, malaria and other pandemic invasive' strains, they demand to be named and faced. By facing them we may come to understand better the attitude, work and message of Jesus; whose power is the sole antidote to lovelessness.

The cultural strain of controlling power

Walter Wink uses a different metaphor to describe 'Caesar'. He warns of an over-arching network of Powers he calls,

> 'the Domination System. It is characterised by unjust economic relations, oppressive political relations, biased race relations, patriarchal gender relations, hierarchical power relations to maintain them all.'[95]

This is the strain that produces the tyrant, the bully and paedophile; and the over-ambitious. It is spawned by fear. The insecure may be especially prone to it, especially if they perceive their need for significance depends on forcing compliance on others. It is seen in those whose ambition spawns a ruthlessness, counting people's loyalty, trust and well-being as unimportant. It treats employees, subordinates and the vulnerable as objects rather than people: to be used and exploited. Nowhere were the outcomes of such destructive power more visible than at the abandonment of Auschwitz-Birkenau in 1945. At lesser destructive levels, this power manifests in a proclivity to manipulation and gossip. This strain is always corrosive of relationship and community.

Authority is essential for every community's governance; intrinsically neutral, capable of fostering good or evil. Over time, destructive power removes the understanding of how community relationships can work. The STASI's 44-year activity in former East Germany sought to excise truth and trust from its communities. It yielded a vile harvest, with long-term consequences. The right type of power is clearly fundamental to any community's wellbeing. There is a choice to be made.

Worldly power ignores the energy people get from being valued. Its lovelessness fractures communities, expecting people to function because of the pressure they feel. Bearers of authority invariably choose to adopt power – either of love or lovelessness, even if they never think in such terms. Those who subscribe to Jesus's summary of the law will incline to follow the path of love; but the insidious infiltration of lovelessness always requires vigilance.

Archbishop David Moxon has said this;

'The good use of power with justice can carry out God's will, but absolute power, without respect for God's law, will corrupt. For us personally, this can mean becoming a control freak, with the consequent damage to our relationships or work style. There must be room for humility, contemplative calm and perspective, self-examination and the wisdom that comes from consultation and good advice.'[96]

Love is person- and community-centred, motivating people to do well and flourish. The power of lovelessness can prompt a number of foci: personal ambition, accumulation of wealth, self-aggrandisement, the gaining of goals regardless of cost or level of demandingness, the building of 'empires', the erection of monuments to personal achievement, survival of an enterprise, or fear of failure or of being let-down. Such power abuses people, using them 'mechanically' as tools, being dismissive of – rather than responsive to – frailty. It discards people, is deaf or unfeeling towards them, and regards them as inferior. It fails to spot human potential – and fails to appreciate, thank, praise or offer helpful correction.

We see it today in our obsession with targets – often ill-judged – and the use of coercive fear to gain results. It engenders yes-men and women, discourages initiative, leeches trust from the work-place, discourages straight-speaking and progressively weakens relational sinews, thence corporate cohesion.

Leaders are put to the test when a crisis breaks out; typically involving conflict or misdemeanour. Whether they like it or not, their true character will here be revealed. If they subscribe to the power of love, they will use the instrument of truth to discern its precise cause, reaching just decisions over what is to be done. By contrast, if leaders subscribe to the power of lovelessness, their first concern might to lurch in a different direction; to protect reputation. This makes them careless of justice, and misunderstand the redemptive power of well-judged, just discipline. This latter trait has been disclosed chillingly, and too commonly, across many nations as patterns of systemic child abuse have been uncovered within organisations.

Michael Williams, a university senior lecturer and head of media ethics, described the power of lovelessness from his experience when head of news at the Sunday Times:

'News journalism is a complex and often chaotic cocktail of adrenalin, risk-taking, egotism and competitiveness. Most of the time it is underpinned by a genuine quest for the truth and a sense of decency, however confused it might seem. But the Murdoch news machine is fuelled by more toxic and combustible ingredients – a culture of fear, unquestioning subservience to the media tycoon's political and business interests and a willingness to push the envelope … I know exactly what the phone-hacking private detective, Glen Mulcaire, meant when he told *The Guardian* that his employers exerted "relentless pressure" and "constant demand for results."'[97]

Contaminated power appeals to the ambitious. Yet it heads towards corruption, incoherence and division. Such aspirations risk ending up with human distress and organisational havoc. They do not work.

The cultural strain of enchantment with historic customs
Tribalism, seen in political and other allegiances, may prompt longings for a return to a mythical 'golden age' – indeed, even today, a minority of Russians reportedly hanker for the rigid certainties of Stalinist communism. This cultural strain is seen in the perpetuation of the Northern Ireland marches, or in extreme form in the tenacious tradition of female genital mutilation in parts of Africa and the African diaspora. This was tellingly described in a Church Times interview:

'It's such an entrenched practice: we talked to a guy a few years ago who was making a film in West Africa called The Cutting Tradition, and he's been sensitised: he knows the implications. But at the end, off-camera, he said: "I'd still like it for my daughter."'[98]

It probably prompts most of us to gravitate socially towards 'people like me'. The insecure – especially those lacking a sense of identity – are prone to this strain. It tends to polarise, thus bruising relational and community development.

We can come to depend on our personal 'historical journey' to define who we are. Our regard for our blood-line can be too dominant, as can our educational and professional pedigree, our lifestyle or choice of neighbourhood. Then our sporting, church, and other social affiliations may equally come to govern who we think we are, and how we wish others to view and understand us. Political and other passions and affiliations seem often to be handed down within families. The strain thus tends to polarise, hindering the development of new relationships and community allegiances in a wider world.

An insidious thing about this cultural strain is that – for most of us – it seems not to matter much.

Count Helmuth von Moltke demonstrated this understanding of identity strikingly in 1945. A Christian lawyer and aristocrat caught up into the High Command of the Armed Forces in Hitler's war, he was assigned to counter-intelligence as an expert in martial law and international public law. He worked courageously and with some effectiveness to uphold Christian values. Then, towards the end of the war after a bogus trial, Hitler murdered him. He had 'testified that he stood before the court "…not as a Protestant, not as a great landowner, not as an aristocrat, not as a Prussian, not as a German…but as a Christian and nothing else".[99]

There is a further problem with this strain. If we depend on historic influences, experiences or achievements for our identity, we build a barrier against those whose identity stands on different foundations. The barrier between the Jews and Samaritans is one example, with clear harm done to the culture in which Jesus lived.

He would have none of it, telling the story of the Good Samaritan with astounding directness.[100] Then, in the village of Sychar, the woman felt it important, immediately, to relate to Jesus as a Samaritan, rehearsing why this made her different. Jesus chose not to pick up on this, showing neither preference for the Samaritan 'mountain' nor for Jerusalem. He switched the conversation to the issue of ordinary human appetites. When Jesus had touched on her unmet appetites of spiritual thirst and – with exceptional gentleness, on her unmet appetite for durable relationship – he was able to reveal his true identity: Messiah. He thus released his Father's 'living water' into an entire Samaritan community.[101] He foreshadowed his eternal role; in Paul's words he was making Jew and Gentile into one, breaking down the dividing wall, the hostility between them, and proclaiming peace to those who were far off.[102]

Sadly, all communities have some experiences of hostility, of dividing walls. I have worked with colleagues from two nations with a perverse dependency on a dividing wall of hostility that reached back into history. I heard personal loathing voiced from each side of those from the other nation; stemming from an oft-refreshed catalogue of atrocities committed by the other nation against theirs, some within their family's memory span. This was probably fed by two factors – fear of similar atrocities in the future – and as a perverse way of strengthening their sense of national identity. Fear and recognition of the 'evil' of the other nation was for them what bound their nation together, above all. Thus one can see how enmity – the fruit of lovelessness – can grip small communities and whole nations, being seen today in extreme form in places such as Sudan, Myanmar and Zimbabwe.

Dependence on historic events *for identity* – disasters and achievements, wide-scale or personal – is both false and dangerous. This seems true for both individuals and communities, through to multi-national alliances. It can become rigidly, non-negotiably, held; a fixation in aspic. Division and hostility are the likely outcomes.

The cultural strain of individualism
Angela Tilby wrote,

'The selfish individualist is curiously sterile, passing through life as though in a glass cage, never really in touch with others.'[103]

Selfish individualism is seen in people's reluctance to demonstrate *belonging*, to consult and communicate with superiors, peers and subordinates alike. It shows up in the anxieties of the ambitious to be the sole recipients of accolades; and in a reluctance, through pride, of believing inherited practice may contain wisdom deserving attention. It nurtures a culture of relational blindness; the inability to see the significance of others, in community, as essential to coherent living. It is typified by greed and raw ambition. It is seen in the luxuriant pastures of bankers' bonuses and inordinate levels of remuneration. It may come from social illiteracy or distrust of others. But whatever the cause, it delivers fragmentation and loss.

Those brought up in a dysfunctional environment, whether of family or wider community, are likely to struggle to relate well with others. They are likely to seek the bogus solution of solitude. Individualism may develop in a number of ways. An unresolved sense of personal or professional inadequacy may prompt it. Equally, an excessive pride in professional competence can push in the same direction. Individualism – as an unhealthy survival technique or an inappropriate tool of power – increasingly pulls people from healthy corporate living into the sickly narrowness of solo lifestyle.

In the narrative of the Fall, Adam's rebellion stemming from arrogance showed individualism at its worst. Indeed, the pursuit of individualism, to which we are all prone, is linked – embarrassingly and invariably – to both arrogance and rebellion.

Individualism prompts us to seek places where collegial constraints seem few. It may be fuelled further by ambition to achieve, from within a position of power. Some critics of the 1997-2010 government have highlighted the prime minister's downgrading of the Cabinet's conventional role, seeing it as harmful to the British governmental system.

In recent years, political writers including David Owen have drawn attention to the 'Hubris Syndrome'. They discern it may come from holding high office over a period; perhaps by being infected by the grandeur or the intoxicating power of office. David Owen tells that 'the phenomenon of something happening to people's mental stability when in power has been observed for centuries and the causal link between holding power and aberrant behaviour that has the whiff of mental instability about it'. He suggested a hubristic career looked like this:

'The hero wins glory and acclamation by achieving unwonted success against the odds. The experience then goes to their head: they begin to treat others, mere ordinary mortals, with contempt and disdain and they develop such confidence in their own ability that they begin to think themselves capable of anything. This excessive self-confidence leads them into misinterpreting the reality around them and into making mistakes.[104]

He goes on to assert, 'The moral is that we should beware of allowing power and success to go to our heads.'[105]

Then in his opening chapter he lists a number of observable symptoms of the syndrome, and includes:

- A predisposition to take actions which seem likely to cast them in a good light – ie. in order to enhance their image;
- A disproportionate concern with image and presentation;
- An identification of themselves with the state (referring here to government heads) to the extent that they regard the outlook and interests of the two as identical;
- Excessive confidence in their own judgment and contempt for the advice or criticism of others;
- A consequent type of incompetence in carrying out a policy, which could be called hubristic incompetence. This is where things go wrong precisely because too much self-confidence has led the leader not to bother worrying about the nuts and bolts of a policy...[106]

All leaders are susceptible to hubristic tendencies as they accustom to wielding power. Brigadier Charles Richardson, a senior member of Montgomery's staff, saw in him towards the war end, a diminishing receptiveness to counsel: he 'grew steadily more aloof and remote.'[107]

Individualism thus harms community life. It diminishes the practitioner, making them liable to increasing – and non-negotiable – folly.

The cultural strain of dogmatism
This is the twin brother of undue individualism; beguilingly leading nowhere.

Dogmatism is unreasonable. It is seen in an un-listening, non-negotiable preoccupation with a particular line of thought, maybe an unbalanced devotion to single-issues. A dogmatist is one who lives by mantras, and cannot see the significance of underlying principles or wider issues. Borrowing words of G K Chesterton, 'he is in the clean and well-lit prison of one idea; he is sharpened to one painful point. He is without healthy hesitation and healthy complexity.'[108]

Dogmatism entices, offering a power over the hearts and minds of others, offering a way forward that connects with popular prejudices. It works by evincing a semblance of truth and appropriateness. Dogmatism greatly helped the monstrous 20th century movements of Communism and Nazism gain their followings.

It contains an element of deceit. It reduces a complex, multi-shaded landscape into black-and-white. Its definitions pretend to clarity, embrace everything, and summarise what cannot be summarised. It works with coercive intent to rally people around a particular agenda, foreclosing proper analysis. It fosters a rigidity of view-point that – when coupled with a degree of arrogance – may gain momentum, then wield inappropriate power. It thrives in the worlds of politics and religion. Dogmatism may breed amongst those having a fixation with power, or with inappropriate historic or other loyalties, preferring fixed ways of doing everything, and amongst individualists who cannot learn from what others are saying. Like individualism, it heads towards solitude, where lovelessness reigns.

Dogmatism grows in a culture where goals are set that reject relational values and the human factor. They bear terrible fruit. Hitler's decision to invade the USSR in 1941 provides an example. The historian Ian Kershaw wrote that he had 'a small number of basic, unchanging ideas that provided his inner driving force'. The historian Andrew Roberts judges that,

'Hitler's self-reinforcing world view was based on the need for Germany to dominate Europe, win *Lebensraum* [living space] for herself and come to a final reckoning with the Jews. These views never altered or moderated, and stayed central to his thinking from the 1920s to his death two decades later. All three could be achieved by an invasion of Russia, and none could be achieved without one.'[109]

I suppose dogmatism has some appeal for most us, providing simple and clear statements of what we believe to be true and important. Yet there are other hazards apart from its proclivity to falsehood. As we shall consider later, a serious problem with dogmatism is its tendency to elevate truth above love, and knowledge above understanding. Dogmatism offers the subscriber a false sense of significance, of their identity, intellect or judgment. It acts intrinsically as an instrument of division and harm.

THE PRIMARY TARGET OF THE FOUR LEAVEN-STRAINS

A nation's, group's or individual's identity are all targeted by these strains. The temptations they offer are as fraudulent today as they were in Jesus's time. He was offered in the wilderness the possibilities of a false identity; from false public acclaim, false power and false status.

Each of his temptations was to covet contaminated power. Each was to adopt individualism. They came from a dogmatic use of scripture.

Fungal mutation and outcome
These cultural strains all impact upon leadership, pastoral and administrative practice. They penetrate cultures, mutating with other strains to deliver discord, incoherence and fragmentation. A particular and severe instance of such mutation is found in Max Hastings' magisterial account of the last year of WWII in Germany, *Armageddon*. War discloses the powers of evil and their consequences in grim detail. Some scrutiny is therefore valuable – such matters are neither small nor inconsequential.

By October 1944 it was becoming obvious that Hitler's war was going to be lost. The combination of the Allies' stricture that unconditional surrender was the only option, and Hitler's demented decision to fight to the bitter end – regardless of consequence – set the scene for the carnage of the last months of the war. Hastings assesses that this latter policy resulted in the gratuitous deaths of 'some five million Germans, as well as those of millions more of their enemies and captives.' (As an aside, Stalin sacrificed one million of his own soldiers in the last month of the war alone, in his determination to occupy Berlin ahead of his allies).

Interestingly, Hastings apportioned blame equally upon Hitler's 'men of honour' – his senior generals, not in the main Nazi party members, and several having exceptional military skills. He epitomises Field Marshal von Rundstedt as the typical 'aloof, unemotional, aristocratic Prussian General Staff officer.' Hitler himself operated with extreme individualism, reaching the position where he heeded advice from no-one.

Chillingly, all four strains seem to have affected these 'men of honour', entrapping their souls. They could find no exit. However noble their original stance may once have seemed, they certainly used *contaminated power* for evil ends as the 'noose' tightened around their necks. Some of the most eminent non-Nazi generals were responsible for mass killings, notably on the eastern front. Some participated in the so-called Court of Honour that despatched to the gallows many involved in the July bomb plot.

These men's *enchantment with historic ways* is seen in their 'semi-detached' concept of honour: the un-breakability of an oath, regardless of implications. Hitler had entrapped them in the late 1930's with a requirement to take an oath of personal obedience to himself. It seems their pride in the Prussian military code and traditions closed their mind to some of the greater realities of life. Tyranny's straitjacket reduced the scope for *individualism* with these 'men of honour', for good or ill. Hitler's unbending individualism allowed little discretion to his commanders.

The effects of *dogmatism* were also evident in the dough of rampant lovelessness. These professional, non-Nazi, 'men of honour' had been surrounded with the dogma of Nazi thinking and propaganda over many years. They failed to give rational scrutiny to the dogma and its increasing consequences to individuals, the nation and the conduct of the war before it was too late. They seem to have deceived themselves into believing that *not holding* the dogma themselves was sufficient in ethical and practical terms, and as military men their role was to concentrate solely on narrow military tasks. Doing *nothing* rather than *something* is a major way in which the lovelessness pandemic infiltrates, confuses, fragments and multiplies. Changing the metaphor, by 1944, the 'cancer' was inoperable through human intervention.

Hastings writes,

'Even if Hitler's decisions were demented and his refusal to sanction retreats condemned hundreds of thousands of men to die, what alternative strategy could be deemed rational, except surrender?'

In this dilemma, the senior generals:

'knew that any course of action could only delay the inevitable. It is hardly surprising that a substantial number of senior officers in the final months suffered nervous collapses or shot themselves. The strain of presiding over carnage which could not save Germany, but which merely deferred the day of reckoning for the Nazi leadership, proved unbearable for many officers.'

Hastings assesses that Hitler's generals, whether SS officers or old Prussian aristocrats, allowed themselves to lapse into fulfilling their duties in a moral vacuum. They abandoned coherent thought about the future and merely performed the immediate military functions that were so familiar to them. Germany's generals in the last months of the war indeed behaved as automatons, amid the whims and obsessions of their monstrous master. Most turned against Hitler not because they acknowledged he was evil, but because they realised he was losing the war.

'Most of the courageous Germans who had dared to oppose Hitler were now dead or in cells awaiting execution, where their grace and dignity did more to redeem the German people in the eyes of posterity than anything achieved by the Wehrmacht on the battlefield.[110]

We can see from this example the scale, depravity and horror of leaven-ingestion whose progress is unchecked. We can see these mutating strands – power-abuse, historic dependencies, individualism and dogma – feeding and reinforcing each other to produce division, fragmentation, chaos and death on an unprecedented scale.

Leaven-ingestion is what happens to individuals. We, and all people, are personally vulnerable to the appeal of these strands. It is spurious, lying in their offering to boost our sense of identity; our self-worth. When the 72 disciples returned from their mission recorded in Luke 10.1-24, they were exulted by the divine power they had mediated and seen. It seems that Jesus then moved swiftly: warning them not to rejoice in this, but rather in their names being written in heaven. Their identity was rooted in Jesus, and his testimony in heavenly places. To Jesus fell the joy of exultation over them! (vs21)

My next three chapters continue with this this theme of leaven's invasive power; its threat to the Church's life through the inherent vulnerability of every person, from the greatest to the least. We shall also explore some implications of the 'principalities and powers'.

The fruit of these big four strains is lovelessness: overlooked, un-named, the great scourge of our world. Its approach is devious. It comes in 'under the radar'. Evil chooses the indirect approach, knowing it will repel if too obvious. It infects the cultures that shape our lives thence infecting us individually. It targets the Church as we engage with our world. We the Church, with our inherited culture and forms, need to take lovelessness very seriously. Only then can we address its vast Sahara drifting upon the world outside.

I know each of the Big Four has infected my own life at different points and different times. I imagine others can make a similar admission. We are affected by the 'air we breathe'; by inherited culture. Both love and lovelessness are born of appetite. We shall consider shortly some of the dynamics of love and relationship, and their opposites, and explore issues of appetite and momentum. But first, we look afresh at how Jesus the Source of love unknown saw and understood such things.

Part 2: Church Vulnerabilities

We have identified four dominant leaven-strains in the world and its power systems. Such culture enfolds us in varying measure. It's in the air we breathe. Without our consent it offers fraudulent norms for community life. This culture strenuously discourages challenge – challenge being abnormal. More seriously it has leached, over decades and centuries, into the Church's structures, systems and customs – without consent.

Whilst each strain is capable of supersession by the more powerful strains of Kingdom culture, they must first be recognised and named. The wrong leaven is counter-life and counter-Kingdom.

Caesar: the leaven-strain of worldly controlling power

5

'*Culture is what happens when no one is looking*'.

Bob Diamond

So spoke the former chief executive of Barclays Bank when addressing the Parliamentary Committee on Banking Standards.[111]

'What a profound statement', blogged American industrialist Patrick Phillips about this aphorism. 'There is simply no arguing this point. Often organizations will introduce tools and practices to change their workforce to be more "efficient", but this does very little to actually treat the cause or even the symptoms for that matter.'[112]

Cultural influence in the Church

Jesus declaimed against bad culture as part of his Kingdom proclamation and demonstration. In today's Church we tend to denounce a great deal – often with a focus differing from Jesus's, as we shall explore later – but seem unreflective of any bad culture attaching to our own Body lifestyle. In the words of Hugh Rayment-Pickard:

'We have only to leaf through a few parish magazines and diocesan newspapers to realise that churches are not properly focused on the colossal and bold ideas in Jesus's teaching. Increasingly, churches focus their energies on trying to make people religious rather than trying to transform society into the shape of the Kingdom.

'Religious activity is regarded as an achievement in its own right. Increases in Sunday attendance and additional acts of worship are taken to be advances in God's Kingdom, while broken people and broken communities are all around us.'[113]

People looking for marriage guidance do not approach someone whose marital life is in disarray. Why should people bother about the Church unless it shows coherence and love. Outsiders notice such things. They affect whether they will even be open to *considering* faith-in-Christ, let alone move towards any Christian commitment.

Incoherence, imbalance and dysfunctionality are the fruits of institutional lovelessness. They hinder credibility and trust.

Such characteristics do not develop suddenly. They emerge gradually, unnoticed and over long periods. Like unseen spores, they affect the host's health and performance. Leaven is an appropriate term, being non-pejorative. Its spores come from the air outside. They represent an uninvited assault by a power other than Christ's.

So now we must ask: who is *looking* at culture's impact on today's Church? Cultural spores do not attach to secular bodies alone. For too long the Church of England has introduced tools and practices to change the institution to be more 'efficient', but this has done very little to actually treat the cause or even the symptoms for that matter.

'Watch out', said Jesus, 'beware of the leaven of the Pharisees and Saducees' (Mt 16.6). He was warning against the cultural strands of Old Temple and respectable Godless pragmatism, transmitted through deceptive teaching (vs 12); then in the Luke 12.1 account, he saw it rooted in hypocrisy. Paul exhorted the Roman church, 'Don't copy the behaviour and customs of this world, but let God transform you into a new person by changing the way you think'[114] – then similarly the Colossian church:

'See to it that no one takes you captive through philosophy and empty deceit, according to human tradition, according to the elemental spirits of the universe, and not according to Christ.'[115]

Is lovelessness – that energised the dark leaven of Herod, the Saducees and Pharisees – to be found within any of our own corporate attitudes and activities, however unconscious and unintended?

Echoing Patrick Phillips' thinking above, Walter Wink is clear we have to address not only the outer forms of our customs, organisation and systems, but their inner spirit as well.[116] It means we *have* to deal with the wrong leaven. It has to be identified with some precision before it can be destroyed. Every year the Jews – in their Passover rituals – faithfully affirm their on-going rejection of 'Egypt'. Having been delivered from its physical bondage, they continue to reject and destroy, ritually, any residual bondage inherent in its contaminating leaven.

One deadly fruit of the principalities and powers that stand behind secular rule is nationalism. Seductive to the insecure, it offers a skewed sense of identity whilst drawing people into an unquestioning allegiance to the State. A parallel phenomenon may occur in the Church. We can have an unquestioning, denominational allegiance because of our skewed sense of identity; unthinkingly giving our denomination a trust that rightly belongs to God. We become 'denomi-*nationalists*' rather than Kingdom patriots. Such mis-allegiance may explain our affection for things as they are, and our unwillingness to review our inherited culture. Whilst we are to love the Church, that love can pervert to idolatry. In examining our own Church body, we must look out for any fraudulent, inherited loyalties. The Church needs critical friends.

So how and where has worldly leaven corrupted the Church's dough without permission, *when no one was looking*? Voices from within the Church alert us to the issues we face. Here and in the following two chapters we consider the possible impact of the Big Four cultural strains.

Caesar's Mindset, Dominating Power

In his remarkable one-line response to a verbal ambush, Jesus took a coin and contrasted God and Caesar. It has fastened in the Church's understanding. We hold the implication that they represent contrasting entities: opposing powers. As representative secular 'Lord' for all-time, Caesar has no intrinsic moral reference point. Caesar does what Caesar wills; sometimes benign but sometimes not. By his chosen independence in aim and attitude, he is always prone to act against God's purpose. Paradoxically, God sees him as his agent, whether Caesar recognises it or not. Jesus is indeed King of Kings and Lord of Lords.

The God-and-Caesar question is not confined to what we are to render to whom. We need, with equal clear-sightedness, to question what we receive from whom. For there are signs that, from its early years, the Church has lost some confidence in its own particularity. We have tended to admire some of Caesar's ways – drawing heavily upon his models of governance – not noticing how his spores attach to leadership and organisational methods. This is the central nervous system of Christ's body. Such cultural ingress causes relational damage, imperceptibly nudging it towards incoherence.

Insidiously Caesar inclines to redemptive language; sometimes ascribing unusual wisdom to the leader. An historic inscription to Caesar Augustus found in Myra, Lycia, declared,

'Divine Augustus Caesar, son of god, imperator of land and sea, the benefactor and saviour of the whole world, has brought you peace.'[117]

Redemptive allusions veneer British general election campaigns today when politicians imply an ability to change society for the better. The power to effect beneficial human change rests, not with human leadership – not even within the Church – but with God.

Caesar works from a humanly contrived position of authority, from intrinsic insecurity. Within his Domination System, people *have* to comply. With Jesus as King, people will long to please him. Caesar feeds on fear more than anything else.[118] He fears loss of position or control. Such fears stimulate power abuse. They subvert the reasonable use of ordered systems and of law. Turning them into weapons of control, Caesar uses them to force compliance and give an appearance of stability. His methods are inherently exploitive, and light on relational values. Their outcome, unless moderated, will be the cowing and de-motivation of people they serve; their coercion into compliance. There is no respect for the person, no affirmation; just insistent demand as the brick-makers experienced in Egypt. Unless checked, communities degrade and fragment. It is in utter contrast to the will and way of Christ.

Caesar tends to assume people are not to be trusted, and of course some are not to be. He thence builds his kingdom upon the mechanics of authority, objectives, targets, and coercive power. Indeed, many of our Church governance systems with their quasi- democratic processes come from Westminster and other secular models. Many have regarded it as inevitable that the early church, as it expanded, would evolve from the New Testament organism into a large organisation. Yet there is no theology, logic or experience to invalidate the pattern of Church-as-organism. Since the Body of Christ signifies nothing less, we should present this reality, as public message, to all organisations that 'being organism' – a living, relational, coherent and reproductive unit – is God's way. It works.[119]

God deals primarily in relationship. He offers everyone a profound confidence in being indwelt, unworthily, by his Son. From this emerges a mutual interaction – observing, hearing, feeling, attracting, knowing, healing, redeeming, nourishing, correcting, equipping, empowering and then sending. He deals with us individually and specifically so that, with new life flowering out of new relationship, realignment begins to take effect. This alignment to life in Christ leads us to where God is at work, and where he is heading. Christian leaders are only effective inside such a reality; a faith-based context. In this place, the only appropriate power is God's. Human constructs of organisation, planning, systems and customs have to be subordinate: silently supportive, enabling and reinforcing what God is doing.

Unless we are a coherent body, formed of trust-based and mutually supportive networks, church leaders will always weary themselves trying to impose Gospel values within inherited non-Gospel structures. Too often it proves impossible. Too much of the Church is working against the grain; seeing no other option but to try harder and risk burn-out. Fr Helmut Schüller, an Austrian Catholic priest, surely spoke for our own Church when he described 'the challenges faced by many overworked priests who oversee multiple parishes' and mourns that,

> 'we can no longer be companions of parishioners' lives..... Instead of knowing their names, there are meetings, meetings, meetings. This cannot be our vision – a Church that is a kind of Starbucks, a sacrament-distributing agency.'[120]

And worse than this, whenever systemic frailties are discerned, we too easily reach for 'best practice' in Caesar's realm: the Clergy Discipline Measure and Terms of Service legislation being examples. Our calling points in a better direction. Ought not we evince Kingdom values to a flummoxed, and spiritually bankrupt secular world? Indeed, if the Church side lines the relationship imperative, we shall display an untransformed Body, largely indistinguishable from the world's models. We offer a stone, not bread.

Periodically the Church appoints commissions to address its component parts. These have covered numerous components of the Body: bishops, cathedrals, the Archbishop of Canterbury's role, discipline, terms and conditions for clergy, and ministerial training for example. Commissions do not look at the whole. Dr John Hartley touched on this in the July 2009 General Synod debate on reducing episcopal and senior clergy posts. He said the motion was not basically about cuts. Instead, he wanted to start a debate about "the big picture", the need for change in the staffing of the Church.[121] Unless the Church has a clear and godly relational frame, commissions will tend to apply local remedies, overlooking any systemic distress in the patient's bones and nervous system.

Fr Timothy Radcliffe, responding to the tragedy of child abuse within his Church, spoke prophetically of the priesthood and power:

'This Tridentine understanding of priesthood is in its turn showing signs of crisis, of which the sexual abuse scandal is just a symptom. Its stiff clericalism and authoritarianism, unsurprisingly perhaps because of our past battles, do not help the Church now to thrive and be a sign of God's friendship for humanity. And so we need a new culture of authority, from the Vatican to the parish council, which lifts people up into the mystery of loving equality, which is the life of the Trinity.

... Painfully, the Lord is demolishing our high towers and our clerical pretensions to glory and grandeur so that the Church may be a place in which we may encounter God and each other more intimately. ... We can discover Jesus's commandments not as a heavy burden which crushes people but as the invitation to his friendship. We can be liberated from harmful ways of using power in the Church, which are ultimately rooted in secularism, and become more like the Christ who was lowly and humble of heart, and we shall find rest for our souls.'[122]

Pope Francis has been given to his Church since he wrote this. Fr Radcliffe's words may speak to us, too.

Caesar bends people and relationships to his own aims and objectives. They are there to support systems and organisations: not the other way round. Ultimately, they may need to be manipulated, threatened and exploited to satisfy established ends – and in extremis, dispensed with. Caesar has power to provide, to constrain; even to harm, but no power to stimulate goodness and none to bless. He can provide a framework for righteousness to flourish, but cannot change people nor change society for good. Any claim or attempt in this latter direction is blasphemous, as we have noted.

This may be why Jesus sought no entry into the corridors of secular and religious power; instead only giving time to secular or religious leaders *when they came to him*. He offered salt and light to all who entered his zone. Then, in launching his Church its charge was to provide, in his name and power, the means for righteousness to flourish: for lovelessness to be addressed redemptively. Therefore, what *really* counts in Christ's body is not strategies, synods, councils and committees, church law, appraisals and effective clergy tenure and disciplinary structures. It is, rather, clear relational networks with believers bonded to the rule of God and thence bonded with each other: structures becoming supportive tools rather than oppressive masters. Their relational patterns will reflect people's rightful roles, allow increasing coherence, foster trust and well-being. They will position the Church in that place where God has a voice and where the Church has a passion for obedience.

Hence, if we think God's redemptive purposes are achievable primarily through the secular powers, Church leaders must get alongside them as much as possible. But if we rather believe that his Body is his subversive agent to accomplish these purposes in the Holy Spirit's power – in a way often incomprehensible to Caesar – we then need to act as salt and light. We should be unconcerned whether those in power are open to our friendship and wisdom, or not. Jesus did not court secular power: neither should we.

Jesus's example surely conveyed this understanding of human psychology and the dynamics of power. For reasons of history and inherited custom, Church leaders present themselves in the corridors of power because of their historic status. Once in such corridors, the challenge to singleness of mind must be acute. Writing on the story of Job, Jane Leach touches on the delicacy of this challenge:

'God, here, is not fazed by questions or by Job's desire to understand – but, if Job is to approach wisdom, a radical re-centring is required, in which he will no longer seek to pull God into the vortex of human understandings of justice but will allow himself to be caught up into a wider vision.'[123]

Even when associating and working with Caesar is appropriate, a real hazard follows in its wake; that of creating an elite. Elites tend to draw together people like themselves. People rise into an elite circle perhaps through marriage, long friendships, or through academic influence or distinction. Such an elite unconsciously shapes itself according to what it perceives will be both acceptable to Caesar, and stand a chance of being heard as a collective voice. Whilst seeking Caesar's favour contrasts with the servant-God's pattern, such elitists stand to lose the favour of those they serve in the Church. Elitism, Caesar's way, presents its members as strong and wise. Yet our God does not make us strong and wise in a way that Caesar would understand. We, like Paul, do well to remain weak and foolish so that the wisdom and power of God, his glory, may be seen through us.

Drawing upon Old Testament prophetic literature, Walter Brueggemann describes the character of 'empire'; in his case the USA's version. It shows the mind-set of Caesar:

'Empires do not grieve, do not notice human suffering, do not acknowledge torn bodies or abused villages. Empires deal in quotas, statistics, summaries, and memos. And memos rarely mention loss; when they do, they disguise it in euphemism so that no one need notice. Empires characteristically do not notice loss because they are able to engage in reality-denying ideology that covers over everything in the splendour of power, victory and stability. Empires do not acknowledge that many such claims are highly contested, and beyond contestation are frequently exhibited as false. But empires are undeterred by inconvenient truths, and rush on to persuasive certitude'.[124]

Only God knows how much this needs to challenge our thinking. It certainly deserves reflection. Sir Roy Strong expressed concerns in 2008 on launching the Village Church for Village Life competition. He wrote of the difficulties of achieving change to church buildings:

> 'Other things surfaced. One was the crying need for a radical overhaul of the bureaucratic processes whereby change was achieved. There have also been unhappy experiences caused by those at the top who have the power to act, but no responsibility for what they land on hapless, penniless congregations.'[125]

The forming of an elite, however unconscious or indeed, well-meaning, bears no relation to the life of Jesus. It is the stuff of life for Caesar and his world but the stuff of death for Christ's body, being bound to block God's purposes whose power is revealed through weakness.

Whilst the need for some Church law and regulation is obvious, we have too much of it; as any churchwarden will testify. It constrains more than enables. As things stand, clergy and parishes are often unfamiliar with, or unconvinced by, the purpose and scope of some of our laws and regulations; maybe dismissive. Breaches that bruise relationships may then occur. If clergy and congregations alike feel aggrieved, enforcement becomes difficult. Grief generally spills out over the 'grapevine'! What then is wrong? Good law should be a friend, yet laws not seen this way become problematic. A harmful culture can develop – even within otherwise healthy churches – that is dismissive of inconvenient law and regulation. Such developments threaten local church leaders' credibility and diocesan relationships. Furthermore, they polarise the problem, pressing a diocese either towards strenuous enforcement, or laxity, with relational consequences either way.

If this is broadly correct, we have to take a view: either decide for a Church that is grace 'heavy' and law 'light', or the reverse? Since *law* moves in to fill a relationship vacuum, the path to an increase of *grace* emerges from the mist. For this, we need to endow our Church with an overriding relational emphasis.

Conclusion
Clearly, a large church body requires order. This demands some systems and some regulation. But the great challenge is to make

them as few and generous as possible; then administer them so as to promote rather than diminish relationship. We need to work out how to do this. The wonder of relationship Jesus intends for his Body needs greater opportunity. Leaven is the theme. We take it further in the next chapters. We need to leave Egypt more decisively.

Old Temple:
the leaven-strain of historic enchantment

6

The Church was born in history. Since that Jerusalem Pentecost, we have been shaped across two millennia by historic events. We depend on history's recorded facts and events for understanding both God and ourselves. God's self-revelation, and his times of intervention – of demonstration and display – are integral to mature faith.

Yet at the same time we are susceptible to the strains of undue historic loyalties; in particular, an 'aspic-fixation' with Old Temple. I refer to the physical and outward customs and forms that derive from – or mimic – the Temple system, nearing its end during Jesus's ministry.

Jesus, the great I AM, calls us to keep our heads in the here and now. He is the God of the present tense. Worldly leaven pushes to consume us with tomorrow's concerns: to become semi-detached from the present. It is in the present that we hear his voice; come to see with his eyes and feel with his heart. Our calling is to be lilies of the field, declaring Christ's beauty in the 'now' moment.

Old Temple's danger is that it hides under the umbrella of historic loyalties; distracting us from the spiritual life revealed in Jesus. Its heady mix of history, beauty, reasonableness and order – posing fraudulently as coherence – makes people comfortable, giving a false basis for confidence. Old Temple's dependence on hierarchy, rank, inappropriate deference, visual expressions of grandeur through processions, robes and ornate liturgy is alive and well today. Highly structured services, superb buildings, ordered and reordered with passing ecclesiastical fashion: all provide beauty for the eye, ear and mind. They have a great power to satisfy. Yet, these happen not to be the tools Jesus chose to use. He did not come to reform Old Temple, but to supplant it.

The Old Temple mindset saw, correctly, that we had to offer faith in God to others through the senses, not just through words. Yet we chose the wrong tools. Chapter 12 comes to focus on this point. Jesus's way of working through the senses could not be reduced to formula or technique. His tools were of the Spirit, not of any inborn artistry of women and men; even though dedicated to God. He used a different set of tools for demonstration and display: *demonstration* of his reality within life's rough-and-tumble, and *display* of unity and God-reflecting glory, through God-indwelt, re-connected, human lives.

This Old Temple cultural strain causes serious difficulties. The Law, misappropriated as a pharisaic weapon, and the pharisaic norms of Old Temple dependency, obsessed Saul. He savaged the early Church. After conversion, he had to confront Peter's infection by this specific strain: separating himself from table fellowship with gentiles because of his fear of the 'circumcision party.'[126] In his humanity, Peter was drawing upon the culture of a 'party' within the Church rather than on the pattern of Jesus who shared his table without reserve.

If Peter was vulnerable to such cultural strains, so are we. This chapter seeks to highlight the risk of familiar things.

Buildings and God's presence

'How lovely is your dwelling place...' opens Psalm 84. 'My soul longs, indeed faints for the courts of the Lord', follows, as well as further similar emphases. This Psalm seems rooted firmly in the Old Temple's life. Yet behind these words, we can see the reality of God's presence is emphasised more than its location. Paul used this deeper truth to help his Athenian listeners, 'Since he is the Lord of heaven and earth, he doesn't live in man-made temples, and human hands can't serve his needs – for he has no needs.'[127] Earlier, filled with the Holy Spirit – in Paul's hearing and with martyrdom imminent – Stephen had said, 'the Most High does not dwell in houses made with human hands.'[128]

Two thousand years later, much formal Church worship appears based on superseded Old- more than New-Testament Temple forms of Christ and his Body. Old Temple forms may not connect with ordinary people; especially with unschooled church-visitors' needs. Albeit with the best of intentions worship can, readily and unnoticed, become performance; regardless of the church tradition. The Old Temple strain can damage the emotional life of Christ's body. Neither sacred place nor sacred space seemed part of apostolic thinking, although both terms are now commonly used.

So from Pentecost on, a sense of God's presence was to be found particularly amongst his worshipping people; not in buildings.

The Samaritan woman tried to engage Jesus somewhat defensively on the niceties of worship's form and location. He would have none of it. 'True worshippers will worship the Father in spirit and truth, for the Father seeks such as these to worship him', he said.[129] And this is an obligation. Perhaps Psalm 51 says something similar, 'For you have no delight in sacrifice [performance?]… The sacrifice acceptable to God is a broken spirit; a broken and contrite heart, O God, you will not despise' (vs.15-17).

Such worship is only possible when God's Spirit opens us up. True worship is intensely personal, which means being very serious about our relationship with God and with others; if need be breaching cultural norms and appearing foolish. Mary of Bethany gave an exquisite example of true worship in her extravagant anointing of Jesus's feet, then wiping them with her hair.[130] Formal worship – in all its beauty and moments of dramatic power – carries risk. We may be drawn by its beauty more than by the one we worship, nudging us into becoming spectators. The personal and intimate can become distant, and any impromptu display of devotion seem deviant.

In John's account Jesus prophesied, 'Destroy this temple, and in three days I will raise it up. The Jews then said, "This temple has been under construction for forty-six years, and will you raise it up in three days?" But he was speaking of the temple of his body.'[131] In Mark's gospel Jesus contrasts two temples; one built with, and the other built without, human hands (14.58). Bishop Tom Wright suggests that Jesus 'is the true temple: he is the word made flesh, the place where the glory of God has chosen to make his dwelling.' He also writes that 'with Jesus's resurrection, judgment has been passed on the Temple, and that Jesus himself is now the place where, and the means by which, the father's presence and forgiving love are to be known. This is the meaning, too, of Jesus comment to the woman of

Samaria that "the hour is coming when true worshippers will not need a particular geographical location, because they will worship the father in spirit and in truth."" He further thinks 'that Jesus saw himself, and perhaps his followers with him, as the new Temple.'[132] I am interested that the prophet Nathan – in telling David that an offspring would be raised up after him who would build a house for his name – may have glimpsed the faint outline of God's purpose in making the 'Son of David' the builder of the house; in being the New Temple itself.[133]

Tom Wright makes the point when he writes of the Temple (as with the Torah) that Jesus's actions and words conveyed,

> 'an assertion that the time had come for the institution to be transcended; in both cases there was an accusation that the institution was currently operating in a way that was destructive both to those involved and, more importantly, to the will of YHWH for his people Israel.'[134]

In this context he embraces Jesus's warnings about a new patch on an old garment and new wine being poured into old wineskins.[135] These warnings portray a 'disconnect' between Old Temple and what is to follow. It needs heeding. Tom Wright then argues a little later:

> 'that, for Jesus, part of the point of the kingdom he was claiming to inaugurate would be that it would bring with it all that the Temple offered, thereby replacing, and making redundant, Israel's greatest symbol.'

Surely, the main reason for the divinely sanctioned destruction of Herod's temple was not because of its considerable corruption, its power and spiritual vacuum – all of which were capable of purging and renewal – but because it purported to be God's chosen place for his future dwelling? God's chosen dwelling place in his emerging plan was different, yet consonant with prophecy. He was to dwell in, and be displayed in, human lives; within the organism of his new Body.

Old Temple works today in rebellion: to reverse God's intention.

Later on, Paul and Peter came to expound on Jesus's new Temple understanding in their letters.[136] God's presence was now to be found in his people, with Jesus as chief corner stone. This plan draws us into partnership with Christ, joining with him through baptism and obedience, receiving the Holy Spirit and connecting coherently with fellow believers. He intended us to be the 'place' where his presence would be palpable and his glory visible. Tom Wright has written:

> 'The [old] Temple was the place, like the tabernacle in the wilderness, from which God ruled Israel. Now the new Temple – Jesus and his Spirit-filled followers – is the place from which and through which God is beginning to implement the world-transforming kingdom that was achieved in and through Jesus and his death and resurrection.'[137]

Buildings and worship

We have inherited buildings as the focal point of Church life and activity. We did not choose it to be this way. Buildings are then valued as a 'spiritual statement', a reminder to the passer-by of the Church's existence. How frail we are to think in such terms. We describe our buildings as places of worship. Across the land, church and cathedral mission statements name worship as their main aim. We regard worship – as a gathered, congregational activity – to be central to Christ's purpose for his Body. Graham Twelftree formed a different perspective from his study of Lucan scripture:

> 'Another comment that Luke might make in a contemporary conversation about worship would be his surprise as to how much worship preoccupies or dominates the life of our churches to the point of defining them and sometimes being the sole focus of Christian activity. From what he has written, Luke is likely to expect mission rather than worship to characterise and dominate the life of the Church.'[138]

Old Temple power rests on the way it may entrap our affections. We easily revere, even love, the historicity and beauty of Old Temple customs and artefacts. Jesus was alert to such things. He warned his followers repeatedly about the teachers of religious law and Pharisees. 'Practice and obey whatever they tell you, but don't follow their example. … They love to sit… They love to receive…'[139] He gave these hefty warnings – against wrong affections – to crowds and his disciples.

He might this way reach the teachers and Pharisees, with redemptive purpose. He warned the disciples because Old Temple entrapment was to be an ongoing hazard to his future Church.

Jesus's withering comments on the outward religious forms of the Jewish leaders, scribes and Pharisees should discomfit us today: for we slip unthinkingly into some of our outward forms like comfortable slippers.

Old Temple depends on straining to please God – on buildings, on form, on tradition, on processions and appearance, on hierarchies, on veneration of place and things, on timetables and events. Its message is 'come to us'. It is clergy-centric. We have surely forgotten: Jesus transcended the Old Temple system in his prophetic ministry. It ended in AD70, never to re-surface in Judaism. Yet, we can look over our shoulders like Lot's wife, and hanker for that life from which we have been rescued.[140]

There was a surprising moment when Jesus rebuked the religious leaders for their attention to scripture, 'You search the scriptures because you think that in them you have eternal life. Yet you refuse to come to me to have life' (John 5.39,40). The word in which they trusted inordinately had become flesh. It stood before their eyes, unrecognised, unheeded. The Anglican tradition holds word and sacrament in balance. Might Jesus conceivably be saying today, 'You faithfully attend the Eucharist because you think thereby you receive eternal life? Yet you refuse to come to me to have life.'?

The building-centric emphasis – on buildings-for-worship – dominates Church culture. It contrasts the relative simplicity of first century attitudes. Any Christian act of worship needs to answer, 'what is this saying or showing about relationship?' This is particularly important today with the media shaping many of the views held by those outside. Television has a stiff challenge to convey something of God's reality. Immanence, love, trust, forgiveness and new creation are hard to convey. The historic buildings we love, the formality, the processions and robes, furniture, fine silver and the style of music that goes with them, are easily conveyed. Too bad these seem to derive from Old Temple perspectives; less discernibly from Jesus. The Church can easily come over as more tailored for the National Trust and NADFAS[141] constituencies than for those on society's wrong side: the prostitute and tax collector. Yet Jesus indicated these latter were just the people who would be barging into his Kingdom ahead of the orthodox. Such strong words should make us a little nervous.

In his day, Amos prophesied:

'I hate all your show and pretence – the hypocrisy of your religious festivals and solemn assemblies. I will not accept your burnt offerings. I won't even notice your choice peace offerings.

'Away with your noisy hymns of praise! I will not listen to the music of your harps. Instead, I want to see a mighty flow of justice, an endless river of righteous living.'[142]

Later on, when under Sanhedrin interrogation for his faith in Jesus, Stephen drew on Amos to challenge their Old Temple hypocrisies; with reckless directness. He then said,

'You stubborn people! You are heathen at heart and deaf to the truth. Must you forever resist the Holy Spirit? That's what your ancestors did, and so do you.'[143]

He understood Jesus's point that 'true worshipers will worship the Father in spirit and in truth. The Father is looking for those who will worship him that way.'[144]

Brian McLaren touches on public worship in *A New Kind of Christianity*:

'Trying to facilitate worship as a public spectacle without forming disciples in the way of love seems to me to be an adventure in frustration. So you can make worship your mission without forming Christ-like agents of love, but you can't do the latter without also forming people who worship.'[145]

Love is the better way. Worship is to do with a person, not a process; upon relationship, not ritual. We must recognise the risks our core building-based activities carry: services and sacraments. They have a perverse power to draw our gaze from the One standing behind sacrament and word; for whom sacrament and word are at best inadequate indicators. Indeed, initiatives on church growth, our increasing focus on church attendance statistics, even the Back to Church Sunday approach, demand some reflection. Our task is to disclose the centrality of relationship – for the best way of living and of discovering God's love – yet our Body-language conveys a message that God is mainly interested in people showing up in Church. Or worse, that living the Christian life equates in some way to church attendance, which pleases God.

New Temple was built so the source of Love might capture our affections, then equip the body for effective engagement with lovelessness outside. Its message is 'we'll come to you' and it is every-member ministry. Mission, after all, is speaking the word and doing the works of Jesus. Now here's a peg on which to hang our identity and our testimony to the world.

Buildings and money

A decade ago Church of England parishes were spending about £160 million a year on buildings. They spent some £40 million on mission agencies and charities, a ratio of 4:1.[146] Is this what we really want? Has property become more important than those we are called to serve? Do buildings dominate our Church life more than support it? And who is thinking about the long term? What will our successor Church be inheriting in 50 years, and at what cost? Which way is the expenditure graph's curve likely to go? And what vast sums will have been spent in the interim? How may we justify our building expenditure when the hungry and sick are dying, and the orphan and widow stand at the door?

Maybe we spend billions of God's pounds – including all those widows' mites – on buildings because we think short-term only, and prefer to hope for the best. For whom are we investing this money – for ourselves, for our successors or for God? Maybe we hope a larger membership will arise to meet such costs? Maybe a greater appetite for historic buildings will grow? Yet few Church members under 40 seem to have much appetite. When will we pause and face these big questions? Will we leave them, irresponsibly, for our successors to face?

It is obvious that major adjustment is daunting. But this provides no argument for procrastination. The first step would be, I suspect, to recognise our actual expenditure betrays our de facto priorities. We may then see 'where our heart lies', and see how New Temple values –

our real treasure – may increasingly be appropriated.

What message does our present priority on buildings convey to young believers and a watching world? The world needs the New Temple model. We may preach the New Temple reality, yet purvey as professionally as possible the Old Temple model with its buildings and sacred places.

Buildings, perception and faith

We all hold images in our minds that govern our choices: the way we live. Any Old Temple preoccupation will harm our imaginings and ability to think objectively. Do we suppose God desires to see people at his Church's centre, connected to him and each other with a love-commitment so strong it has superseded lesser priorities; hallmarked with a willingness to suffer and lose everything? Would he desire a commitment demonstrated by a discipline to listen and obey, and our selves being our instruments of worship, adorned with delight in seeing his power, in pleasing him and enjoying his presence? Is the fragrance of our individual and corporate lives reaching the dark corners of lovelessness?

Old Temple entices our imaginations along a different logic-path. We might start with the common portrayal of church buildings set across the landscape, offering a sign of God's reality and involvement. This may be near-blasphemous: for what human construction, set on God's earth, can offer a greater sign than is inherent in his landscape? For what, then, are these buildings there? Well, they are there primarily for worship. So our worship becomes focused on formality and ritual, set times and a complex of supporting organisation: but capable of receiving a far greater emphasis than James's orphan and widow.[147] Then what is the main vehicle for our worship? This has of course to be the Eucharist. And because it is so important, it has to be administered by a priest. Thus may a priest come to think this is the most important thing he or she has to do; and in any case, this privilege has actually become the defining mark of their priestly call.

A FALSE 'COMFORT ZONE'

An underlying attraction behind the Old Temple is its spurious offer of security in the absence of vision. We do not readily grasp the revelation of New Temple and its power. We turn to the old forms for a sense of identity, and to feel 'at home'. Old Temple can hanker after physical means of presenting God's reality, rather more than God's means. It subverts the reasonable use of community gathering, of buildings, of music, of sign and symbol. These can metamorphose into being the end more than the means. Being anchored in 'beauty', they gain an unquestioning affection and compliance. Whilst God is surely against none of these things in themselves, their prominence bruises the spirit. Old Temple can offer an undefined and unaccountable spirituality rather than that intimate, holy and sacrificial relationship found in Christ alone. It may appeal more to the 'cultured' and educated, but less to others. It is not relationally centred. It offers lesser things as the core of Christian attention, risking people missing God's main point. For this reason, it may be short of nourishment, degrading communities by spiritual starvation – offering inadequate scraps to those starved of love – the marasmic.

Whilst uncomfortable to think in such terms today, many of Jesus's teachings about religion caused offence and seemed extreme. The idea of many centuries of honoured practice unravelling is worrying, yet that is much more God's problem than ours. We may have no easy answers, but he knows what is best and transformation is his great redemptive speciality. The minimum response that may be required of us is that we should acknowledge the imbalance honestly, and seek understanding as to how profoundly such imbalance may offend God and disturb his purposes. Only then may we be open to his wisdom.

Devotion to outward forms

In the Anglican Church, the identity of priestly leadership seems too dependent upon eucharistic presidency. Even worse, being 'a communicant member of …' is often cited as essential for employment by a Christian organisation or church, indicating a preference for a non-relational view of faith. A New Temple alignment might require applicants to show a serious discipleship: engaging habitually in close, mutually accountable connection with fellow believers, eager to grow in Christian commitment and understanding. Whilst communicant membership of a church is essential, it guarantees little of itself. Disciplines of life ought to give the Church more significant indicators of personal character.

Nicholas Henshall has written on what makes a 'successful' church:

'The terrible recognition, perhaps, that a "successful" church, even or especially at Christmas, is not one that is full four times on a Sunday; and that the Gospel is not measured by the glory of our buildings, the beauty of our music or the magnificence of our liturgy. It is measured by the quality of our love. In John Bell's words, "the master's privilege – to kneel and wash servants' feet before they feast."'[148]

Jesus's devastating comments on the outward religious forms of the Jewish 'establishment' should certainly bother us.

Cardinal Christoff Schönborn, Archbishop of Vienna and president of the Austrian bishops' conference, set a ground-breaking example in his own cathedral when leading a service of lament and reconciliation in response to the scandal of clerical child abuse.

'The cardinal, dressed in a simple black cassock, walked unobtrusively down the main aisle accompanied by his vicar general and cathedral priest, both wearing black suits and clerical collars, and by the initiators of We Are Church.'[149] [The service had been initiated by this Austrian reform movement.]

Buildings and relationship

Old Temple works against the development of Christ-like relationships within the Body. In their book *'The Responsive Church'* Nick Spencer and Graham Tomlin identify the unhelpful psychology of 'the congregation' in today's church life. They desire the Church to provide a place of belonging, where people can find relationship and intimacy with others, and a place to discover God together. They identify the problem being,

'the monopoly of the idea of congregation as a synonym for church. In 'congregation' mode, most people who are not involved in performing actions up the front wait passively in the pews to be served up something interesting. There is little sense that the people in the church really matter, or that anything would be missing if one of them didn't turn up one day ......

'Congregational worship is good for a corporate 'act of worship', but it is lousy for relationship.'[150]

These words show how customary activities can empty church life of relational significance. Dr Peter Brierley has commented on 'Fresh Expression gatherings, with just half of them taking place in church buildings. "The genius is that you get informality in an institutional setting."'[151]

It is particularly important to ask what the Eucharist is saying about relationship. In a series of talks on the Lord's Prayer, Bishop John Austin Baker made this point:

'We have lost the plot. What is the Eucharist now? A ritual in which we take a sip of wine and a tiny morsel or wafer of bread. It is in every way unlike an ordinary meal, and so it does not carry the spirit of fellowship which marks normal eating together. Instead of the meaning coming naturally we have to keep telling ourselves what it is all supposed to be about. The Sacrament needs to come back into the world of daily bread. It needs to be reinstated as simply something that a family or friends do when they eat and drink together, to be a domestic celebration like those of Judaism from which it originally came.'[152]

Dr Michael Winter has also emphasised the essential relational dimension in handing the faith on to children,

'The second factor [to be considered] is the absence of a supportive community to sustain a young person's faith if an adequate decision has been made (ie. of personal commitment to Christ). The average parish is not a community, it is too large, and attending its liturgy is rather like going to the theatre.

'We should learn from the Jews. Their annual Passover provides a year-by-year invitation to belief. After the child's question, "Why is this night different from other nights?", the father tells them about the Exodus and its significance. Because it is a supper party at home with about a dozen participants, this is also a perfect community to support a young person's commitment to

God. Actually, it reminds me of the Last Supper: could this be a coincidence?'[153]

Graham Twelftree makes an even more arresting statement in '*People of the Spirit*' in his analysis of Luke's view of the Church, in his gospel and the book of Acts:

'If we asked Luke what part the Eucharist should play in Christian worship we are likely to be surprised, for he does not show the Christians celebrating the Last Supper. Thus, we have already noted that Luke has given no evidence to support the view that the Eucharist was an instrument of grace or that the Church is to be understood as gathered round the Eucharist. As important as eating together is for Luke, it is a corporate expression of the joy of its life not its cause or means of cohesion. Thus, what Luke would probably say to us is that Christians eating together is the joyous remembering of their companionship with Jesus, no more and no less.'[154]

Lastly, Catholic layman Brendan McCarthy has written of his experience of faith lived out with priests within his family – Catholicism as a religion of the hearth:

'While I can appreciate high liturgy, I have been spoilt; no solemn Mass can ever come close to a charged moment across a kitchen table.'[155]

The demand on Clergy

The stress levels parish clergy reportedly experience may have a range of causes. It seems possible that Old Temple demands of time, focus and fund-raising becomes an unacceptable burden, impeding their call to New Temple leadership. The increasing number of multiple benefices must add to the burden. The cost borne by clergy and their households may be greater than leaders readily imagine. No doubt some serious analysis of clergy burdens would greatly help our senior leaders in their shepherding task; perhaps, best by asking the questions habitually rather than launching yet more questionnaires.

Old Temple depends on straining to please God, on buildings, on form, on tradition, on appearance, on hierarchies, on veneration of place and things, on timetables and events. Its message is 'come to us' and it is clergy-centric.

New Temple depends on intimate relationship with God, on building an agape-based fellowship of people hungry for God, on teaching, nurture and listening to one another, on equipping the Body for effective mission and ministry in the loveless places outside. Its message is 'we'll come to you' and it is every-member ministry.

> 'We must return to the notion of being the household of God, getting back to wholesome values, being a space, and giving time, for relationships to develop into a genuine sense of committed belonging, which in turn fosters the nurturing of other families and the universe itself.'[156]

Parish ministers need release, and help, to make disciple-forming and commissioning their main New Temple priority. Culture needs changing. Our present hindrances are not small.

Conclusion

If coherent love is to be the core value of Christ's church, the theme of agape-relationship will govern all church understanding and practice: love's task being incomplete until it secures relationship after God's model. Grace, then, needs to be central. In my experience grace is, oddly, almost exclusively spoken of in the context of what God has done and still does towards us. I doubt we give sufficient attention to grace's outworking through believers' engagements in the gristle of daily life. How may we become truly gracious? When James wrote of pure and genuine religion, he said, 'in the sight of God… it means refusing to let the world corrupt you.'[157] Caesar's and Old Temple's inherent lovelessness soils what was born to be lovely.

Our attitudes to law may be influenced by both Old Temple and by Caesar's mind-set. The Pharisees gave extravagant emphasis in their Old Temple forms to the accumulated law and regulation of their tradition: it was for them the route to Old Temple health. Then in the ensuing two millennia, the Church has unthinkingly borrowed from Caesar's fear-based dependence on law to accomplish his purposes. Old Temple and Caesar – each bearing relational consequences, nurturing fragmentation, fear and dysfunctionality – collide with Paul's revelation of grace.

And what of the cost of both strains to clergy well-being? The reported stress levels clergy now experience doubtless has a range of causes. Yet the demands of Old Temple and Caesar are likely to contribute much to their burden. Their demands of time, attention and fund-raising are not conducive to New Temple leadership. Equally seriously, they are likely to hinder loyalty to the institution and its leadership. This theme of clergy pressure is pursued later on. Without doubt, objective analysis of clergy burdens – perhaps conducted independently – would assist our senior leaders in their shepherding task.

Individualism and Dogmatism:
culture and the person

7

Lovelessness powers the leaven of Herod, the scribes and Pharisees: the 'powers that be.' It impacts inevitably on community; on relationships.

The added strains of individualism and dogmatism reinforce Caesar's and Old Temple strains. They nurture incoherence, division, and then dysfunctionality: fruits of lovelessness. It is no small matter that any creep towards institutional incoherence denies God's character. Yet the driving influence behind such outcomes tends to avoid recognition and evaluation. Although capable of serious harm, these strains are barely seen as significant issues in today's Church. Cultures perpetrate norms. If noticed at all, these two strains can seem normal; and quite acceptable.

Both individualism and dogmatism, coming from within a person, are prone to be fed by pride, and impelled by a determination to *succeed*. I know this well from my own excursions in this direction. Both ignore that we are made as relational beings: purposed for life with others. Both degrade a culture.

THE LEAVEN-STRAIN OF INDIVIDUALISM

Individualism: The dominant feature of the Western societies that encourages individual freedom at the cost of traditional family ties and social cohesion, and stresses individual initiative.[158]

By excessive individualism we mean the belief that the prime duty of the individual is to make the most of her life, rather than to contribute to the good of others.[159]

Individualism and team-work

The Church acknowledges the need for teamwork. Ability in or potential for team-work is an issue in the selection process for ordination training, and for a long while certain benefices have been earmarked for team ministry. Yet the imprint of individualism lingers on in the Church's DNA. The parochial system silently fosters individualism in its leadership. It is thence unsurprising if it is glimpsed at senior and national levels.

Very often, clergy – through no fault of their own – will have less experience and understanding of community life than many of the people in their care. It is surprising that the Church's preparation of those moving towards ordination and beyond, generally offers scant experience of close inter-dependent community. Theological College community life is valuable, but does not involve significantly the shared tasks and disciplines of serving others in the community outside, over prolonged periods. Equally seriously, it may hardly allow objective judgment of an individual's relational ability in the context of demanding team activity.

Individualism and professionalism

Individualism works intrinsically against professionalism. It inclines to 'know best.' It is disinclined to look for, let alone submit to, 'best practice.' At all levels in the Church, a pattern of procedural mistakes being repeated can be seen; suggestive of a lack of procedural analysis, a lack of known best-practice models and a felt need to 'move on' to deal with other matters. Individualism lies at the root of such institutional frailty. Professional leadership *demands* rigour in analysing organisational frailty, and in identifying – then disseminating – good practice. Any malfunction or crisis, properly handled, can yield substantial dividends.

Individualists will be disinclined to admit to mistakes or perplexity; disinclined to seek advice or to learn significantly from their struggles.

Individualism and social attitude

Individualism can also foster a sub-Christian attitude to 'sameness and otherness.' Most of us incline to gravitate towards kindred spirits:

people like ourselves. Social stratification still affects our nation, not least between the educated and less educated. Sadly, the Church too often reflects this in the way it works, attracting the educated end of the spectrum much more than the less-educated, for whom it easily presents too high a threshold for them to cross. Jesus's social patterns were refreshingly different. It would be hard to imagine a greater spread of unlikely and unlike people when Jesus chose the twelve, as many have noted.

Jesus's main social contacts seem uncontrived, either occurring randomly or initiated by others. The thrice-mentioned teaching that 'in Christ there is neither...'[160] is sometimes linked superficially to secular notions of equality and human rights. Yet it is plainly to do with our relational habits. God's pattern goes for *otherness* more than *sameness*. Within the gifts of marriage and parenthood, male and female otherness provides healthy challenge, stimulus and growth in the other. Otherness affords a rich benefit.

The *otherness* of the Creator and created has the incalculable potential of redemption. We dare not partition our lives into God's bit and ours. Whilst lives need refreshment, exercise, rest and fun as well as 'work', we are never to live in disconnection with the Father; off-duty means out of relationship, for which we have no licence. Whether sitting at a well to slake our thirst, or enjoying a wedding celebration, we are 'on-call' for partnership in God's hidden purposes. We are to mingle with the loveless as well as the lovable as we go along.

We can become unwisely selective in our human contacts. As John wrote, 'if we walk in the light as he himself is in the light, *we have fellowship with one another.*'[161]

John Austin Baker summarises such thoughts trenchantly:

'Small cells of the *un*like-minded, however unimportant they are by worldly standards, who want to explore into God together, and come to a new and shared understanding, must have the arrogance to decide to do so, whether others will hear or whether they will forbear. If the lions are too cowardly, the mice must be brave. Then the Word will unite where words have only divided.'[162]

What does this say about our Church structures? I suggest a great deal. It may affect the formation of ordinands, their choice of theological college or course, the selection of training-parish and the lifestyle of ordained ministers. It may make the difference between a priest's commitment, or otherwise, to deanery chapter meetings, training days, continuing ministerial education and indeed diocesan clergy conferences – quite apart from their appetite for team ministry.

Individualism's cultural power is insidious, damaging the movement of Christ's body.

'If you want to go fast, go alone. If you want to go far, go together,' says an African proverb.

THE LEAVEN-STRAIN OF DOGMATISM

Dogmatism: The tendency to lay down principles as irrefutable, without exhaustive consideration of evidence, of related issues or of others' opinions; a stubborn and narrow-minded way of thinking, sometimes arising from prejudice and bigotry.

We now consider this fourth cultural strain in relation to the Church. One of the most remarkable features of Jesus's recorded words is how removed was his style from the modernist approach we regard as normal. In our teaching, preaching and writing we lean heavily on precise definitions, on systemised approaches to various topics, on logic and proofs. We marshal our words with the intent of drawing our listeners into precise acceptance of all we say. We are pressing for uniform acceptance of every detail, wanting to clone people's minds. In so doing, we are living in a world of facts, knowledge and argument.

Yet Jesus, living in a relational world, acted differently. He scattered seeds profligately, content these would germinate in the listeners' understandings in God's good time. Whilst there were fundamental constants – drawn from the law and prophets – on which his teaching rested, he gave them no *theology* as we would know it, and no *knowledge* of the sort so pervasive in today's educational culture, let alone any structure for systemised thought. He had no wish to make his followers knowledgeable or clever. He helped them absorb wisdom so as to gain *understanding.* He imparted understanding of how *life* should work out in God's world, for 'in him was life and the life was the light of all people.'[163]

His teaching was like a large impressionist painting. Each parable or message of wisdom was a few daubs of colour painted with a broad brush. Each was sufficiently clear to make an impression, be memorable and convey one or more significant point. The parables were sufficiently tantalising for the listener to want more. For those drawn to hear much of his teaching, they found they were being shown a large and comprehensive picture; an impression of a world under God's rule and an insight on how to get there, belong and engage in it.

His life showed the way: his teaching and parables provided explanation. Staying in his company allowed people to accumulate wisdom.

In contrast, a clinical treatment of 'truth' generates knowledge that accumulates and may contribute to arrogance, power and self-righteousness. Such a dogmatic approach was foreign to Jesus.

Brian McLaren has put it like this:

'The belief that truth is best understood by reducing it to a few fundamentals or a single "sola" (only) insight is, to me, at least questionable if not downright dangerous.'[164]

It seems evident that the strain of dogmatism can attack the Body's theology and, most significantly, pervert understanding of how truth and love relate with each other. The governing theme for all Christians needs to be that 'Jesus is Lord'. It gathers us into a profound unity on the most important central truth for the world and the Church. It provides all we need for establishing our individual and corporate identities. The danger of dogmatism for the Church is its tendency to produce other rallying-points, prompting kindred spirits to associate on the basis of lesser themes. And lesser themes – too fondly advocated – become dominant themes, even 'greatest single issues.'

If Christians pursue truth over love, we may contrast the consequences like this:

If we believe God's primary characteristic is:

	Truth	*Love*
which has its basis in:	facts, logic, law, regulation and definition	reality in relationship
that require of the individual:	intellect and effort	openness and allegiance
and of the leader a format of:	discipline	pastoral oversight
all of which will appeal to:	the intelligent & articulate	the needy
and may stimulate:	pride and individualism	humility, gratitude & community life
Conduct will be focused on:	morality	pleasing God
tending to result in:	judgmentalism	love for the loveless
making a community of:	the few	the many
marked by:	an unattractive self-obsession	Christ-possession
with a likely outcome of:	division and loss	unity and coherence

It is worth looking further at the dissonance between those opening aspirations; for knowledge, or for understanding. Knowledge as we have seen is a clinically objective word leading to 'cleverness', whilst understanding is a relational word taking a different trajectory, leading to wisdom through relationship.

Knowledge
Brian McLaren has described how knowledge fits in:

'The Church, then, in Paul's mind, must be above all a school of love. If it's not that, it's nothing. Its goal is not simply to pump knowledge into people, but to train them in 'the way of love', so that they may do 'the work of the Lord', empowered by the Holy Spirit, as the embodiment of Christ... Not simply a place where you hear lectures and amass information, but a community where you see living examples of Christ-likeness and experience inner formation. If taken to heart, this simple shift in metaphors from house of worship or religious institution... could catalyse a true renaissance in our Church life.

... Why should people go to the trouble of being part of a church if it does a thousand other things well, but falters in this one primary calling.'[165]

Angela Ashwin has written in similar vein:

'... a deep and prayerful knowledge of God is about love, not facts, and can never be possessed. Arrogance makes brainpower into an idol, but truly to know God is simply to understand in our deepest being that we are loved (1 Cor 8.3).'[166]

And again, Bishop Peter Forster follows it in his review of hitherto unpublished writings of Professor C F D Moule:

'Moule was distrustful of exegesis that is too quickly generalised into theological or doctrinal statements. He emphasises that the New Testament does not provide direct information from God, but that its proper function is to witness to Jesus Christ, so that in him we may find God, and through the Holy Spirit be guided by God'.[167]

Finally, Fr Daniel O'Leary has written of experiencing the divine everywhere:

'Knowledge alone, ideas and concepts do not change us profoundly. Pure experience does. It is always focused, concentrated and non-dualistic. It attracts, persuades and convinces. After it we see things differently ...

'Our experience is pure when we hold no preconceived notions. You cannot really experience reality with the judgmental mind because you are dividing the moment before you give yourself to it. You are not free to receive. You are in control of the outcome. Your fearful mind is in charge; you are not yet vulnerable enough.'[168]

Knowledge clearly carries particular dangers that may catch us unaware. The pursuit of knowledge may not be what it's stacked up to be, certainly within God's Church. The creation story may hint at this sort of problem. The representative Adam and Eve were invited to eat the fruit of any tree in the Garden, including the tree of *life*; but eating of the fruit of the tree of the *knowledge of good and evil* carried an outright prohibition. Disobedience then meant loss of access to the tree of life. I am interested that no further reference to the tree of life is found in scripture until John the Divine's vision of the New Jerusalem. Jesus, in offering eternal life, represents that tree of life – and sharing in his risen life, the pursuit of wisdom and godly understanding, is eating of the tree.

Understanding
The Church's raison d'être is relational. It has no other. If we hold the themes – of love and truth, of wisdom and knowledge – in imbalance, there are consequences. If we over-emphasise truth, we shall be less able to lead church members in the relational direction of understanding and wisdom. Furthermore the Old Temple and Caesar strains may serve to amplify the difficulties.

As has been noted, Caesar's influence nurtures fear, and fear's only known antidote is perfect love. We must recognise reality. Things work both ways: and *perfect fear casts out love*. Fear is immensely destructive, able to divide communities and corrode relationships. All wisdom, all understanding, derives from God; the Spirit offers us 'the mind of Christ' himself.[169] Wisdom and understanding are healing agents in relationships. So, following the Church's calling is to pursue such essentials, allowing them to colour all we do.

Old Temple inherently distracts. It weakens our hold on New Temple: the living Jesus who works through relationship. It may conspire with those who love beauty more than true relationship, locking them into a state of spiritual emptiness; of spiritual misunderstanding.

And an imbalanced emphasis on truth is likely to demean love, draining it of practical meaning. This will distort the character of both, for individuals and the Church as institution. If we come across as obsessed with law, dogma, custom, knowledge and morality, we should not expect to attract many people.

Damage to the Body
Each of these cultural strains is divisive, wanting to draw us in the direction of division. They deceive us into an unjustified conviction that the course we pursue is right.

Individualism, by definition, works against community. It is very enticing, offering to yield results, yet producing fruits of division and incoherence.

And dogmatism is similarly deceitful. It purports to convey truth forcefully, yet does little to feed understanding. Understanding brings coherence and strengthens community, whilst dogmatism divides.

God's love has to shine on such strains so they die.

Damage to the individual
Our sense of identity affects personal well-being. Poor parenting or other sources of lovelessness touch us all in varying degrees, skewing our sense of identity.

Both strains work to subvert our sense of identity. They deceive us by offering a beguiling, but spurious, foundation for understanding ourselves and hence living our lives. Exercising Caesar's power, individualism and dogmatism can each make us feel significant or important; and Old Temple dependency can make us feel secure and orthodox.

Jesus was very clear on the importance of the foundation, telling of 'a man who dug deeply and to lay his house foundation on rock ... (Luke 6.48).

Lesslie Newbigin described Jesus's own sense of identity in his comment on John 15:

'.... He planned no career for himself. He sought no "dentity" for himself, no "image." He simply responded in loving *obedience* to the will of his Father as it was presented to him in all the accidents, contingencies, and interruptions of daily life, among all the public ambitions and fears and jealousies of that little province of the

Roman Empire in the time of Herod and Pontius Pilate. Only thus did Jesus "abide" in the love of the Father. So the disciples will "abide" in the love of Jesus by following him along exactly the same road. He will not be concerned to create a character or a career for himself. He will leave that to the wise husbandry of the Gardener who alone knows what pruning, what watering and feeding, what sunshine or rain, warmth or cold is needed to produce the fruit he desires.'[170]

The public ambitions and fears and jealousies described are the fruits of the four cultural strains, furthering the work of lovelessness. A relationship shaped in obedience provides us with the secure foundation of identity we need to further the work of love.

We must eye the strands of our enwrapping culture with sober realism and heed Jesus's warning afresh.

We should ponder that most evil event the world has seen. We must note how the confluence of these leaven-strains, working through the religious leaders, shaped events leading to Jesus's execution. We may see how the dominant rigidity of Old Temple priorities and systems eclipsed the prophets' disclosures of God's underlying intentions and his governing characteristics of love, compassion, mercy and truth. We see how those authorities embraced the option of destructive power. Richard Bauckham has observed that:

'the chief priests who ran the Temple and claimed to represent God's rule over his people, grossly misrepresented the nature of God's rule. Instead of differing from the way the kings of the Gentiles ruled, they imitated it.'[171]

The strains of dogmatism and individualism seemed to entwine to reinforce the other cultural strains. So this toxic confluence of leaven caused the custodians of God's cosmic purpose, their nation, to 'reject ... and kill the Author of life'.[172]

The experience of Saul
The testimony in Paul's letters and in Acts points to all four cultural strains having a devastating impact. Having gained the high priest's authority to cover his violence, he was the embodiment of *destructive*

power. He consented to mob-killing, hounding some to death. Many times he had believers punished (tortured?) in the synagogues to get them to curse Jesus. He went 'everywhere to destroy the church, going from house to house, dragging out both men and women to throw them into prison.' He came to utter threats with every breath and was eager to kill the Lord's followers, scattering believers across the eastern Mediterranean. He admitted to violently persecuting God's church, doing his best to destroy it.[173] We see an equivalent irrational cruelty today in the jihadist group calling itself Islamic State.

Saul's need for a sense of identity was shown in an inordinate *historical dependency* – pride in the outward forms of an extreme and legalistic Judaism, and in the purity of his Jewish lineage:

'I was circumcised when I was eight days old. I am a pure-blooded citizen of Israel and a member of the tribe of Benjamin – a real Hebrew if there ever was one! I was a member of the Pharisees, who demand the strictest obedience to the Jewish law. I was so zealous that I harshly persecuted the church.'[174] 'I was far ahead of my fellow Jews in my zeal for the traditions of my ancestors.'[175]

Evidence of his *individualism* is more implicit than explicit. His misplaced zeal seems to have moved him away from the moderating of any peer group. 'I was *far ahead* of my fellow Jews in my zeal for the traditions of my ancestors.' Although he was careful to obtain Jewish leaders' authority for his persecution of believers, the evidence suggests his initiatives and energy were fired from within and in this sense he was not under direction.

Evidence of his *dogmatism* is similarly implicit. His irrational use of terror-tactics stemmed from an unreasonable desire to enforce precise – even extreme – pharisaic viewpoints. So strong was his dogmatic zeal, he elevated the demands of perceived truth above those of love. He was blind to God's command to love his neighbour as himself. Whilst this occurs but once in the Torah,[176] as Jonathan Sacks has pointed out, 'love the stranger' appears upwards of 30 times. Only an extreme dogmatic infection can have blinded Saul the scholar from understanding that his God's governing characteristics were mercy and compassion.

We see how these mutually reinforcing strains deformed a man of intellect and religion. Yet the time came when he viewed this culturally-induced deformation as ordure: to be rejected so he could gain Christ and be one with him.[177] This great theologian, who developed our understanding of love's great theme more than any other apostle, was rescued by and joined to Love from an epicentre of lovelessness.

The picture emerges of someone with an irrational conviction of his own rightness, in belief and in action. Gripped by a chilling pressure to impose his understandings on a whole community of faith, violence became his instrument of persuasion. His disregard of the cruelties and suffering he perpetuated seems psychotic. Cruel power had become essential to him. Unlike the Paul he became, he seemed to travel alone – it was *his* show. There were no signs of an inner faith, rooted in love. Joy had no place in his religion. The fruits were terror and destruction.

Paul experienced his own Exodus from the leaven of Egypt. In God's mercy he was endowed with Kingdom leaven. In his story we see, writ large, the love-powered culture of the Kingdom overwhelming of the culture of Herod, the scribes and Pharisees.

A 20ᵗʰ century warning from Bonhoeffer

Dietrich Bonhoeffer gave a devastating critique of the wrong leaven's power to infiltrate the heart of a Christian community:

'In the community of the Spirit the Word of God alone rules; *in human community of spirit* there rules, along with the Word, the man who is furnished with exceptional powers, experience, and magical suggestive capacities. There God's Word alone is binding; *here,* besides the Word, men bind others to themselves. There all power, honour and domination are surrendered to the Holy Spirit; *here* spheres of power and influence of a personal nature are sought and cultivated. It is true, insofar as these are devout men, that they do this with the intention of serving the highest and the best, but in actuality the result is to dethrone the Holy Spirit, to relegate him to remote unreality. In actuality, it is only the human that is operative here. In the spiritual realm the Spirit governs; *in human community*, psychological techniques and methods. In the former, naïve, un-psychological, unmethodical, helping love is extended towards one's brother; *in the latter* psychological analysis and construction; in the one service of one's brother is simple and humble; *in the other* service consists of a searching, calculating analysis of a stranger.'[178]

21st *century reflections*

This is by no means a new challenge to the Church. Consider, for example, the issues faced at the Reformation by Luther and others. Phyllis Tickle wrote, in her foreword to *'A Generous Orthodoxy'*:

'What Luther had sought, we now know, was not insurrection (though he got it); it was his faith's beating heart, the God centre, *around and over which the centuries had superimposed church as protector and interpreter.*'[179]

This seems a polite way of referring to 'principalities and powers' – the Church coming to act as Lord more than Servant, without seeing or minding the enormity of its ensuing deformity.

Brian McLaren describes a kind of group-think that can emerge and take over a group, 'possess' it, drive it. He then writes even more directly about Jesus's responses:

'Just as he draws out and drives out hidden demonic invaders, Jesus must draw out, expose, name, reject, and banish this systemic, transpersonal evil – incognito beneath robes and crowns, hiding in temples and palaces, camouflaged behind political slogans and images on coins, covert in policies and traditions, seeming to "possess" groups so they think and move in an awful choreography …….. This transpersonal evil can possess, oppress, sicken, and drive insane whole nations, religions, and other social networks just as personal demonic spirits possess, oppress, paralyse, and convulse individuals.'[180]

Here is the challenge for the Church. Any system, custom or cultural attitude that harbours lovelessness and hinders the Kingdom's advance must be faced objectively with Gospel authority. The unauthorised incursion of leaven-strains into the Body's life must be taken seriously. We must stop looking the other way.

An appraisal of our culture, and the roots of its formative strands, with Terry Eagleton's 'clinical cold-eyed realism'[181] born of love, is thus our urgent challenge.

CONCLUSION TO PART 2

Individualism and dogmatism will tend to self-propagate through example – damaging individuals, families and communities. They incline to use Caesar's power and to divide. It is likely that those of us who feel under-confident of our identity, worth or role in life may be drawn to such imbalances. Yet, the principalities and powers are lined up behind the unconscious and sub-conscious – working deceitfully, through the fraudulent norms of worldly culture.

We have thought about the effort demanded of clergy to buttress Old Temple and cope with Caesar-like demands. The further interweaving of dogmatism and individualism into Church life reinforces the harm. Fruitlessness in mission and ministry stemming from division, fragmentation and incoherence in the Body are likely outcomes. What Jesus was doing on the cross should arrest our attention. Walter Wink encapsulates it brilliantly:

'They nailed him to the cross, not realising that with each hammer's blow they were nailing up, for the whole world to see, the affidavit by which the Domination System would be condemned.' (Col 2.13-15).

'What killed Jesus was not irreligion, but religion itself; not anarchy, but the upholders of order.'[182]

Caesar's power gives the appearance of logic and legality. It masquerades as both useful and necessary in our fallen world, yet will both damage trust and fail to stimulate it. Godly power binds the Body together; worldly power shatters it.

Old Temple loyalties claim the fraudulent authenticity of historic bench-marks. Yet they do not deliver. They favour *form* more than *interior reality*: the *impersonal* more than the *personal*. When people hunger for the bread of relationship, they offer a stone. Old Temple has no power to heal, no power to build weight-bearing relationship. It diverts attention and understanding away from God's New Temple.

Jesus alerted to the dangers in both the religious system *and* the law's domain – Old Temple and Caesar. 'But beware! For you will be handed over to the *courts* and will be flogged with whips in the *synagogues*. You will stand trial before *governors and kings*...'[183] And again, using equivalent terms, Jesus warned against the spirit-numbing unbelief arising from the unthinking adoption of Old Temple and of Caesar's secular or humanist mind-set, 'Beware, be on your guard against the leaven of the Pharisees and the leaven of Herod'.[184]

The Powers we face are real. The four invasive strains mutually reinforce. They are deceitfully toxic. Their spiritual assault, anti-God, propagates lovelessness at every opportunity. Their power roots are elusive, and in human terms exceptionally hard, if not impossible to confront, expose and euthanize.

Walter Wink stresses that we, the Church, need:

'to escape idolatry, not this planet. We do not seek to rid ourselves of subsystems and structures in order to secure an individualistic paradise on earth or an afterlife in heaven. We seek rather, to relate these systems to the One in and through and for whom they exist, and in whom all things hold together. (Col 1.16,17)'[185]

The needs of the world, the life of Jesus and the work of the Gospel are only fully understandable if we recognise lovelessness as *the root of the deepest and most destructive human pain of all*. The enchained Paul knew that his relationship with Christ and the ensuing benefits put all temporal pain in its place:

'I want to know Christ and the power of his resurrection and the sharing of his sufferings by becoming like him in his death, if somehow I may attain the resurrection from the dead.'[186]

Our Church needs to relate our inherited 'subsystems and structures', named by Wink, to the One who is utter coherence. We may thereby anticipate a greater experience of God-ordered and Christ-fragrant community for increasing numbers of women and men.

Perhaps we may conclude that we need, as Church, to see the power of Christ's love and of the Holy Spirit's intervention in the totality of our systems, structures and customs. The problem has to be addressed, but is beyond our human wisdom and power to overcome. But that, we always knew, is the message of God's redemption.

Part 3: Embracing Love

The core question is: how might love be given a greater entry into our structures, systems and customs? We enter this large landscape by reflecting on God's strategy for implanting his leaven – the power of love – in the world, across history. We then note how, over time, certain divergences have crept in, unhindered. This opens the way to review the Church's structures, systems and customs; some aspects obvious, others less visible. But all are important. This is not really about detailed spanner-work, technical adjustment or tuning. It is about deeper themes that govern the way we live as Church. It is about the Church aspiring to be Christ's Body. Do our relational patterns deliver godly benefit?

Kingdom Leaven

8

'God is a relationship, not an explanation.'
Anthropologist Tanya Luhrmann[187]

The launch of the Kingdom had a long preparation. It is part of the long story of the two opposing powers that had been around from the start. One purposed the destruction of relationship, and death. It has oppressed and bound the created order: corrupting human choices. As patterns of tainted decision-making repeated, worldly cultures emerged; each offering fraudulent reference points for living, embedding false *norms* ever more deeply in societies. The fraudulence centres on enticement to follow attractive paths that lead to relational destruction and death. No human wisdom or effort can overwhelm such power. A telling example of such fraudulence today is the increasing political pressure on western governments to legitimise euthanasia. It masquerades as kindness to suffering individuals, and maybe their immediate families.

God faced the problem from the beginning, following his own timescale. As Clement of Rome wrote:[188]

> 'His purposes cannot be hurried. No stage can be left out. The whole process must take place. But let us be in no doubt that inevitably his purposes will be fulfilled.'

God is working his purposes out, yet grace constrains him. In addressing our cultural bondage, we see his non-negotiable commitment to mercy; and to love the unlovely. Whilst worldly culture emerges in community life – mysteriously and silently, eating away at relational connection – his supplanting Kingdom-culture is counter-intuitive and depends on human resolve. It, alone, can ferment coherent life. The other's fermenting power provokes instability and incoherence, paradoxically disclosing a self-condemnation. This plausible cultural power depends on community for its traction. Yet, lacking any creative power, it can only work towards that community's destruction.

Out of Egypt

God's story of leaven began when Egypt had enslaved and infected the Israelites with its culture. As his great exodus plan got under way, he had to separate the embryonic Israelite nation from Egypt: physically, culturally and spiritually. The Israelites had all been born into slavery; into an unchosen pagan, corrupt culture.

Their domination by all things Egyptian must have wrung the corporate life out of them. Slavery's cruelty, its gross demands, prevents any flourishing of community life. Across four centuries, memories of an earlier life disappear. Imaginations of a better life are disabled. The aim of a small captive people shifts to survival: how to endure each day, and how to moderate the impact of systemic, long-term cruelty. The experiences of captivity in Babylon (Is 3.15) and, in modern times, of black slavery in the Caribbean and American plantations, all speak of this. As I write, the plight of a 30 year-old woman is in the news. A man and woman have apparently held her captive, with two other women, in a London house. Reports say she has been there for her entire life, in servitude. They tell of her probable inability to adjust to life in the outside culture.

At the same time, the murderous tyranny of Kim Jong Un made headlines. Demonstrating vividly how the bondage of 'Egypt' erases understanding of how to live, The Times reported thus:

'The absoluteness of North Korea's tyranny is its defining characteristic …

The personality cult of the leader isn't just extreme: it's unlimited, and *it's the only culture North Korea's people have.* The regime has survived for 65 years – through war, famine and economic collapse

– not by skill in statecraft but by enslaving its subjects in mind as well as body. Only a people without access to books, films, news, the internet and travel would find unremarkable the institution of necrocracy, rule by the dead. That is literally what North Korea has. Despite having been a corpse for 19 years, Kim Il Sung remains the country's "eternal president".[189]

The Israelites needed a full release from their equivalent bondage. They had to sign up to what God was doing. They had to enact their personal and corporate rejection of that culture. God placed this necessity upon them. They had, simply, to locate and destroy Egypt's leaven before they could leave the land. They then had to repeat this God-given ritual and discipline annually, which yet continues after 3½ millennia.

They would not know how to live together in their sudden release into freedom. They landed in Sinai with a slavery-induced vacuum of no- or thin-culture: wholly inadequate for an extraordinary freedom as a newly birthed community, let alone as God's chosen people heading for a Promised Land. They had first to receive a new culture's seeds.

Planting and growing a culture
God's setting for his cultural implant was powerless desolation, in the wilderness as a holding-ground. They would be safe from marauding powers, safe from the influences of a resident population, but lacking sustenance for survival without culture – hence no norms, no model of independent community life. It was a forty-year unleavened experience.

His big lesson for them was to do with relationship. As Exodus records,

'Then I will live among the people of Israel and be their God, and they will know that I am the Lord their God. I am the one who brought them out of the land of Egypt so that I could live among them. I am the Lord their God.'[190]

He revealed himself as compassionate, offering dependable relationship from which material provision followed. There was an emphasis on corporate worship, commitment to obedience and acceptance of dependency to secure and nourish this relationship.

In this new setting, he set about teaching them how to live as a people of his very own possession, to be holy and separate from the other peoples, to be his.[191] He was to induct them into accepting a common purpose (to be a nation), with a Promised-Land destination and a dependable leader (Moses). They were to be given a framework for practical living, for relationships to work (the law); and a framework for nurturing community life, for justice and dispute resolution (a network of leader-judges). At the same time he gave strong warning against being tainted by the culture and customs of the people he was to clear from the Promised Land.[192]

Centuries later, Stephen described the giving of the law on Sinai as 'Moses receiving life-giving words to pass on.'[193] We have come to see how God has pitched his interventions throughout history to deliver *life in all its fullness*. So it was, here in the wilderness law- giving. Tom Wright writes that:

'the intention of the law (to give *life*) is finally and gloriously achieved when, by the spirit, God gives resurrection life to all those who belong to the Messiah, Jesus.'[194]

The long haul of nation-building

God was equipping his chosen nation for its vocation. Yet even after forty years, his task was incomplete. Before Joshua entered the Promised Land, Moses prophesied, 'your children, who today do not yet know right from wrong, they shall enter there.'

Centuries later, Peter evoked this moment in Hebrew history when reminding his readers, 'Once you were not a people, but now you are God's people; once you had not received mercy, but now you have received mercy.'[195]

Stephen chided the Sanhedrin by reminding them of their ancestors' refusal to listen to Moses in Sinai, rejecting him and wanting to return to Egypt's fleshpots. Having experienced a corporate deliverance of unprecedented magnitude, they reverted immediately to extreme public idolatry.[196] Then through ensuing centuries, the Jews battled with cultural contamination. In spite of forty years' testing in Sinai and subsequent exiles, and the gift of their law and prophetic warnings, severe cultural contamination provided the context of Jesus' ministry.

Whilst not God's last word, the Law established cultural foundations for his chosen people that could be tested and strengthened, could succeed and could fail. Within it they could learn and develop as they chose, through many generations.

In this pattern, individual lives and received culture would inter-act. Personal attitudes and habits would slowly shape culture, and cultural norms shape individual and family lives; both affecting individual and corporate well-being. Individuals could work at the revealed disciplines of life. They could hold thought, speech and action together as a coherent whole, and form habits according to what does and what does not seem to work.

Through long centuries wisdom accumulated, prophets emerged and spoke, times of disobedience came with further bondage ensuing, and faith waxed and waned. Yet the golden thread of God's love and faithfulness was visible throughout to those with eyes to see.

Although God had delivered his people from Egypt's leaven, their emerging culture needed time to be nurtured. It was a crafted process. Hosea makes this clear, even if they had to *return to Egypt* to learn. Furthermore, God is interested in relationship above everything:

'Yet it was I who taught Ephraim to walk, I took them up in my arms; but they did not know that I healed them. I led them with cords of human kindness, with bands of love. I was to them like those who lift infants to their cheeks. I bent down to them and fed them.

They shall return to the land of Egypt, and Assyria shall be their king, because they have refused to return to me. The sword rages in their cities, it consumes their oracle-priests, and devours because of their schemes. My people are bent on turning away from me. To the Most High they call, but he does not raise them up at all.

How can I give you up, Ephraim? How can I hand you over, O Israel? ... My heart recoils within me; my compassion grows warm and tender. I will not execute my fierce anger; I will not again destroy Ephraim; for I am God and no mortal, the Holy One in your midst, and I will not come in wrath.

They shall go after the LORD, who roars like a lion; when he roars, his children shall come trembling from the west. They shall come trembling like birds from Egypt, and like doves from the land of Assyria; and I will return them to their homes, says the LORD.'[197]

The phrase *returning home* is pregnant with meaning. God was intending more than re-founding or re-habilitating a nation. He was preparing an invitation for them, to *really come home,* to an eternal Kingdom.

Whispers of the Kingdom

The idea of an eternal kingdom is first mooted through the prophet Nathan, in God's covenant with David. God purposed an offspring from David and would establish his kingdom and its throne forever.[198]

The psalmist saw this Kingdom's reality:

'The LORD has established his throne in the heavens, and his kingdom rules over all... They shall speak of the glory of your kingdom, and tell of your power, to make known to all people your mighty deeds, and the glorious splendour of your kingdom ... Your kingdom is an everlasting kingdom, and your dominion endures throughout all generations.'[199]

According to Daniel, the hitherto brutal King Darius made a remarkable decree that all his people should tremble and fear before Daniel's God: 'for he is the living God, enduring forever. His kingdom shall never be destroyed, and his dominion has no end.'[200] (We shall know God is releasing fresh power when Darius' present day successors find themselves saying such words: I believe possible with God.)

As the prophets sought the mind of God, his message of an enriched future appeared through the mist. It would stimulate appetite. They would come to learn how to live relationally. Isaiah wrote, for example,

'Many peoples shall come and say, "Come, let us go up to the mountain of the LORD, to the house of the God of Jacob; that he may teach us his ways and that we may walk in his paths." For out of Zion shall go forth instruction, and the word of the LORD from Jerusalem.'[201]

Indeed, as we track through the Old Testament we see striking evidence of a small number of people with lives leavened by the yet-to-be disclosed Kingdom; living faithfully in wrong-leavened, toxic cultures at high risk and sometimes heavy cost. Within the idolatrous empire-centres of Egypt, Babylon and Persia, Joseph, Daniel and Esther manifested Kingdom values strikingly in their different ways. And beyond this was Jeremiah who was inspired to send the exiles a letter, not about surviving, but about purveying Kingdom leaven in undeserving Babylon. They were to seek the city's peace and prosperity, and to intercede for their captors, to this end.[202]

God had laid foundations for a good culture. We see a pattern forming for realising his Kingdom.

- First, his power and glory were displayed to demonstrate his presence – his reality.
- Then, within his encounters he invited relationship.
- Thirdly, he warned, declaimed against any opposing culture.

This threefold approach is seen, again and again, as the decades and centuries followed.

God allowed them time: maturity comes slowly, even for those who seek it. He is in it for the long haul. He does not hasten. His canvas has the width of a whole life experience. A 60-year-old gains understandings that he could not assimilate 30 years earlier. In the same way, God set a time for the Hebrew nation to grow its distinctive culture. In the process, their story was forming.

The Kingdom is launched

Then, 'when the fullness of time had come, God sent his Son, born of a woman, born under the law.'[203]

The time for change had arrived. Although a faith culture had formed that granted a sense of identity, of belonging to God and his purposes, it was not yet exportable. The nation's leadership fomented a suffocating culture: the leaven of Herod, the scribes and Pharisees. It constituted bondage. In Paul's later words, they held to the outward form of godliness, but denied its power. Such people were to be avoided.[204]

God's people had known deliverance, his times of intervention in power. They had their law and scripture, and inherited some respect for its teaching. What they lacked was the ability to resist the pull of surrounding cultures. By the time of Jesus, they could not discern their suffocating culture's characteristics. They were powerless.

Their inherited cultural framework needed supplanting. They needed rescue from bondage. Jesus saw the corruption of the leaven of Herod, the scribes and Pharisees: that black leaven of death, incapable of reform, enshrouding his nation. It was his ministry's context. He sent his disciples out as sheep amongst wolves, warned them of court proceedings and floggings, and told them not to be afraid of those who wanted to kill them.[205] He warned that the elders, leading priests, and teachers of *religious law* would reject and kill him.[206] The custodians of a law that purposed life were resolved to *kill* the source of *law* and source of *life*.

If Israel's vocation to the Gentiles – the wider world – was to be fulfilled, something had to be done. God acted. They needed no new laws, save one: *that you love one another as I have loved you.* They needed the ability to supplant the culture holding people in bondage. They needed the power of God's love, the power of the King. Jesus was to demonstrate it; a power the world had never see.

John the Baptist had proclaimed the Kingdom's imminence.[207] Jesus now announced it from the outset. In becoming the new Moses, he had to warn his followers repeatedly to distance themselves from the Jewish authorities' dominant culture. The disciples would not know how to live together in their dramatically new context, and had to receive the seeds of a new culture for this promised Kingdom. Cultures press upon us in ways we do not notice, regenerating with hidden momentum.

We must see and absorb how Jesus communicated the new reality of the Kingdom: how he handled his mysterious leaven. John trumpeted the impact made on him by just one man, Jesus. Whilst living in Jesus's company, he had watched and listened through storm and calm, with crowds and alone, seeing clamorous support and vicious undermining, and then his brutal death and beyond. John testified how Jesus's persona, his presence, overwhelmed him. Its radiance energised his life and hence his writing; it all rested on what he had seen, heard and felt. Even so, any understanding we gain through John's words is far, far less than John's ears, eyes and senses had received. Words are never enough.

So the Word did become flesh and dwell amongst people such as John, and he passed on what he had seen and felt: his lengthy and weighty experience of Jesus. And experience *has* to be conveyed, not taught. Thus the way Jesus lived – his lifestyle – was the foundation on which John's faith and writing rested. It was 'out of this world', with an innate, unique authority. Glory became visible; shining on his Son.

Jesus revealed his glory in his first miracle at the Cana wedding. His disciples believed in him. In the following pages, John described something of glory's dynamic. It is to be sought; but for God's honour, not our own. Disability and death yield opportunity for the display of God's glory. Jesus anticipated it was for us to display, so that we might be one as the Godhead is one.[208]

For the people of Israel, it was now not so much a matter of conventional learning – of more words – but of seeing, feeling and receiving. God revealed his power and glory in this one incomparable life that demonstrated love's incomparable power. Its like had never been seen. Display and demonstration was God's main approach. It still is.

So it is that belief comes through seeing the life of Jesus and seeing his works; not through the instruments of persuasion and argument.[209] It was handed on this way[210]: showing and seeing, more than words. Jesus gave understanding more than knowledge, by living confidently as Son rather than living individualistically. His intimate dependence on his Father and obedience in sometimes appalling circumstances *was* the message; with example its channel. His example showed that, because of his Sonship, the Spirit's power flowed in unexpected and unusual ways; a natural consequence of relationship. Jesus then used words – not as his primary channel, I would argue – but to explain, and add weight, to the message people were receiving with their eyes and feelings, and absorbing in their understandings.

The display continued for some three years: the whole spectrum of wisdom, truth, authority, love, joy, peace, grace, patience, kindness, goodness, faithfulness, gentleness and self-control. A new power lay behind this dazzling display in a human being, able to display God's fullness without loss or hindrance. Whilst God's power had appeared at specific times, in specific ways, in moments of history, he now invested his presence and power in a human being. John the Baptist was clear, 'the one whom God has sent speaks the words of God; to him God gives the Spirit without limit'.[211]

People saw the power in his *presence*, his prophetic speech, and his serving and healing. They saw him revealing God's heart as he raised up the faltering, and in unnumbered kindnesses. They noted his miracles and occasions of supernatural knowledge. This power's hallmark was love.

The value of the *display* was limited to those who saw it or heard of it, and were able to receive it. There was nothing religious about it. It was an extraordinary revelation of what one human life could be like; a new way of living. It depended, not on cleverness, status, law, schemes or plans, nor on coercion or manipulation, but on intimacy with the God-who-is-real. The glory of his life drew people towards him. It was the reverse of fear.

In launching God's Kingdom, Jesus followed the same patient pattern of the Godhead in launching a new nation out of Egypt; a threefold demonstration and display, of his power and glory, of a beckoning relationship, and hostility to – denunciation of – the opposing culture.

As Timothy Keller has observed, Jesus's 'message attracted the *worst* of people: the sinners, outcasts and those without hope,' but repelled the great majority of *religious* people.[212]

Unknown to his followers, their three years with him were leading to a further God- initiative, then a future beyond imagining. They were being prepared for change: not a re-gathered life in the wilderness, but a re-gathered life in a battlefield. He was investing their lives with new understandings of life's frameworks, even though they could scarcely make sense of it.

A remarkable aspect of Jesus's life was its paucity of attention to what we call strategic planning. Our world's leaven presses us to give it high priority, bringing 'today' into line with tomorrow. Whilst governed by his Father's overriding purpose, Jesus seemed to work the other way round. He held lightly to tomorrow's plans, shaping 'today' according to what emerged, and what he heard his Father say. He planned to go on to Galilee, but the interlude with the woman at Sychar delayed him by two or more days. Another time he planned not to go up to the Temple with his disciples, but then the Father caused him to go. Again, his friendship with the Bethany family must have pressed him to join them when Lazarus fell ill, but the Father held him back because of the Divine timetable. We need the wisdom of God in our planning, but the attentiveness of Jesus in the decisions of the moment: the route to fruitfulness and displayed glory.

These understandings gained by the disciples centred on coherent, love-filled relationship. It was exceedingly precious, a treasure, needing to be passed into our communities and onto future generations. Paul spoke of Jesus's indescribable life being made visible in our bodies like treasure in clay jars.[213] This treasure of Christ-centred relationship was to be imparted through the chemistry of relationships; a sign of ultimate reality. The primary outcome of such a relationship is example. It cannot be contrived; it happens. It would challenge, influence, instruct, motivate and guide in a unique way, unattainable through other means.[214] Indeed all types of leadership call for relationships that deliver outcomes.

This extraordinary potential of relationship shown in scripture cannot be over-emphasised.

How did Jesus purvey Kingdom leaven?

From the start, Jesus denounced to his disciples the leaven of Herod, the scribes and Pharisees. 'Unless your righteousness exceeds that of the scribes and Pharisees, you will never enter the kingdom of heaven.'[215] Luke recorded that 'when the crowd gathered by the thousands, so that they trampled on one another, Jesus began to speak first to his disciples, "Beware of the leaven of the Pharisees, that is, their hypocrisy."'[216]

His declamations were also made fearlessly before the general public. His litany of 'woes', his altercations with the scribes and Pharisees as they intervened from within the crowds, and his chiding and rebukes within social events, were significant parts of his ministry. Those parables that shone a spotlight upon their corrupt culture were particularly direct. 'When the chief priests and the Pharisees heard his parables, they realized that he was speaking about them.'[217] Jesus was not emollient. He did not aim to be 'nice.'

Having shone his dazzling light on the bad leaven's power – devious and pervasive – he manifested in his person the infinitely greater power of God's new leaven. His life displayed God's reality, and his words addressed the reality of everyman; their inner pain and lostness. All people have been exposed to tyranny's shades of lovelessness. All crave for justice, and to be valued. All crave for wholeness and for a governing life-purpose; cravings intrinsic to that condition of *lostness* Jesus diagnosed. He therefore spoke of judgment, demonstrated love, ministered forgiveness and healing, and offered unending life in the Kingdom as the only reasonable life-purpose.

Lost individuals inevitably import lostness into our world's institutions and organisations. Such lostness has become increasingly evident in Britain since the 2008 banking crisis erupted. Many of the large institutions of state have shown themselves to be in serious trouble through mismanagement of both people and finance. Evidence has surfaced, in all of the professions, of people at the top whose dominant life-purpose seems to be the accumulation of wealth. Many have revealed an unformed sense of accountability; a disregard of the wellbeing of subordinates or those they purport to serve, and of law and ethics.

And yet, we know the Kingdom is good news for all. We *know,* for we too are victims – and perpetrators of – lovelessness, in its various guises and in varying degrees. We know because we have discovered the Kingdom represents, for everyone, the only life-purpose that gives what 'it says on the tin'. Its good news nonetheless contains the essential ingredients of *judgment* – here being no such thing as non-accountability; and of forgiveness – there being the real phenomenon of mercy. The unjustly treated *will* receive justice. In utter contrast, whilst the culture of this world purports to give people value, and to make them more complete as persons, it moves to damage and destroy.

Jesus spoke truth in introducing his Kingdom, not just to ordinary people, but equally to the principalities and powers that purloin God's world, using organisations and institutions to exercise dominion. Judgment is therefore something the Church needs to trumpet. It's a missing word in today's vocabulary. It is for redemptive, not coercive, use. It opens the route to truth, light and freedom.

How did Jesus equip his apostles to purvey Kingdom leaven?

Jesus's primary gift to them was his presence, evincing the power of the Spirit – palpably the power of God's love – in a simple human life that lacked status, privilege and any human authority. In the sight of all the people that 'mattered', he was an utter – yet mystifying – nonentity. Such power in an otherwise inconsequential person was nigh unbelievable.

On this basis, as his ministry began, he invested considerable time in preparing his disciples for eventual apostolic ministry. His tools were example, teaching, training, experience and revelation.

Which of us, in adulthood, has spent three years in an exemplar's itinerant company, with eleven fellow novices? These were dense years of puzzlement, wonder and emotional stretching as they shared his life. Thus was divine understanding embedded in their depths.

There was still more. As he developed as a Spirit-filled man, they watched him sustaining intimacy with Father, learning to hear his voice and learning to discern the specifics of his unfolding will. Too often example's potential is underestimated and undervalued; at best relegated to matters of morality and manners. Jesus's example was a priceless gift.

He conveyed the wisdom of heaven, addressed misunderstandings, faced their failures and affirmed them. He demanded much of them, as did his Father of him. Above all, he prepared them to go out under his authority, in the Spirit's power, and do the things he had been doing.

We can learn from his way of conveying understanding; of preparing the raw dough for the Kingdom's leaven. He essentially taught the crowds through parables, through the evidence of his character; both endorsed by miraculous signs. He sowed seeds in parables that, with Spirit-stoked appetite and the Spirit's watering, would open up understanding and a desire for more. Yet his teaching gave them minimal knowledge or information, as the world would classify such things: just seeds of understanding and a framework for living. He interpreted the parables to his disciples when necessary, but gave little in the way of knowledge. He interpreted his actions and dealt with their questions, cajoled and corrected – and above all, affirmed and encouraged – whenever opportunity presented.

All the while they were watching and listening, puzzled and enthralled, misunderstanding, questioning and doubting. They watched and absorbed how he related to all types and conditions of women and men. They saw him with a betrayer, a woman caught in adultery, a rich young ruler, desperate beggars, the demon-possessed, rough soldiers, the Bethany family, those shadowy hostile agents often standing at the crowds' edge, his 'well-heeled' supporters, and so on.

They watched across the full range of his activities: entering the temple, walking through fields, entering homes, enjoying meals and celebrations, in a storm at sea, through nights of anxiety and facing crowds. They saw him reacting to crises, to grief, to falsehood, to exhaustion and to threats. They observed the look in his eye, his tone of voice and gentleness of touch. They would have understood his dealings with the Canaanite woman that words alone may barely convey.[218] They watched him raise the dead, heal the sick, feed the hungry and cast out demons. These accumulated events – witnessed by tens of thousands – were scored into memories and doubtless, oft reflected upon. His life would have prompted emulation, producing benefit way beyond anything attainable by word and parable.

The divine Jesus's self-emptying encourages me to believe that his example was supremely about living as a Spirit-filled man: as human being, under God the Father's authority and direction, and in Holy Spirit power. A particular feature of his example was in listening obedience; of learning this obedience through what he suffered.[219] They saw how he walked in his Father's company, how he prayed and how he discerned his Father's priorities day by day. This is how the Father sent him to work: and as the Father sent him, so he was to send the apostles as he imparted the Holy Spirit to reside in their lives.[220]

This vast deposit of understanding conveyed through example was not coincidental. It was purposeful because he was to send them out just as he had been sent. It then seems his example was to be conveyed by equivalent example down through the generations of believers who were to become disciples: God's adopted means for handing down understanding. This might explain why the gospels and epistles contain scant instruction on working in the Spirit's power, on healing and casting out demons, on speaking in tongues and using the other gifts of the Spirit.

Example is thus of first order importance in God's work, the power of his example being implicit throughout the Gospel narratives. It is implicit in the expression 'follow me'. It is implicit when Jesus said: 'Take my yoke upon you, and learn from me: for I am gentle in heart and you will find rest for your souls.'[221]

Holy Spirit power is a norm in Jesus's Kingdom culture – its expression, its flow, a natural outcome – except we hinder it. We saw how community unbelief hindered Jesus at Nazareth. The Spirit-endowed life releases holy spores into the air people breathe, attaching to, and empowering our world's dough-lumps.

Accepting the yoke demands close relationship. It begins a profound learning process. Whilst that is a key message of the text, my eye falls on the succeeding clause 'I am gentle and humble in heart'. How were his followers to learn gentleness and humility in heart? How can one possibly teach that? Not through words or training, but only I think through example.

The Gospels mention *example* but once; at the end of Jesus's ministry:

'After he had washed their feet ……. he said to them, "Do you know what I have done to you? You call me Teacher and Lord – and you are right, for that is what I am. So if I, your Lord and Teacher, have washed your feet, you also ought to wash one another's feet. For I have set you an example, that you should do as I have done to you …."'[222]

Example is nonetheless implicit in some of the most remarkable events in the Gospels, the missionary journeys found in all three synoptic gospels.[223] In preparing them for sending-out, he said that students are to be like their teacher, and slaves like their master.[224]

These training missions are amongst the most under-preached gospel events in my experience of Church life. The reasons may be complex. Some might say the occasions were unique to the 1st century, or to the ministry of the Son of God. Some might be diffident about Jesus's diagnosis of evil-spirit manifestation and prescribed application of God's power. Others might simply baulk at the strangeness of it all, viewed against 21st century western Christian culture.

How then did the disciples know what to do? It seems Jesus did not teach them in any present-day sense. They had watched Jesus, assessed the activities of evil spirits, noted his way of responding to the unexpected, and pondered his use of power and his Father's authority. Jesus, who was later to say, 'as the Father sent me, so I send you,' anticipated this commission – for training purposes – by sending them out two by two, with authority over evil spirits and authority to heal.

Prior to the Passion, nowhere is the primacy of example more evident than here. I would assert that example was the chief method by which Jesus imparted understanding – *know-how* – to his followers. Its significance is hard to exaggerate.

An important feature of example is its inherent versatility. Each recipient draws from it – interprets and emulates it – according to their unique personality, experience, present understanding and set of needs. In the Body it may be a silent work of God through his Spirit. For some, example will stimulate a series of questions, a revelation or a strand of thinking in new directions. For others it may grant precise answers to unresolved questions, trigger an aspiration, or stimulate a deeper wonder at the glory, wisdom or love of God. Or again, it might offer hope of a love break-in to deal with a deep rooted lovelessness. Twelve disciples will draw down benefit, tailor-made to themselves, in twelve different ways; sub-consciously, over time. Those of us with memories of wasted school-lessons know that verbal teaching does not necessarily have such effectiveness. Those who use words to teach will emit a stream of them – maybe theoretical more than real – maybe tailored more to their own personalities and experiences. Whilst not valueless, they lack example's potential for multiple, three-dimensional planting in the understandings of unlike people.

A great part of Jesus ministry was devoted to enlarging his disciple's understanding in preparation for their subsequent apostolic ministry. Example, not speech, was his main tool. John's prologue helps us see this:

'In him was life, and the life was the light of all people' (1.4). *His life gave the illumination – not just his words.*

'The light shines in the darkness, and the darkness did not overcome it' (1.5). *His purpose included vanquishing darkness, supplanting the wrong leaven – his life, more than his words being the prime tool, and having power.*

'The true light, which enlightens everyone, was coming into the world' (1.9). *His life did the enlightening, not just his words. It was a 'display'.*

'But to all who received him, who believed in his name, he gave power to become children of God' (1.12). *Relationship was his aim, achieved through his living, not just his speaking. This was a 'demonstration'.*

'So the Word became human and made his home among us. He was full of unfailing love and faithfulness. And we have seen his glory, the glory of the Father's one and only son' (1.14 NLT). *God disclosed in Jesus how a human life was to be lived – the ultimate fulfilment of the law of love. His unfailing love, faithfulness and glory were observable – not just received in words. Here was the ultimate 'display'.*

'God's unfailing love and faithfulness came through Jesus Christ. No one has ever seen God. But the unique One, who is himself God, is near to the Father's heart. He has revealed God to us' (1.17,18 NLT). *Jesus mirrored the Father, demonstrating perfectly how to live in relationship, in all directions – within the Trinity, with friends and followers, responding in love to neutrals and the hostile. 'Display' meant revelation of God.*

Ultimately, all his teaching and parables amplified his lifestyle, reinforced the message of his example. His conversations, prayers and reactions to hostility were key elements of his example.

Lastly, revelation was a further conduit into the disciples' understanding beyond example, teaching, training, and experience. When Peter proclaimed that Jesus was Messiah, Jesus replied that 'my Father in heaven has revealed this to you. You did not learn this from any human being.'[225] Earlier Jesus had thanked his Father for 'hiding these things from those who think themselves wise and clever, and for revealing them to the child-like.'[226] Human initiative cannot cause revelation. Revelation-initiative belongs to God alone. 'No one truly knows the Father except the Son and those to whom the Son chooses to reveal him.'[227] How then may ordinary people become open to revelation? Of course, God in his sovereignty may reveal specific things about himself to whomever he wills regardless of circumstances. But scriptural evidence encourages me to see that meeting and being together, with Christ in the midst, gives a most likely setting for revelation: where expectancy and trust allow God to act.

Summary

As the Father sent Jesus, so he sent his disciples. What then was the deposit of understanding that Father had given to Jesus, and Jesus had planted in them?

Dominant in our usual summary of the detail of Jesus' life beneath the strategic level of incarnation, redemption through cross and resurrection, and empowerment of the Holy Spirit will be the episodes of healing and other miracles, his teaching with and without parables, and his preaching.

What we have alighted on is God's gracious endowment of wisdom he wishes to give his Body – beyond teaching, training, or words – conveying it silently and subconsciously through example into disciples' understanding. It was his foundational gift. From Pentecost, the Holy Spirit increasingly picked it up; replicating and reinforcing it as they practised obedient intimacy. Planted deeply in their subconscious as well as their conscious minds, it provided a well of insight and wisdom. Its provision came at a price for Jesus, and his disciples. Their three years of close living and working together was very tough by any standard; but necessary, to transfer it and see it locked into their souls.

Since Jesus neither taught nor trained it into his disciples by verbal means alone, so it is with us. As part of God's redemptive strategy, Jesus purposely and precisely modelled how his followers were to continue his work. It had to be displayed, demonstrated and revealed. Thus could Jesus say, 'I tell you the truth, anyone who believes in me will do the same works I have done, and even greater works, because I am going to the Father.'[228]

We see the centrality of relationships in all God's revealed patterns. His emphasis upon love, and commands to love, are enmeshed with his desire for outcome in relationship, cohesion and harmony. Indeed his revealed character may be summarised by the words *love* and *coherence*, for all his attributes resonate with or derive from them. Truth, for example, carries no necessity for love or coherence in itself; yet neither love nor coherence has substance except they embrace truth.

Jesus was supplanting a culture leading to death with his Kingdom culture. He was supplanting cultural norms with the radical norms of the Kingdom.

We have a single vocation, as individual Kingdom citizens and as Church, to be conduits of Kingdom extension. We have a divine pattern to follow, through the Spirit. The Father used this pattern in launching a new nation out of Egypt. The Son used it in launching a new Kingdom out of the kingdoms of this world. It is for us, too. Empowered with his love we must anticipate displaying signs of that power and his glory, and anticipate drawing others into relationship. We must also anticipate denouncing repeatedly our world's beguiling culture.

The eventual, complete establishment of the Kingdom is for us a certainty.

'Then the seventh angel blew his trumpet, and there were loud voices in heaven, saying, "The kingdom of the world has become the kingdom of our Lord and of his Messiah, and he will reign forever and ever."' Rev 11.15 (NLT)

Inherited
Divergencies

9

'The kind of outsiders Jesus attracted are not attracted to contemporary churches, even our most avant-garde ones. We tend to draw conservative, buttoned-down, moralistic people. The licentious and liberated or the broken and marginal avoid church. This can only mean one thing. If the preaching of our ministers and the practice of our parishioners do not have the same effect on people that Jesus had, then we must not be declaring the same message that Jesus did.'

Timothy Keller[229]

When comparing our received 21st century Church patterns with those of Jesus's lifestyle, surely necessary to Kingdom leaven, the obvious contrasts are in their relational dependency. In our world, organisations inherently swerve towards the impersonal: towards lovelessness. It often goes unnoticed. Moreover, the Church is not immune to this influence.

In this chapter, we look at the problem from three angles. First, we refresh ourselves on distinctive marks of Jesus's ministry. We look secondly at issues of organisational coherence, inevitably drawing from Jesus's Kingdom teaching. And lastly, we face the imbalances of the Big Four:

Caesar and God, Old Temple and New Temple, and that zone – between Law and Grace – where individualism and dogmatism fight their bitter battles.

MARKS OF JESUS'S MINISTRY

We can identify six distinctive marks of Jesus's ministry, each shaped by love. As we seek to be formed as his Body, his Church needs to appropriate them today. His ministerial disciplines, priorities, and emphases were these:

1. His sustained intimacy with his Father, with an associated relinquishment of initiative.
2. His sustained irradiation of love upon the receptive and hostile alike – rooted in listening, observing and absorbing, then imparted by deeds, words of encouragement, silence, warning, and *rebuke.*
3. His profligate investment of time and attention, upon a modest number of very ordinary women and men, across three years.
4. His use of example as his primary means of imparting understanding.
5. His consistent diagnosis and declamation against the leaven of Herod, the scribes and Pharisees.
6. His channelling of the Holy Spirit's power and activity, disclosing the perfect coherence and integrity coming from his unblemished Trinitarian relationship.

First, Jesus's sustained intimacy with his Father, with an associated relinquishment of initiative

As we noted in Chapter 2, the strength of his intimate connection with his Father, with his resolute obedience, is the only way to make sense of his lifestyle model. Certainly, the evidence suggests that everything substantial Jesus said or did was received from the Father. He only took lesser initiatives as he strode along his Father's path.

Secondly, his sustained irradiation of love upon the receptive and the hostile alike – rooted in listening, observing and absorbing, then imparted by demonstrations of power, deeds, words of encouragement, silence, warning, and rebuke

Love always draws. Matthew described Jesus's *drawing power* in geographic terms.[230] It was extraordinary. Once word got out of his teaching, announcement of Good News – substantiated by his profligate healings and deliverances – people took to the road. They headed on foot for Galilee in often-unmanageable numbers, perhaps

12-15,000.[231] They came from Jerusalem, parts of present-day Jordan, Lebanon and Syria; from up to 100 miles away.

He related in love with those offering hostility. He met with Herod, the Chief Priest, Pilate and the Sanhedrin as a body; and there were the scribes, Sadducees and Pharisees who glowered at him from within the crowds. He met with the scribes and Pharisees who visited him or invited him to a meal, as well as those who came out of the crowds. His door was ever open, never slammed in people's faces. He spoke truth to power without fear. He did not engage in personal attack.

He related in love with his followers. In the gathering intimacy of his company they were drawn into a relationship like none other: a dauntingly demanding relationship that did not admit half-measures. This was the only way he could ready them for a Kingdom leaven that would overcome the world.[232]

Thirdly, his profligate investment of time and attention upon a modest number of very ordinary women and men, across three years

He was focused on the disciples. They were the ones to whom he would entrust the work of the Kingdom. How we use our time is the primary indicator of where our priorities lie. The gospels make plain that, within his messianic mission to the Jews and thence the world, his main time-priority was with his disciples. In those bare three years of ministry he was equipping them for spiritual war, not getting them ready as an organisation.

Theirs was a shared life, through a wide range of circumstances and events – through acute danger and uncertainty, betrayal and abandonment – through death and resurrection.

Fourthly, his use of example as his primary means of imparting understanding

Jesus's primary teaching tool was example, as was argued in the previous chapter. It is also today's primary teaching tool; almost wholly overlooked. For three or so years, a humble, love-dominated life was demonstrated, with power. He conveyed Kingdom-reality in holy-presence, deed and word. It was validated by a palpable glory.

Fifthly, his persistent diagnosis of, and declamation against, the leaven of Herod, the scribes and Pharisees

It is easy to miss the extent of his habitual declamations. The Gospels testify that cultural denunciation pervaded Jesus's spoken ministry. He did so in some parables, overtly or obliquely. He did so in his teaching by exhortation and warning, on about nine occasions. Then he did so, on some twenty recorded occasions, when engaged by scribes and Pharisees with questions or accusations, often connected with his healings and acts of mercy. It seems his Kingdom proclamation was purposefully contrasted with focused declamation. Light's glory is thus seen most vividly in contrast to the bleak darkness offered by the prince of this world.

He did not challenge secular or religious policy-making. Instead, he publicly defined the bad leaven, unclothing its patently absurd folly. It is doubtful if Jesus would have spoken today against going to war in Afghanistan, against fracking, phone-hacking, unfairness in the detail of social benefits, or against the detail of questionable genetic research: all being outcomes, not causes, of bad leaven. His incarnational pattern was to contrast, vigorously, the bad cultural influences with the leaven-values of his Kingdom. Resolutely apolitical, he targeted those leaven-powers generating lovelessness with great clarity, avoiding gratuitous insult.

Some may incline to back away from using this approach if they think that friendship disallows it: the cultural influence of 'niceness.' It is of course costly.

Sixthly, his channelling of the Holy Spirit's power and activity – disclosing the perfect coherence and integrity coming from his unblemished Trinitarian relationship.

The Trinitarian relationship evident throughout Jesus's ministry added immeasurable substance and veracity to his person and ministry. It seems to have been the dominant factor in the glory displayed to those with eyes to see, and to be significant for us in understanding his great High-Priestly prayer. Chapter 12 examines this further.

* * * *

These marks of Jesus's ministry are very challenging. We see in them God's ongoing threefold pattern of engagement with a world distorted and soiled by bad leaven. He demonstrated God's presence – his reality – by displaying the Kingdom's power and glory in his person. Secondly, he invited relationship through encounter. Lastly, he warned: defining, and declaiming against the pervading culture. The incarnation was God's intervention to release all people from an alien culture that enslaved and carried us in the direction of death. His strategy was to engage that culture, supplanting it with the greater culture of the Kingdom. He demonstrated and purveyed love's revolutionary power; and exposed the fraudulent power of lovelessness. He did not focus on individual needs alone.

We now weigh two means by which worldly leaven impacts upon the Church as institution. In the last section of the chapter, we dwell on inherited divergences in terms of the Big Four leaven-strains. We shall first consider incoherence.

INCOHERENCE AND COHERENCE

Incoherence creeps in unobserved; this first-fruit of lovelessness becoming a purveyor of lovelessness. Any divergence from Jesus's patterns risks incoherence, with ensuing fragmentation and dysfunctionality.

Whilst serving within the Church's governance system I saw the impact of leaders over the led. I saw a Christ-like humility and sensitivity working against a more worldly culture to bring unexpected benefit. Bishop Keith Sutton was Bishop of Lichfield from 1984 to 2003. Relationships were central to his ministry. A humble man, he was loved by many for a range of good reasons. I was particularly struck – and instructed – by the way he differentiated between judgment and discernment. He was consistently un-judgmental, yet not soft. He instinctively followed his conviction of God's redemptive purpose. He saw, and related to clergy, as the persons they might yet become rather than as the persons they seemed to be in the present. He had no time for slick caricature. With this stance, he gained the respect and trust of many; not just for his approachability and kindness of spirit, but for the godly wisdom and counsel that these relationships were then able to channel.

In contrast in other circles of senior church leadership I have seen or learned of inherited Church systems and customs working unnoticed against Kingdom values, leaving distressed individuals or parishes to flounder into an unknowable future, with difficulties unresolved. On occasion, I saw power used in Caesar's way (as I saw sometimes in the navy), with good intent but sorrowful result. I caught glimpses of the bruised and hurting being overlooked, and the bully respected. I can only surmise these incidents arose because leaders had somehow missed the point that leadership has to be relational. Loveless leadership has consequences. It does not work.

Strong-sinewed relationship brings coherence. Relationship is therefore what matters most in governance. Relationship-building involves knowing people, being known and *earning* trust, and offering a Jesus-patterned example. It means giving unconditional pastoral care, noticing – then lifting – burdens from backs. It involves training and nurturing people where they are, enabling and equipping them. It demands wise judgment in matters of conflict or misdemeanour, and wise perception in 'career' decisions: selecting, ordaining, appointing and preferment[233]; skills that are considered further in Chapter 11. It means a sensitivity, and openness to change when custom or Church systems disclose a bias against relational-building.

Crises – particularly those involving discord – are baffling to those inclined to views of inherent human goodness. In my experience they are drawn to diagnose *personality clash* in preference to *wrong-doing*. Whilst human misunderstandings can cause ructions and need resolution, my experience suggests that, when crises flare up with bitter hostility and divisive recrimination accruing, specific and discoverable wrong-doing is likely to be at the root. It is seen in wilful character vilification, campaigning against a person, undermining through words or entrapment, or simple bullying. In such circumstances, if personality clash is taken to be the cause – especially where evidence of specific events and actions has neither been sought nor recorded – mediation will seem a desirable tool to look for compromise and a middle way. Whilst mediation may help in situations where someone seems unable to see another person's point of view, I am wary of the personality clash diagnosis. It can be a cop-out, allowing an illusory explanation whilst perpetuating harm. When such attitudes are adopted, crises seem a bore. Trying to sort them seems to waste senior-clergy time, akin to clearing drains when more important things clamour for attention.

If so, divergence from Jesus's example could hardly be greater. He 'read' the human landscape with compassion and accuracy. Have we not noticed that, in the majority of encounters in Jesus's ministry, he faced one crisis after another, attentively and with compassion? In his Father's company, his judgments and perceptions were matchless.

With our understanding of human fallenness, we should expect crises routinely. We can then grasp them as opportunities to bring God's mercy, wisdom and healing into a community. This ministry of healing – physical, psychological and relational – is central to the vocations of ministers and the Church itself. The emergence of a crisis is therefore helpful, indicating dis-ease whose cause – or even existence – was not otherwise apparent. It is as valuable for episcopal leaders and parish ministers as a patient's symptoms are for their doctor; a hitherto hidden malaise could not be articulated, diagnosed or treated. The gospel and apostolic accounts suggest a well-handled crisis can result in a situation better than if it had not happened. Peter's grievous denial of our Lord was more than trumped at the beach breakfast by Jesus's pastoral response. His relationship with Jesus deepened beyond measure, and his preparations for apostleship completed. The apostles were crafted though Jesus's expertise in facing and settling crises.

The contrast between the models of organism and organisation is explored in the next chapter; the Church needing to aspire towards the former. These models are significant when we consider how godly authority is best used in Church affairs.

The best-selling novel, '*The Shack,*' attributes to Jesus an interesting comment on hierarchy and authority:

> 'Once you have a hierarchy you need rules to protect and administer it, and then you need law and the enforcement of the rules, and *you end up with some kind of chain of command or a system of order that destroys relationship rather than promotes it. You rarely see or experience relationship apart from power. Hierarchy imposes laws and rules and you end up missing the wonder of relationship that we intended for you.*'[234]

The relationships of organism are what work, and what we need. Unless we form a coherent body, based on networks – sinews – of coherent relationship, church leaders will always weary themselves trying to insist upon Gospel values within inherited non-Gospel structures.

Secular organisations are prone to self-serving elements that demean true leadership. The Church is not immune. Unthinkingly we accept and endorse hierarchies, rank and its attendant deference-culture: keeping people at arm's length, and disabling them from speaking truth to power.

Tom Wright tells in one of his commentaries of such issues being faced decisively, during the 1940s, in the constitution for the newly united Church of South India. He quotes from Lesslie Newbigin's autobiography, '*Unfinished Agenda*':

'The chairman raised the question: what shall we do about canons, deans, archdeacons and the like? "I paused," said Newbigin, "with my pen ready to write down the decision of the committee. Nobody said anything for a while; then a single voice said 'Abolish them.' Since nobody challenged this proposal, I wrote down the one word: Abolished."

'That cheerful iconoclastic approach to "offices" held by some within the ordained ministry of the church was a response to the needs of a new situation. The newly formed body *saw no need to perpetuate the kinds of subtle distinctions that had gradually become taken for granted in the older churches which were joining together.* And, though Paul clearly envisaged the need for something we can call "offices" within the church (see the "bishops and deacons" in Philippians 1.1 for instance), he seems to go out of his way to avoid giving us the same list twice, just in case we should suppose that he had an actual hierarchy in mind – which is of course what this chapter (1 Corinthians 12) is intending to rule out.'[235]

Today we have, perpetuate and even revere, a *de facto* hierarchy. It thus becomes normal to view clergy and laity as less important than the hierarchy. The most sensitive and important human issues – not least relational connection and understanding – being bludgeoned by bureaucracy, distanced by synodical processes and a surfeit of formal meetings. Such domination of leaders' diaries offers the illusion of achievement whilst defrauding the community of more important relational opportunity.

Signs of fragmentation

There are many signs of fragmentation. The clerical-lay dichotomy, unhelpfully dispersed functions of oversight and leadership, and excessive party loyalties are particular examples. There are also the single-issue factions – each offering alternative leaders.

o *The clerical-lay dichotomy.*

This rank-based phenomenon may be more acute than most clergy easily recognise. It demotes laity to trivial roles. It encourages clergy to adopt a self-protective pattern of meeting together; buttressed by a deference-tradition that Church leaders seem seldom to recognise, let alone challenge. Deference develops in a soil where a rightful respect for leaders, and a desire for unity, confuses clergy and laity into forgetting that – in the pattern of Jesus and the apostles – love has to embrace a mutual willingness for straightforward truth-speaking, and rank-free patterns of meeting together. Without this last element, mutual accountability fades within the Body; and unaccountable power ascends. Over-emphasis of ordained ministry under-values the lay role. Two misconceptions may lie at the cause. Firstly, that the most important place for ministry is within the church; even the church building. In God's intention, it is surely the world outside. Secondly, that clergy are God's front-line troops for penetrating the undergrowth of our loveless world. In every way, this is wrong.

Laity – including the ordained – are God's primary agents. They need to be recruited for battle: then trained to demonstrate and speak God's love in his battle against the dark powers. The main battleground is in those communities where Jesus's followers already work, live and socialise. Any division of believers between those who are ordained and those who are not is a fault line running right through Christ's body. In its extreme forms, the clericalisation of the church is a scandal; most certainly an agent of dysfunctionality and fragmentation.

Then there is the imbalanced emphasis over lay and ordained vocations – a first order theological – and ecclesiological – issue waiting to be addressed. Whilst ordained vocation demands proper attention, where is the equivalent effort and investment at, say, deanery and parish level on lay vocation; vocation into the highways and byways of neighbourhood and workplace, over and above any emphasis of church lay leadership roles? Why for example did we invest in Urban Industrial Mission without establishing an ethos that here was a task for every lay person? Where are the equipping strategies? And why do we support Bishops at considerable cost in their House of Lords duties if we do not offer recognition and support to Christian laity exercising influence at high levels of responsibility in all public forums? These, after all, are better placed to talk authoritatively on a range of specialist issues.

Dispersed leadership.

The Church's systems have tended increasingly to relieve bishops of significant components of their engagement with clergy: spiritual and professional nurture, training, parish appointments, ministerial review, pastoral care, encouragement and ministerial development, counselling, active involvement when things get difficult and in a small number of cases, discipline. These have shifted over time, unnoticed, from the centre of a leader's portfolio, causing relational loss and fragmentation. Arguably,

- or reasons of structure, consistent nurture is barely offered except perhaps in a minister's early years by an incumbent and a diocesan officer, if they are fortunate;
- training in the full dictionary sense seems rarely given in the Church's culture, either for leaders or parish clergy;
- appointing has become unstraightforward – sometimes perhaps more driven by the need to fill a gap than by rigorous analysis of parish needs, a priest's capacity and character, and by a commensurate unwillingness to gap a post rather than appoint unwisely;
- encouragement from a bishop is likely to be somewhat random and distant – indeed some may never receive it;
- counselling has often been dispersed to diocesan teams – whose hands seem full. (Has anyone analysed patterns of need behind the substantial recourse to counselling by ministers, nationwide?);
- involvement in difficult times is likely to come from archdeacons,

if offered, and less often from bishops – indeed I have heard clergy say they would not turn to bishops or archdeacons in the first instance, if they needed help of any sort;

– and discipline is now being outsourced from bishops to those from a secular background, probably distant from the context of alleged misdemeanour and perhaps without any pastoral remit.

Core elements of episcopal leadership have thus been pushed beyond the immediate reach – even visibility – of most bishops. (And there is risk in a recent initiative to establish a national system of HR officers: the temptation to expect HR advisers to get involved in management decisions may need watching.)[236] Equally, new ways for releasing parish clergy may need to be found.

Furthermore, the synodical system may focus too much on details of governance and management; and insufficiently on concepts, ideas and initiatives, the precursors of objectives and strategy. It has become a hard place to exercise leadership. Clearly, bishops need to demonstrate a proper accountability to their flock in a way where challenge is permissible and effective: yet the present system chokes the Church with its 'leadership-lite' surfeit of boards, councils and committees, unthinkingly misappropriating lay effort in the process from its local place of mission and ministry. New ways must be found to release bishops from chairing meetings whilst giving them freedom, within agreed strategy, to offer direction and oversight.

o *Alternative leadership.*
The Dioceses section of the Church of England Year Book tabulates the Church's appointed leaders. There they are, so that is it; or is it? That is the formal view of leadership, but the view from the incumbent's desk may be different. The question is, upon which person or group does she or he depend for their ministerial stimulus, for their reading material perhaps, for their encouragement and shaping? For there is an array of alternative leadership too easily airbrushed out of strategic thinking, found maybe in special interest groups, church-political groups and other para-church organisations.[237] This sign of fragmentation

deserves serious attention; not so much for what it is saying about this alternative leadership, as for what it is saying about the given leadership in Christ's Body.

At the very least, these alternative leaders may have significant inputs for the formal leadership's consideration. Alternative leadership represents some degree of loss from a Church that deserves all the allegiance and support it can get.

Signs of dysfunction

o *Bureaucracy.*

Many people, even Prime Ministers, talk of the need to reduce 'red tape'. The problem with such talk is that red tape is a product, not a cause. It is born of relational inadequacy. It is a work-around, trying to achieve coherence by organisational means rather than through relational repair. With good leadership in place, engendering trust, people will be receptive to guidance and will wish to bring about good solutions accordingly. With weak leadership, or dysfunctional oversight systems, trust withers. Appetites for compliance weaken. 'Caesar' then moves in with his apparatus of power. The mass of regulation increases, and coercive techniques adopted to ensure compliance. All the while trust weakens further, demoralisation sets in and initiative atrophies. Stalinist Communism offered instructive demonstration of this process.

Every denomination and congregation needs grace's imprint across its life. Yet grace's flow depends on the connection of relationship and common purpose. In ordinary life, we may glimpse grace when mutual commitment between two parties is born, forming relationship glued by trust. Where such commitment exists between leaders and led – whether in nation, institution or family – conformity to common aims and activities is the likely outcome. Calm and well-being result. I can testify to this truth of from my naval experience. When a ship's company is well-led and well-managed, recourse to the 'law' reduces. When 'grace' puts it into the hearts of the crew to do well, law and regulation still stand, but are hardly needed to achieve standards. The law is thus fulfilled as a natural consequence.

o *Clergy support.*

We start with a juxtaposition. Management Today named a young professional businesswoman, Lamorna Trahair, as one of "35 women under 35 to watch". She is a Director of a company running substantial adventure activities in Mongolia, India, Africa and South America. A published interview goes like this:

'Although Lamorna is only 23, a wise and mature attitude has seen her and the team through the first few years of start up. When asked how the team is managed, her response is typical of the inclusive, relaxed style she exudes, "there is a mutual respect, if one person has a task that needs getting done there and then, people muck in because we know that when people say it is important, then it is." This is also reinforced by good communications, easier Lamorna admits with a small team. Communication is one of her golden rules of business, she says, "this is an ongoing challenge, particularly if you are working in another part of the world. We strive to make everyone, wherever they are working, a real part of the team, making sure we know what everyone is up to and that they are supported keeping that a priority. We always make sure that there is a number to call from overseas with someone on duty at all times to talk about anything, from the mundane to a crisis." Good communications are key for all organisations but as they grow she admits they will get harder, but even more important

… Lastly, as a small company they have recognised and embraced the need to connect as a team on a personal level. They meet up at the pub for drinks or have a meal together to maintain and develop a close and supportive network. Lamorna explains this is for one very important reason above others, "when the **** hits the fan, then we know how each other will react and deal with it, as we know them outside of work as well. It gets harder as we get bigger, but relaxing and letting your hair down outside of work is just as important." Hearing her say this I wonder how many companies have forgotten that their workforce are people first and that getting to know what really makes them tick could have a lasting and positive impact on their business, especially in times of crisis.'[238]

This picture of corporate care contrasts starkly with one parish priest's experience. Emerging from depression's darkness, he wrote:

> 'Sadly, my experience has been one of struggling in a "vacuum of care". Partly this has been the result of my seeming competence and confidence in ministry... The Church is going through an extensive period when stipendiary clergy are increasingly trying to do "more with less". Additionally, on top of just keeping the show on the road they are having to engage in demanding pastoral reorganisations as parishes are reconfigured for ministry in the twenty-first century and so as to function parochially with fewer stipendiary clergy. ... Not only has there been a reduction in staffing for the day to day functioning of the parishes – costly enough – but this reorganisation has been attempted in parallel with those existing demands with no external or additional resources being put in place during the transition.'

Bricks and straw spring to mind. He continued,

> 'My overall impression is that there needs to be a more robust, proactive, pervasive and institutionally embedded approach to on-going clergy development, support and care... I suspect that many clergy (on their second or third careers) will have come from organisations with more robust systems of staff development, support and care. Does the Church live up to its duty of care?'

o *Discord.*

Discord in the Church may be public or hidden. I have heard of ugly discord within bishops' meetings as well as in clergy chapter meetings. Disagreement is part of the stuff of life, and was certainly part of the apostles' experience. Somewhere along the line it turns into discord, perhaps when attacks become personal, when those bearing a larger responsibility suffer character assassination, and whenever animosity is unchecked.

Mutiny is a military hazard. No-one in the Church is likely to mutiny: it's not that sort of body, and other coping systems will be found for grievous discontent. And yet ... that does not preclude a mutinous spirit developing. The military experience of mutiny's causes may therefore have a wider application.

Richard Woodman wrote of two US aircraft carrier mutinies in the 1970s:

'These point most cogently to the root cause of *all mutinies*: a detachment of the captain of any vessel, irrespective in size, from the mood of his crew, *all* of his crew, not just those with whom he has most in common or sees most frequently.'[239]

What should concern the Church, and indeed any large body, are some barely-asked questions. Do its leaders know the feelings of those they serve? How may bishops gauge the mood of their diocese, *all* of their clergy, not just those with whom they have most in common or see most frequently? How may they know the corporate mind of parish clergy and church officers? These are surely first order questions for church leaders. The answers are unlikely to be found through synods, councils, licensings, confirmations or correspondence.

o *Distance of the leader from the led.*

Knowledge is essential to shepherding. Jesus said, 'I am the good shepherd. I know my own and my own know me, just as the Father knows me and I know the Father. And I lay down my life for the sheep.'[240]

The shepherd spends much time with his sheep so that he knows them really well and they know him. For Jesus, cascading relationship starts in intimacy with his Father through the Spirit, and replicates in his relationship with his sheep. Yet the Church, with its inherited ways of working, too often tries to shepherd with slim or patchy knowledge of the sheep; perhaps not grasping that shepherding demands relationship. Close and confident knowledge of clergy is fundamental to the episcopal role.

A retired diocesan bishop has written:

'My current view is that despite the long history of national-affairs-involvement episcopally, there is little likelihood of prominent bishops cutting much ice via the media. As in some earlier ages it is small local groups who might affect a neighbourhood. So bishops need to be much nearer to them, for training and nurture.

'What I now observe (from the parish and deanery level) is that the (church) authorities, including their training advisers, do not see the clergy and leading laity in action in their localities – and thus the mistakes they make which quite simple training would cure. When the authorities do come local it is they who do the talking. In the armed forces the leaders are close enough to spot and correct mistakes quickly. How can the C of E bridge this gap is the question I wrestle with.'[241]

If children grow up with inadequate experience of family life, their development of relational skills will suffer. Time together is essential. Example cannot take effect without it. The Church's system perpetuates an equivalent deprivation. Teaching seems more dominant than training, isolation is the norm and extended times working with others are rare. Individualism rather than teamwork seems commonplace and acceptable; indeed, it is fostered institutionally. The frameworks for discipling ordained and lay Christians seem sparse.

o *Irksome in-trays and crises.*
The Church has bought heavily into secular thinking and systems. Its leaders can become so encultured by the way things are, they become unaware of some big questions around. Archbishop Rowan Williams was reported saying that 'words were not always the best tool for understanding God.' When asked what the Church would look like if it took God seriously, Dr Williams expressed frustration at having to deal with "institutional fire-fighting" rather than being able to concentrate on answers. When he had time to think about it, however, he began to realise that the Church talked too much. If it could learn the value of silence,

it would be closer to "getting God right" than when it was being endlessly chatty.'[242]

Another Church leader has observed that the bulk of his time is consumed in what are essentially bureaucratic tasks – such as a vastly increased workload in making clergy appointments, dealing with correspondence, complaints ...[243]

Another, when interviewed by the Church Times, mentioned his dismay about clerical indiscipline. He went on to say

'episcopal life is like white-water rafting. You're always worried what set of boulders will next upset you.'[244]

But are not these elements – 'fire-fighting', 'white-water rafting', clergy appointments, correspondence and complaints – the stuff of Kingdom ministry, of first order importance in a leader's role? For whether at the level of the Anglican Communion, national Church or diocese, dealing with 'fires' is part of a bishop's healing role, so well expressed in the ordinal. Then, *so far as any parish is concerned*, the appointment of a priest is the most important decision the bishop or diocese may make across a span of decades. It will either enhance the work of the Kingdom or diminish it; no small matter. If the associated systems are cumbersome and difficult, then should not leaders use their position to address the issues corporately in the national bodies? If not, who else should be taking care of such things?

Much of a bishop's non-routine correspondence either presents a pastoral opportunity, or reflects some systemic dysfunctionality in the Church that ought to be acknowledged and addressed. Correspondence is a part of Christian ministry. It is communication, and therefore significant in relationship building, in affirming and commending. Even a dull letter confirming a diary date may be lightened with a personal post-script; conveying a value disproportionate to its cost.

And complaints! In the world, wise business leaders treat them as no-cost gifts: warning of dysfunctionality needing attention. So, these assuredly have value to a bishop in his primary task. Doctors should not be perturbed by the number of symptoms brought to them. The ordinal confers, 'a special responsibility to maintain and further the unity of the Church'. Indeed the bishop is tasked to promote unity, peace and love among all Christian people, and especially among those they serve. Of course, crises are time consuming; and cases of discord can be infuriatingly opaque. Yet they enable first-order creative work for a Church leader. Sadly, the Church seems yet to develop a proper system here. Without one, playing things 'off the cuff' and consulting as many people as possible will tend to be the tragic consequence. A great deal of Jesus's ministry was triggered by crises; the unexpected. God seems to work this way.

Empathy with the fragile, faltering or besieged parish leader is an essential attribute of church leaders, not least those in senior positions. Hebrews emphasises God's unlimited empathy in Jesus:

'Since, therefore, the children share flesh and blood, he himself likewise shared the same things, so that through death he might destroy the one who has the power of death, that is, the devil, and free those who all their lives were held in slavery by the fear of death. For it is clear that he did not come to help angels, but the descendants of Abraham. Therefore he had to become like his brothers and sisters in every respect, so that he might be a merciful and faithful high priest in the service of God, to make a sacrifice of atonement for the sins of the people. Because he himself was tested by what he suffered, he is able to help those who are being tested.'[245]

The enormity of the desolation and brokenness endured by Jesus prior to resurrection and victory is unmatched in history: the Son of God judicially degraded and murdered. Nonetheless, both Peter and Paul had to pass through vales of desolation, brokenness and death. Their ministries were deepened in the only possible way. Ordination candidates and applicants for Christian leadership appointments ought always to be asked, 'What is your experience of brokenness?' Unless a church leader has known desolation of spirit and brokenness – even failure – it is hard to see how they can minister to those who come their way. Archbishop Michael Ramsay wrote to clergy: 'It is doubtful if any of us can do anything at all until we have been very much hurt, and until our hearts have been very much broken.'[246]

o *Attitude to laity.*

What does volunteer commitment and lay training investment add up to within the Church of England? For example, how many million lay-person-weeks a year are devoted to PCC, deanery, diocesan, and general synods and their associated meetings? And, additionally, what is the cost and travel time? In parallel, how much people-time, effort and money is devoted to identified opportunity for outreach and service beyond the parish church's social perimeter?

These are critical questions, for committed laity appear to be are drawn back, in large measure, from the front-line; then directed into time-consuming busyness, more to do with institutional maintenance than God's mission to the world. Do Church leaders ponder such data? How may a difference be made?

Mark Oakley asks 'whether lay Christians *are being equipped and encouraged* by a Church that can focus its vocation more around the altar, retreat house or synod than the workplace, home, or the nurture of children.'[247]

Ronald Searle drew a memorable cartoon of two old women who owned a sheep. They spent half the year shearing and spinning the wool, then knitted a thick garment for the sheep to wear in the coming winter.[248] It speaks of an organisation that has lost sight of its 'product's' whole point.

INFLUENCE OF THE 'BIG FOUR':
Caesar's power, Old Temple attachment, Individualism and Dogmatism

The Church of England has strengths: but its institutional, relational patterns are not amongst them. Indeed, such frailties work actively against the Church's great commission. The God who is love is served by a Church with a relational deficit – substantially unaddressed.

Questions of imbalance, incoherence and dysfunctionality – affecting trust and relationship – have dominated this chapter. Although largely a part of our inheritance, and hard to address, they mar the appearance of Christ's body. The underlying issue of relationship needs urgent attention, and a priority given to facing the scourge of the Big Four: Caesar and God, Old Temple and New Temple, and Individualism and Dogmatism. Their hidden power fiercely opposes Christ's gospel. Jesus did say, 'every kingdom divided against itself is laid waste, and a divided household falls.'[249]

The problems are acute, yet have to be entered at the right point. *Relationships* are that right point. We have a substantial investment in engaging the distresses across the nation and the wider world: in social justice, in education, in health and healing, in tackling poverty, in nurture, outreach and mission. Yet we seldom notice our own relational deficit. Fr Timothy Radcliffe addressed RC clergy in Dublin on this point with particular clarity:

> 'Painfully, the Lord is demolishing our high towers and our clerical pretensions to glory and grandeur *so that the Church may be a place in which we may encounter God and each other more intimately...* We can discover Jesus's commandments not as a heavy burden which crushes people but *as the invitation to his friendship.* We can be liberated from harmful ways of using power in the Church, which are ultimately rooted in secularism, and become more like the Christ who was lowly and humble of heart, and we shall find rest for our souls.'[250]

In such a context, Jeff Astley draws from Ephesians 2.13-17:

> 'Not only does Jesus make and proclaim peace, however, he also "*is* our peace". The image is that of breaking down a dividing wall... The result (vv 19-22) is a Church that serves as a re-founded temple, but which is also – like a body (Christ's body) – an organic, growing thing (compare 4.4-16). As such, *it is called to be the supreme example of reconciled, joined-up living.*'[251]

As we examine our inherited culture – traditions, customs, structures and systems – some particular obstacles to the flowering of the Kingdom's culture come into view:

- *Our unreformed parish system with its buildings and boundaries, its unaddressed demands, and its rich soil for individualism, for the proliferation of law, regulation and bureaucracy – and for clergy exhaustion.*
- *Our unreformed theological training system with its academic word-based culture.* Jesus formed disciples with a rigour seldom seen today. The statistics of the past century alone suggest that clerical formation has, for inherited reasons, lost its edge. Thankfully, some change is afoot.[252] Nonetheless, a key question is: where is training to be found in close interdependent community; a community doing front-line Kingdom work? How is example of Christ-centred living to be seen – really seen – in our Church's social and organisational patterns? To be even more provocative, for what D-Day is our clergy's training preparing them, and for what D-Day are the thousands in the pews being prepared, Sunday by Sunday?
- *Our endless church initiatives, our proclivity to individualism and dogmatism, and our failure to make the world envious of our relational coherence in Christ, all too easily work against our governing purpose.* We make it improbable that we shall attract very much interest from those outside – let alone the entry of the tax- collector and prostitute. Jesus's intimate obedience to his Father, and relinquished initiative, drew people towards relationship. In contrast, today, our focus has shifted.

Many features reflect a Church formed for a bygone age and bygone culture. Some are inordinately costly and substantially dysfunctional. They hinder the spread of Kingdom leaven, rather than channel it. How may change be effected? Do we need to develop a new language that makes major adjustment seem reasonable? Is it possible to locate entry points for change, where we can name and address relational hindrances, and where a process of relational transformation may be triggered? In the following two chapters, we consider how and where Kingdom leaven may be given space to supplant the other sort.

But first we must acknowledge that imbalance, incoherence and dysfunctionality signify lovelessness within the Body. They harm the wellbeing of those we serve. They discredit the Body. The watching world has had its fill of lovelessness, and recognises it readily.

Institutional lovelessness counters any message of redemption the Church might otherwise convey.

The world's needs, Jesus's life and the Gospel's purpose are only understandable if we recognise lovelessness *as the root of the deepest and most destructive human pain of all.* We must ingest the force of God's command to love him with all our hearts and our neighbours as ourselves. It is his highest purpose and greatest aspiration. And his Body is at the centre of the cosmic power struggle between love and lovelessness.

We, the whole Church, need to decide what we ought – or wish – to bequeath to coming generations.

Visible Structures

10

Organism: *a system or organisation consisting of interdependent parts, compared to a living being.*

Organisation: *an organized group of people with a particular purpose, such as a business or government department.*[253]

People sometimes say that Jesus founded his Church as an organism; and it turned into an organisation. This seems to be generally regarded as an inevitable result of size; a fact of ecclesial life. This is challengeable. The apostolic pattern of leadership and pastoral oversight, seen in the New Testament, is relational. Apostles and congregations knew each other; the resultant mutual trust and affection could run deep.[254]

Dictionaries indicate a particular distinction between the two words. An organism is a received arrangement with inherent life, born of a creator; not self-determined. An organisation, on the other hand, establishes itself with human ingenuity and initiative; for good or ill. Viewed this way, it is easy to see an organisation's vulnerability to Caesar's, and other, strains.

If the Church manifests relational dis-ease, as informed witnesses testify, it must mean we have fled the divine model of connectedness.[255] We have adopted Caesar's model unthinkingly. If so, however hard we try to Christianise it, it remains susceptible to bad leaven. The antidote is the Kingdom leaven of love: of relationship. We need to open the windows and receive it. We now explore how we might embody love more deliberately in our Church's visible structure. Then in Chapter 11 how we explore how love might be given more freedom to range across the Church's unseen processes.

Caesar's model does relational harm in many ways. It is likely that the silent adoption of a *rank* system by the Body has inflicted the greatest single harm to its relational sinews, distorting its shape and affecting mobility. Rank was unknown in the early Church. The great apostle Paul resisted its very thought, seeing himself as 'chief of sinners' and 'least of all the saints.'[256]

The rank system damages an organism in at least three ways.
First, it locks individuals unwisely into a defined field of deployment.
Rank encourages its holder to be protective of its status, powers and activities. Clifford Longley has written that,

> 'The lesson of the past 50 years is that the traditional hierarchical system, the so-called three-fold ministry of bishop, priest and deacon arranged in a pyramid of control and prestige, is no longer fit for purpose.'[257]

Picking up this argument that the three-fold ministry is no longer fit for purpose, we first consider bishops. It is obvious that all parish clergy, not just bishops, exercise episcopal ministry: that of leadership and oversight. Not only does the Church seem in denial of this fact, it can even award diocesan leadership, innocently, to those who have yet to gain any experience of leading and overseeing parish churches.

Then, the role of priests or presbyters occupies a zone of unclarity. Different understandings prevail and are sometimes asserted dogmatically. As one Church we should hope for an agreed meaning for the role of its primary, stipended servants.

The role of deacons has migrated almost entirely from its New Testament origins. Today's deacons must struggle to explain their purpose to anybody.

As things stand, most people probably define a bishop as one authorised to Confirm, and a priest as one authorised for Eucharistic presidency. If so, how distant we now are from the modelling of Jesus and the apostles. Maybe the time for fruitful change has arrived.

Secondly, rank locks the whole body into a hierarchical structure.

Hierarchical authority structures, suggestive of different levels of human worth and of spiritual stature, foster deference. They hinder relationship, keeping people apart. feed cravings for recognition, approval or status; thereby fostering a false sub-culture of *failure versus success*. It promotes clericalism and demeans the role and vocation of the laity: rank-less, at the bottom of the ladder, and of questionable value.

An institutional, relational shortfall means that clergy are bound to acquire a governing self-image. A truer self-understanding only comes from strong relational sinews. They will thus tend to be discouraged rather than encouraged. The fragmented pattern of oversight produces a fragmented rather than a disciplined and tested, coherent knowledge of each minister. It is bound to result in pastoral confusion: to whom would clergy turn for help? The scandal of increasing clergy stress – related to money, buildings, reducing congregations and *the surrounding culture of dogmatic unbelief* – is real, and calls for action. Like the Israelites, too many are struggling to make bricks with insufficient straw.

The hierarchical structure does not deliver.

Lastly, the rank system contains spiritual hazard.

Jesus launched the greatest movement the world has seen without writing a single word or bothering much with formalities. As we have considered, clericalisation has treated the clergy rather the laity as the front-line troops. Such a posture has disabled and marginalised, even infantilised, the laity. In a subversive and subtle way, rank considerations depend on the sub-Christian notion of 'promotion' with all its attendant snares. In our humanity we are tempted to look for techniques that seem to facilitate promotion, rather than simply getting on with obeying the Master's voice. Promotion issues tend to stoke appetites for acclamation and success – whatever that means – rather than faithfulness.

Dietrich Bonhoeffer viewed rank's distortions like this:

'Every cult of personality that emphasises the distinguished qualities, virtues and talents of another person, even though these be of an altogether spiritual nature, is worldly and has no place in the

Christian community; indeed it poisons the Christian community. The desire we so often hear expressed for "episcopal figures", "priestly men", "authoritative personalities", springs frequently enough from spiritually sick need for the admiration of men, for the establishment of visible human authority, because the *genuine authority of service* appears to be so unimpressive. There is nothing that so sharply contradicts such a desire as the New Testament itself in its description of a bishop (1 Tim 3.1ff). One finds there nothing whatsoever with respect to worldly charm and the brilliant attributes of a spiritual personality...

'The question of trust, which is so closely related to that of authority, is determined by the faithfulness with which a man serves Jesus Christ, never by the extraordinary talents which he possesses. Pastoral authority can be attained only by the servant of Jesus who seeks no power of his own, who is himself a brother among brothers submitted to the authority of the Word.'[258]

Paul described James, Peter and John with whom he met in Jerusalem, the 'pillars of the Church.' A mutual accountability and respect is evident, without hint of authoritarianism or undue deference. It offers an insight into the difference between role and rank.[259]

Rank has to be seen for what it is.

It looks as if the Church was designed for 'solo-flyers', not body-members

I define solo-flyers as those who seem only able to work on their own; those who find the time-investment and checks-and-balances of teamwork uncongenial. Secular organisations may have space for solo-flyers, but there should be no room for them in the Body's organism. Solo-flying denies its miraculous complexity and inter-dependence, its corporate strength and attractive coherence. Solo-flyers are unarguably signed-up to Caesar's rather than Christ's way. They head for lovelessness.

The stained-glass-window Jesus may seem to have had a solo leadership-style and lifestyle. He did not, at all. He lived in Trinitarian community: close connexion and collaboration with Father and the indwelling Spirit.[260] His missionary, training model was partnership.[261]

An impartial outsider, reviewing how Anglican ministry is ordered, might well conclude that the Church intentionally seeks solo-flyers: then trains and deploys them accordingly. It should then be no surprise if solo-flying is most priests' general expectancy and practice; all the way through a forty-year ministry. The signs of excessive care to 'match-make' a curate's placement, the pattern of single curacies rather curate teams learning together, then the experience of sole-charge parish posts for most clergy for the rest of their ministries support this conclusion.

As clergy move through such ministry, the temptation is likely to be an excessive protectionism of the way they do things; a reluctance to accept suggestion or seek advice; a high view of their own authority, with a commensurately low view of their overseer's authority; an inclination to play to their strengths and neglect of their frailer areas; and a proclivity to individualism and dogmatism. Such a model is unlikely to inspire unity or interdependence in a congregation. It is unlikely to permit entrepreneurial and collaborative mission initiatives with other parishes and other denominations. In Desmond Tutu's words, 'a person is a person through other persons; you can't be human in isolation; you are human only in relationships.'

The Church's encouragement of parish vacancies – rather than a gapless supersession model that allows a professional handover – is damaging to coherent ministry, and wasteful of garnered wisdom. Its roots probably lie in the individualism that solo-flying nurtures.

As may be expected, the bad leaven draws us in the direction of division and fruitlessness, producing organisation rather than enabling organism. Bad leaven produces no community model for the needy world to emulate.

It looks as if the Church does not know what the laity is for

An organisation has aims and objectives. If the Church acts as organisation, it will be anxious about statistical trends, and will reach for 'mechanical' ways of reversing them; especially membership and financial trends. Targets emerge, and overseers will probably tend to increase demands on parishes rather lift burdens: how else to get results? (Interestingly, the Egyptian oppression of the captive Israelites was channeled through unbearable brick-making targets.) Not only is this Caesar's way, it denies the central reality of Kingdom leaven. It ignores the way leaven works, through empowerment, reproduction and silent growth.

When acting *as organisation*, the Church sends out mixed messages of what congregations – the laity – are for. It can seem the organisation needs to draw the *best* of the laity – whatever that means – ever further into its embrace. The busyness of councils and committees gives the illusion of developing and using the laity well, whilst actually distracting them from their main purpose. Then, if so demeaned, and lacking the challenge of vocational stimulus, they may feel they are only there to finance the Church.

In the Church-as-organism, the laity are to be served, and equipped to penetrate the world and its culture outside; not exploited just to keep the Church running. Culture presses us to prefer organisation to organism.

What then can be done?
Two points seem important.

First, once we recognise the extent of wrong culture's infusion, small adjustments are no solution. Our God is a God of big solutions. His wresting of Israel out of Egypt, and confronting the principalities and powers at Calvary at immeasurable cost, make this plain. The time for lesser changes may have passed. The Church ought now to anticipate – or, at least be open to the thought – that our radical God may now wish for radical change.

Secondly, Christ-patterned aspirations point the way forward. The detail of how we get from where we are, to where God calls us to go, is first a matter for prayer. It is for Church overseers to discern the godly stages through which the Church must pass. The promised land is not simply the place of salvation for individuals. It is the place where Kingdom leaven is given full rein and full reign. There it can permeate, then energise the dry bones of structures, systems and routine: to give Body-life.

The Body is hungry for godly decision.

And what is the urgency?
Robin Greenwood has judged that,

'the clock is ticking, time is running out for inherited patterns of Church – however we look at it – theologically, spiritually, pragmatically, emotionally and financially. My observation is that, often against their own preference, most of the primary energy of bishops, archdeacons and lay administrators is consumed by the reactive round of bureaucratic activities required for the maintenance of the present Church. Conversations with regular worshipers, many of whom have reached retirement age, can reveal both a sense of anxiety that the Church will fail dramatically unless something is done and an unwillingness to see changes to inherited patterns of Church which have become a comfort in an unfamiliar world. Although it is often denied, a high proportion of stipendiary clergy in particular, at the sharp end of this crisis, is suffering stress-related illnesses. To what extent are such church leaders colluding with a culture of overwork...?,[262]

Above all, there is an urgency because of the dominating leaven of Herod, the scribes and Pharisees. It presses hard on our God-loved world, from every side. The world's cultural systems are not neutral; not parking places where the uncommitted may linger safely. They are, today and tomorrow, spreading bad leaven's spores with virulent power and urgency. There is an urgency to respond because of the Great Commission's urgency.

WHAT, THEN, MIGHT BE OUR PRINCIPAL ASPIRATIONS AS CHURCH?

This book's arguments point to these aspirations; Christ-patterned and purposeful:

First, the demolition of rank
This might mean that all titles of Bishop, Archdeacon, Dean, Prebendary, and Canon are killed-off. We need to echo Paul in his decisive sloughing off his inherited Old Temple stuff:[263]

'I once thought these things were valuable, but now I consider them worthless because of what Christ has done. (NLT)

'More than that, I regard everything as loss because of the surpassing value of knowing Christ Jesus my Lord. For his sake I have suffered the loss of all things, and I regard them as rubbish (dung, in KJV), in order that I may gain Christ.' (NRSV)

It would equally mean the demise of pre-nominals. The Most, Right and Very, the plain Reverend and the Venerable are worthless – both in today's world and in New Testament terms – only we do not see it. More significantly, we need to face the fact that rank defines people. As Nick Page observes:

'One of the real tragedies of the Christian church has been that just placing someone in an official position automatically granted them respect and honour. Nobody thinks that way, not nowadays.'[264]

Rank assigns them a non-negotiable value, increasing at each rung of the ecclesiastical ladder. Many of our senior clergy model a Christ-like grace and humility, and do not see themselves in this way at all. The problem is our system, not our leaders. It may quietly tell onlookers we are out of kilter with our example, Jesus: who emptied himself, took the form of a slave, humbled himself, became obedient and experienced the desolation of powerlessness.

It would mean appointing women and men to *roles*, not rank. When that appointment ends, they should revert to being simple members of Christ's Body, open to any new appointment to which the Spirit leads. We saw this change being prototyped by Lord Hope, who became a rural incumbent after relinquishing his archbishop's role. There have been others.

One might call the diocesan leader a bishop; but as a role description, not title. The field would then be open to devising a coherent network, cascading through the diocese, of proven leaders at different levels, exercising episcopal oversight of clergy and congregations. Objective and informed assessments of church leaders' episcopal giftedness, of a single parish or larger groupings, would then become possible. It would allow confident knowledge of ministerial giftedness and aptitudes; then appointment of ministers to larger and appropriate levels of oversight, according to their evinced capacity. Further benefits will be argued later in the chapter.

Secondly, ministerial partnership

Following the incontrovertible New Testament pattern, *leadership is leadership-in-partnership*. Jesus ministered not individualistically but self-evidently in his Trinitarian partnership. Father and Spirit were party to all he did, saw and heard – his partners of reference. Solo ministry was not Paul's pattern. As well as his intimate dependence upon the Godhead, he travelled with others, ministered with them, and wrote his letters with co-signatories. By this means, what he learned on the road, his associates saw and learned too. Often in danger, and learning together through the experience, they would have known mutual support, encouragement and shared hope. The midnight worship and prayer-meeting of Silas and Paul is extraordinary (Acts 16.25), as were its consequences. Had Paul been flying solo, a lesser outcome is probable. Leadership can be a very lonely experience, yet God did not intend it to be so. Statistics on clergy isolation and stress are likely to bear this out.

We need a new norm: that no stipendiary minister will ever be required, or allowed, to fly solo. The present trend towards multi-parished benefices has placed unreasonable pressures – indeed, disablement – upon clergy. It has aroused much public concern, but no Church-wide strategic response. Whilst indicative of a parish system no longer fit-for- purpose, the Church might ameliorate the problems by insisting on this new principle: that every parish priest in England has a colleague. Hitherto the Church system has pressed clergy into fitting in with parish requirements. Now may be the time to press parishes to fit in with reasonable clerical apportionment. It is not a matter of increasing clergy numbers, but reshaping deployment patterns. If there are two incumbents with adjacent benefices, one of five and the other of seven parishes, they might merge into one. Unless the two clergy would prefer it the other way round, the senior would be *primus inter pares*; but each would offer primary care to designated parishes.

This would of course be a long-term process. It is possible that most of today's clergy offered for ordination because of the 'norm' *of* solo-flying; maybe, for some, an intuitive reluctance to work alongside others. So the Church would need, at the earliest moment, to change its institutional stance, formally and publicly. A primary exploration, in a selection conference for ordination training, would look for solid evidence of each candidates' relational skills. Jesus's summary of the law assuredly allows little choice. Those candidates who suffer from excessive, anti-social levels of shyness must be discouraged from applying. All clergy should aspire to engage confidently and warmly with new acquaintances as a sign of the Kingdom. In what other way can the Church come to offer leadership to churches so that wardens, PCCs and congregations grow increasingly together; move from organisation towards organism?

Curacies would invariably need to be served in parishes or benefices where priests work in partnership with neighbouring priests, able to model collegial leadership and ministry; and preferably with half a dozen curates being trained together for their mutual challenge and encouragement. Working closely together with others – essential to Kingdom culture – needs to be displayed, taught and learned. Jesus showed it needed three years of remarkably close attention.

Clergy need a deep induction in living a shared life if they are to draw their flock in this direction. Understanding shared-living requires both example and experience. Words and factual knowledge do not deliver very much. A major shift in Church investment would be necessary. A great benefit is arguable if conventional theological course training were to be halved, and the time given to tough, challenging shared-living experience. We may be talking of six months before the selection conference: for testing and training, and six months as part of pre-ordination training.

Quite apart from its inherent value, this approach would give bishops a greater confidence in candidates' character and ability before recommending them for a selection conference, and for ordination, respectively. These two six-month opportunities could be divided into two or three month placements. These should not be at the choice of candidates. Opportunities for shared-living placements might be found in secular or Christian enterprises. Examples might found be at home or overseas: with a L'Arche Community, with a charity for the homeless, or one working amongst AIDS/HIV-affected families, or one working for prisoner rehabilitation, for orphans or the dependent elderly, or one working amongst refugees, or the starving or the war-torn. Today there are many such mission organisations across the world, probably seldom used for this purpose. This way, the Church would assuredly never be the same again: its Body-life would 'risk' transformation.

The West Malaysian Bishop, Ng Moon Hing and his wife Siew Lan established a sacrificial pattern of discipling in his previous parish ministry. He has since offered the model to his diocese. It speaks to several of the issues in this book – living together, using example and experience as powerful tools in the transmission of wisdom and understanding.

'In a small way I have tried to disciple some people while I was a parish priest, he writes. For several years his bishop would send a theological college student to work under him for two months' long vacation field work. To every student who came to me, I gave the same instructions:

- The student must stay with my family in the vicarage.
- He/she must eat what my family eats – simple meals only (pity them), except on his/her day off or when receiving other invitations.
- He/she must join my family in family worship and devotion as a 'member' of the family.
- He/she must be ready to get up and work with me at odd hours whenever there was an emergency.
- He/she must carefully observe when and how I prepare my sermons, do my devotion, relate to my wife, relate to my children and their home-work, relate to church members, lead PCC meetings, conduct services, handle issues, relate to my church staff, spend my time and money, food and drink pattern and consumption etc.
- He/she must be willing to travel with me to all outreach centres and rural places for ministry. This includes eating, staying and using the facilities in the rural places.
- He/she must read all the files and Bishop's instructions and assigned books.
- He/she must be willing to communicate and exchange views and ideas with me, including scripture, theology, politics, spiritual matters, economics, medical topics, business issues, topics related to the physical, psychology, arts, science, etc.

'I believe a Discipler is a transparent person. He must be who he is at home, in church and in society. The little things count and speak loudly for a discipler. His disciples will watch him and possibly imitate him. There is great danger and it is very vulnerable to open oneself so wide, but it's worth everything when it involves Biblical Discipleship.'[265]

Here is a way of teaching and nurturing the young, pressing and equipping the future Church to purvey Kingdom leaven.

Our Church needs to covet such an approach; grasping the need to slacken its dependence on courses, words and the accumulation of raw knowledge. Wisdom and understanding are more important. They struggle to penetrate such channels. Most certainly, any resistance to team-work and living together – opposing the lifestyle Jesus showed us – has to be identified before any candidate moves towards possible ordination. Such resistance is scarcely discernible in interviews: it can only be tested practically.

Thirdly, sharing life together

It is hard for congregations to live together well. It is hard for congregations to engage readily with adjacent congregations; and it is very hard for congregational members to feel particular warmth for their diocese. The organisational mindset is like reinforced concrete: hard to change. Only God can do the supernatural through the Spirit, and he alone can change our hearts of stone to those of flesh. He can grow us as an organism. Yet he can only do this with our cooperation. We would need to commit ourselves to journey into a life-together within the Church as far and deep as is possible.

It would be a costly commitment. Time needs to be given, food shared, and homes opened-up. Churches in SE Asia, greatly helped by climate and local customs, live out much of their church lives in public spaces. They meet, eat, talk and pray together in street-side cafés and food-stalls: breakfast, lunch and supper are their opportunities. Of course, the most creative way of sharing life together is in outreach ventures. Living closely together goes against the grain of our inhibited western culture. Yet its potential rewards are great:

- Whether home, sandwich-bar, pub, children's or old-people's home, sports arena or building-site, it moves healthily from church-building-centric life to where other people live, play and work.
- Under good-exampled leadership it fosters openness, mutual understanding and accountability, trust, burden-sharing, celebration; and above all, accountable discipleship. It further offers tailored through-ministry training that the tradition of sector ministry cannot begin to emulate. Professional knowledge, understanding and competence is developed in the most cost- and time-effective way.
- It recaptures space and opportunity for example to do its great work. Present day cultural trends have squeezed – even squeezed out – many life-together opportunities in the home, school and work place. The Church needs to demonstrate to Caesar's IT-obsessed world that investment in relationship – providing space for example – is a Kingdom benefit of exceptional value.

There is a cost to conventional church life. Time is too readily filled with endless committee meetings – squandering time and offering scant nourishment – sometimes life-numbing. Whilst a well-conducted meeting provides rich opportunity for the life-sharing already described, experience suggests that such gatherings tend to reflect organisation, not organism. They can create the illusion of an importance they do not have. Such meetings need objective assessment, perhaps culling.

Good overseers will review every agenda, looking for ways of deciding lesser issues by email or telephone, rather than by meeting. They will see every occasion of gathering as a Kingdom opportunity: for burden-bearing, encouraging, equipping and laughter.

Fourthly, expertise in relational healing
If love is God's great theme and unity his standard, all church overseers – of dioceses or single parishes – need a substantial competence in responding to misdemeanour, conflict resolution, reconciliation and relational building. The Christian arts of wise judgment, encouragement, affirmation, cajoling and rebuke need a long preparation. Each of these skills and arts demands a substantial induction in human psychology that is not always evident. Giftedness

in pastoral counselling should not be relegated to 'experts'. It should be organic to the role of episcopal oversight: for the ministry of 'inner healing' and building up of Christ's Body.

Crises provoke dismay and fear on the human plane. But the New Testament points to their being pivotal opportunities; for change or development, and outcomes more beneficial than if they had not emerged. Rich opportunity then opens up for God to bless individuals and communities. If the community is in harmony and sharing life together, example will strengthen good practice, sub-consciously and effortlessly.

IMAGINING THE OUTCOMES

I now draw on the things I have seen, heard and read – over time, across the world and across cultures – some noted in this book. I have tried to check every perception, each idea, with the template of godly relationship; of Christ-engendered coherence. I have tried to avoid prescription in the detail. There are experienced practitioners and responsibility-bearers far better equipped to look into that. I have however sought to understand and define some pivotal points – issues of governing significance – that, if embraced, seem to offer the possibility of a range of benefits tumbling out.

God deals in pivotal points, pivotal moments. Jesus's simple request, 'please give me a drink', triggered the evangelisation of the Samaritan village of Sychar (Jn 4). Peter and John's decision to attend the temple for prayer at a particular time triggered a sequence of events yielding unforeseeable fruitfulness (Acts 3). These are what we must look for in our individual pilgrimages. This is what I have aspired to do here, aware that only God can initiate.

What then might be God's entry points for change? Perhaps they are the demolition of rank, the reshaping of ministerial lifestyles in partnerships, the increasing pattern of living-together, and the urgent acquisition of expertise in relational healing across the Church. Such decisions, and fresh commitments, might allow the *Body* to develop a different lifestyle. God can free us from customs and trappings that have enchanted us; from subservience to traditions, structures and systems – to serve him, each other and those outside more fully.

He can give us, clergy and laity alike, an openness to change for the sake of the Kingdom and the energy to do so.

In a newly recovered lifestyle, there might be one bishop (fulfilling the role) – not Bishop (defined by rank) – for a diocese, appointed for a fixed term, and then a review. He or she would be selected from a pool of candidates, with proven relational skills, and with episcopal skills clearly evident in their parish ministries. Across the diocese, selected clergy would be given roles of episcopal oversight, working within a cascaded system of ministerial networks. Dependent on the ministerial strength of a diocese, the bishop might have responsibility for say eight episcopal overseers; and they in turn have responsibility for up to eight episcopal overseers, of lesser responsibility, who lead and oversee groups of, say, six to ten ministers in partnership.

Typically, the pattern of the bishop and his episcopal overseers might be to spend a full day and evening, perhaps every two months – one-to-one with their assigned eight – talking, ministering to each other, praying, laughing, eating, walking-the-hills, playing with the children, fixing a broken chair, watching a film. Then, once a month, the nine spend half a day together: worshipping and praying, sharing experiences of encouragement and discouragement, of lessons learned, of books read and resources discovered; and when appropriate inviting wisdom on intractable problems. This proposal suggests a glad investment of five full days a month, in every case, for the oversight, care and building up of the Body. It is very hard to think of better ways of spending five days a month, if we wish to put relational nurture back in the centre of Church life; where it ought to have been for centuries. The Kingdom benefits are surely inestimable.

Some churches are already embracing this sort of approach. Writing about 'Fresh Expressions' in *The Times*, Ruth Gledhill reported the development in a new model church in Buckinghamshire:

'Latimer's is an example of how "fresh expressions" phenomena are calling a halt on the long-term decline in church attendance, and, in some places, actually setting it on an upward trend. In two years, numbers have grown to between 150 and 200 attending during the week and on Sunday are bursting out of the barn. Latimer's ordered a big top, due to be delivered next month. Many are meeting weekly in smaller groups around Buckinghamshire in what are being termed small "pastorates", functioning groups of Christians living in community who know each other well.

"'The idea is to identify leaders of smaller groups who will form groups of confident believers, people who will not retreat into some little cosy Christian subculture but will engage with the real world. They then will also spawn other little groups," explains Nancy Gifford, of the Oxford Centre for Apologetics. "Latimer's has everyone from builders, those seeking work, to sporting champions, venture capitalists, civil servants, teachers and workers for NGOs."

'As with Holy Trinity Brompton, ... key ingredients of Latimer's success seem to be prayer, food and, perhaps most important of all, a strong sense of community.'[266]

Here we see local *episcope* being exercised effectively 'at ground level'. A profitable next stage would be to reconfigure dioceses along equivalent lines, in that unevenly-layered, episcope-sparse zone between churches and the diocesan leader; with cascaded oversight, friendship, understanding, example and trust all being let off the leash.

The opportunity exists for friendship to infiltrate the Church's systems, unconstrained by rank and mindless protocols. Time invested in relationship is seldom wasted.

Many reasons seem to justify such a substantial investment of time and effort:

- It follows the relational pattern of Jesus.
- It reverses the present priorities of time given to committee and formal meetings, as opposed to *people*.
- The bishop becomes better informed on the clergy and congregational wellbeing than is remotely possible with existing structures and systems.
- The message is gently broadcast that *people count.*
- Mutual understanding and harmony across a diocese increases.
- All clergy are likely to feel better known and valued, and feel part of a living organism.
- That the Body's strength depends on relationship more than rules and regulations, on human contact more than paper-work.

- It may develop new norms of spiritual and ministerial understanding, and of professionalism – not least in areas of administrative technique and time- management.
- ... thereby permitting a reduction of *sector* posts, including investment in Continuing Ministerial Education.
- Together with partner-ministry, isolation and loneliness reduce as mutual support and accountability take effect.
- ... resulting in the likelihood of fewer clergy health casualties and disciplinary occasions.
- The influence of gifted ministers, not least bishops and episcopal overseers, is likely to increase through these networks.
- Bishops will be able to gain a more certain knowledge of his or her clergy; better equipped to discern suitability for preferment and other key appointments.
- As such a system takes hold, so it will become possible to cull those tangled patches of bureaucracy – in particular, moulding the synodical and appointing systems to serve a trust-based organism rather than a distrustful organisation.
- *Above all, it would signal a decisive shift away from relationships constrained and chilled by Caesar's controlling appetites, and Caesar's fears. It would enable a relational revolution, bringing relationship to the centre of the Body's life – and more than this, release the power of example to channel godly wisdom and understanding through the whole Body – God's method from the start.*

Ancient patterns and customs have their charm, but unless they reflect Kingdom values, they hinder the flow of God's purposes. We, as Church, must name and face them. The grip of such enchantments needs to be broken.

Unseen Processes　11

'History shows that quasimystical movements among the laity [in reference to the Oxford Group movement] do not flourish where the invisible side of institutional religion is vigorously maintained.'
Evelyn Underhill [267]

Time and cultural process have harmed and hindered episcopal work-patterns, and bishops' standing in Church and society.

Women and men who enter ordained ministry, together with their families, make many sacrifices. They entrust themselves to an organisation that ought to be an organism. As with all organisations, its systems and structures may gain a fraudulent loyalty – a subtle, self-serving pressure for the organisation to serve itself more than the people for whom it exists.

Chapter 3 postulated a universal truth; for those entrusted with care for nations and smaller communities, for families, individuals, God's animals and plants, and God's air, oceans and soil: *treat that which you oversee well, and it will flourish.*

In the received way that episcopacy – leadership and oversight – works, both bishops and clergy are hindered and disadvantaged.

Pressure on parish clergy has been mounting in recent decades for many, well-ventilated reasons. A casual reading of the early church narratives makes it clear that the 'pressure' the apostles felt could be extreme, by any standard. Paul wrote to the Corinthian church,

'We do not want you to be unaware, brothers and sisters, of the affliction we experienced in Asia; for we were so utterly, unbearably crushed that we despaired of life itself.'[268]

Jesus had warned that this would be so. The paradox is that a portion of the pressure in England is not from external sources or persecution, but from Church-induced *organisational* pressure. The evidence has been visible for a while. The Report 'Affirmation and Accountability' was comprehensive.[269] It brought matters to Church-wide attention, and it suggested ways of reducing clergy stress, sickness and ill health retirements. Six years later there was follow-up research on its implementation. Jonathan Williams found that not all dioceses shared the original Report's ethos over 'putting in place systems which could alleviate clergy stress and breakdown.' There was 'still a bit too much of the "pull yourself together" mentality' usually coming from the top. ... 'Clergy are not going to seek preventive help if they feel it will be seen as a mark against them and brand them as someone not able to cope.'[270] Such an ethos is suggestive of Caesar's.

More recently, the national network of bishops' pastoral advisers noted the high level of counselling take-up by stipendiary ministers; in some dioceses mounting to over 20% of diocesan clergy within twelve months. Whilst counselling has a wider scope than matters of acute professional stress, available evidence should prompt a robust Church-wide response. Such has yet to be seen.

A minority of clergy might not have felt much 'organisational' pressure themselves, nor identify with this assessment of stress. They may have been helped by gaining the esteem and attention of bishops, or by confidence in their own ministerial or academic 'achievements', or conceivably because their personal public-relations skills have built them excessive self-belief. A parish minister's well-being within the Church's institution should nonetheless be of particular episcopal interest. An unnoticed structural evolution – impelled by *Caesar's* influence on our received culture – has disadvantaged bishops and parish clergy alike. We have clearly turned to bureaucratic rather than relational solutions to genuine problems.

A BROAD ANALYSIS OF A CHURCH-WIDE RELATIONAL SHORTFALL

In a functional Church, the overseer and parish clergy will know each other well. Mutual respect spawns mutual understanding, empathy and trust. The bishop is able to be a true pastor. He or she will feel confident in affirming and in holding to account, in building up and in rebuke, in helping and directing – always through personal connection where the tone of voice and twinkle in eye is observable, and the warmth of godly concern felt. Yet this can only happen when each knows the other well; impossible when a bishop has care of clergy in three-figure numbers, with Christ-like sure-footedness, for many more than say twelve. Over centuries, such distancing has come to make episcopal relationship a mirage. The wisdom imparted to Moses by his father-in-law – of a cascading pattern of oversight[271] – has faded from our corporate memory. There are really only two possible approaches.

First, the Institutional Approach

This asserts that the rank and status of bishops is unassailable, that episcopacy may only be shared in small, anxiously-guarded ways. It expects that the pattern of dioceses, and diocesan hierarchies, has to be sustained apart from modest, periodic adjustment; then only through energy-sapping, mind-numbing process. This is what we have seen. And we have seen a growth in suffragan and area bishops, but with no obvious improvement in levels of mutual affection and trust. How could it be otherwise, when the numerical ratios are still inadequate for robust human connection? Indeed it has, by default, spawned and reinforced the 'solo-flying' culture.

It gets worse. The most important decisions for Church effectiveness and clergy well-being are those to do with wise judgment and perception; of individuals and their potential. These depend on a deep and mutually trusting relationship. It would require time and substantial personal contact. If these are not available, wise judgment and perception descend to the level of hunch, *good-egg* reputation and rumour; becoming in time fixed as cultural norms.

Churchill and others were not sanguine about D-Day's prospects in 1944. Montgomery was a missionary bishop's son and man of faith.

He faced a fearsome military task unprecedented in scale and long term implications. Yet he saw that, with two million men under his command, rightly judged appointments of subordinate commanders was pivotal. He spent something like a third of his working-day on such deliberations and decisions, despite all that pressed upon him.[272] Generals were killed or injured, or required a break with exhaustion, were promoted or transferred, or had perhaps failed professionally. Montgomery saw that, with right appointing, strategy would work and battles be won; but with ill-judged appointing, the struggle for Europe might fail. It would have been easy for him to spend his time on more visible and public activity, but he did not.

Plainly, if parish appointments are well judged, Kingdom leaven can do its work. Yet the reverse is equally true. A bishop can hardly have a more important duty. If a bishop did nothing else in his entire episcopacy but give rigorous attention to all types of selection and appointment, as well as to the undergirding reporting system, his bequest to the work of the Kingdom could be transformative. Appointments can affect priests for the remainder of their ministries, and bless or hinder the life of churches for decades. A wide accumulation of prior episcopal perceptions and decisions determines substantially the pool of candidates in the frame for any appointment. At worst, a feebly derived pool will mean enfeebled decisions. This candidate pool fills slowly, one decision at a time, across the Church. It is shaped by selections for theological training, by decisions to ordain, by decisions to appoint training incumbents, by appointments of curates, and their later appointments to parish or benefice. There are also critically important preferment decisions.

All these decisions are of first order importance for the Body's health and fruitfulness; with the potential to provide a pipeline of strong episcopal overseers. They are equally important for the contentment, and confidence, of clergy in the Church's handling of their lives. They are of primary episcopal concern. Yet these are the *Unseen Processes*. With the erosion of time, they are guided decreasingly by informed, focused, episcopal gaze. How can they be other, when lesser, yet hereditary, tasks swamp episcopal time and attention – and when the number of people he ought to know intimately is patently absurd?

The organisation, infected by *Caesar*, responds in the only way it knows how. It establishes a range of time-consuming committees, bodies, single-tasked individuals: spawning systems, procedures and paperwork as if these were the stuff of the Kingdom. The truth is that systems have leached bishops of the possibility of confident, relational oversight. Diocesan Directors of Ordinands (DDOs), Selection Committees, complex statutory appointment processes have all been spawned to do the oversight work, with hunch and rumour making their contribution unless there is exceptional vigilance. Even though godly people may manage these processes, they inhabit structures framed under *Caesar's* influence. It is impossible for a committee, large or small, to acquire that close personal knowledge and understanding of a person, and of the character of a potential post, that true episcopacy demands.

Thus, instead of searching out relational ways of enhancing episcopal capability, we have adopted *Caesar's* structures, systems and associated bureaucracy. This has emasculated episcopacy. With such components moved largely out of reach, with only the appearance of authority, leadership and oversight remaining.

To begin with, the Church's responsibility for the nurture and well-being of clergy seems ill-defined. Its duty of care for clergy in stipendiary posts is broadly accepted, but the pattern of care – and the Church's responsibility – for clergy and spouses when stipend stops is harder to define. At this point, does the Bishop continue to bear responsibility, is it left to a central Church body, or does the individual disappear from the Church's radar; indeed, does this minister still belong to the Church, or not?

Observation suggests that retired clergy are adequately covered, but what of those who cease work because of stress or physical ill-health, because of unemployability, professional mishap or misconduct? Sometimes there will need to be a parting-of-the-ways, but if so, a decision needs to be taken and communicated. Jesus's pastoral care of Judas Iscariot ended when Judas's rejection of Jesus became final; Jesus despatched him into the night. Yet for all his other misfits and immature followers Jesus was determined to nurture, rebuke and bless.

Responses to clergy casualties are particularly important if they stumbled more from human frailty than evil purpose. Bishop Keith Sutton looked through his redemptive lens. By no means soft on wrongdoing, he was non-judgmental of the person involved. Whilst not suggesting a superficial attitude to wrongdoing, serious mistakes might not be the end of the road. With wise nurture, incontrovertible contrition and repentance – a conversion – might be lead to a fruitful life greater than can be achieved any other way. This was Paul's story. Such people may be few, but there are others: some, whose faltering and mistakes call for wise sensitivity. Perhaps some in this category ought not to have been accepted for training or ordination in the first place. Some may have received inadequate training and nurture in formative posts. And some may have been given an inappropriate appointment, where reasonable standards were beyond their reach. Loss of position and livelihood, for such reasons, is distressing enough, but when the distress settles upon spouses and children, the Church's alarm bells should ring. Equally, when a priest commits some serious offence, the family's predicament should arouse immediate concern and attract substantial – even long-term – pastoral care.

Whenever an incumbency fails, or some parish tumult erupts, or people perceive the Church authorities to have treated a minister unjustly, there will be a cloud of witnesses. Every negative perception, as well as harming God's ministry in that place, can touch the Church's reputation surprisingly widely; even without media reportage. The pain of a parish mishap will affect a congregation and wider parish. Friends and families will become aware of it, some in places across the nation. Institutional reputations shift. Stories slowly reinforce or reduce a general perception.

We have touched on some important, but largely unseen processes of the Church's governance; selection for ordination training, for ordination, for curate-placement and appointment to parishes. Beyond these are the unseen processes of handling discord, of disciplinary responses, of preferment or non-preferment, and of clergy oversight. Whilst appropriate confidentiality is of the utmost importance, clergy have a right to know – indeed, feel – that matters of their future development and well-being are secure within a professional and accountable system. The *universal truth,* already postulated in chapter three, emphasises that when it works well, people will flourish. If clergy lack confidence in its working, the chill of lovelessness will touch the Body.

So we now look for ways in which love may be embodied more fully in these unseen processes.

Secondly, the relational approach

A relational analogy may help set the scene. A strong family exemplifies the life of an organism: coherent, mutually nourishing and nurturing its members, healthy and strong, laying generational foundations. Its demands on the community are small; its contribution substantial.

By contrast, a dysfunctional family can have a dismal set of symptoms. We are too well aware of the impact of dysfunctional families on community wellbeing. Demands may be placed on a variety of external professionals: police, social workers, doctors, health visitors, child psychologists, school heads, school mentors and probation officers. Fostering, ASBOs and custodial sentences may be necessary responses. Sir Paul Coleridge, the senior Family Courts judge, estimated that t*he cost of family breakdown to the public purse is calculated as £46 billion a year in social work, court time, health care, housing and so on.*[273]

A dysfunctional family may force such interventions to contain its negative effects. Community wellbeing, and that of vulnerable family-members and neighbours, depends on it. Thus, instead of exporting benefit into the community, a dysfunctional family is only able to import costly assistance or constraint. Intervention may be more likely to minimise damage than stimulate lasting benefit. Relational wreckage marks the typhoon trail of lovelessness. The family organism has failed. Organisation, with all its limitation, has had to move in; yet the outcome remains distressing, less than the best. Organisation cannot generate love, heal, or nurture durable relationships.

These polar points may help us wonder where our Church stands, as a relational Body, in the line between the two poles. We know of our command to love, and believe in love's power; yet somehow we prefer to live as organisation as well as we can, rather than consider the serious call to coherent relationship. We might come to see the evidence around us with new eyes. We may conclude that diocesan sector ministries, the archidiaconal roles, our dependence on copious church law, rules and regulation, our structuring of parish share, our synodical system, our distant relationships and the unhealthy, lingering culture of parish freehold together define a dependency upon organisation rather than the relationships of organism.

We now look at aspects of organisational life with narrower focus.

Accountability

Everyone feels uncomfortable if those with authority over them live in an accountability-free zone; one reason why our revealed message of judgment is so important.

All unseen processes carry risks. They can appear deficient in accountability. With inadequate accountability, those in authority can accumulate power and then abuse it. Trust in the unseen processes inevitably becomes a dominant factor, for all clergy and congregations' futures depend substantially on them. Long-term Bodily wellbeing is affected. Confidence may be gained in three ways:

- by giving evidence that those in authority themselves receive appropriate oversight – have sometimes to give account;
- by giving a fuller explanation to those affected of how the processes work;
- and by working hard to prevent *hunch* and *second-hand opinion* gaining entry and influence.

The oversight patterns advocated in the previous chapter allow professional judgments and perceptions to develop with a greater dependability and coherence than can be expected of existing patterns.

Relationship versus bureaucracy

As the episcopal role has weakened in the unseen processes, so has bureaucracy moved in. It always will, as surely as water flows downhill. Good relationships foster good communication and develop trust; characteristics of organism. With inadequate relationships, organisation moves into ascendancy. Not able to engender trust, it operates on the principle of distrust; requiring reports, evidence of performance and accomplishment, numbers and statistical analysis. The paper and ink industries can hardly believe their good fortune. In the meantime, increasing burdens are laid on clergy, wardens' and treasurers' backs. Jesus viewed the Pharisees as specialists in this field.

The cascading, relational patterns suggested in the previous chapter offer the possibility of growing a tradition where a high standard of godly oversight is attainable. When trust and professionalism combine, episcopal leaders could gain and use accurate perceptions of clergy and congregations with increased confidence.

Perception and judgment

These essential functions of leadership need to hold in tension a realistic acceptance of human wickedness, and a conviction of God's redemptive grace. Jesus was clear about both.

'When he was in Jerusalem during the Passover festival, many believed in his name because they saw the signs that he was doing. But Jesus on his part would not entrust himself to them, because he knew all people and needed no one to testify about anyone; for he himself knew what was in everyone.'[274]

It is helpful here to separate out these two key functions of leadership. As we look for ways in which love may be embedded more substantially in the Church's life, I would elevate *perception* and *judgment* to a very high level. Wisdom and skill in these fields have a greater impact than anything else on coherent Body-life and the individual's sense of wellbeing. Conversely, nothing is more destructive to these elements of Church life than the cruelties of misperception and misjudgement. Such manifestations of institutional lovelessness, when they occur, can cripple someone's ministry and harm congregational life for the long term. They deliver injustice in places of vulnerability and pain. They therefore deserve to be treated with the greatest of care, and with high professionalism.

Perception is appropriate in assessing the character of individuals, and maybe, congregational life. It involves examining, over time, a wide pattern of evidence; words heard and read, deeds and activities, fruitfulness or otherwise. A view of the spiritual actualities of a person or group – reputation, authenticity and depth – is formed, with a Christian lens. It is the stuff of primary decision-making, of placing the right person into the right role in the right place at the right time. It is one of the most important episcopal tasks. It requires rigour in all those involved. The last chapter's cascaded relational patterns allow skills to be developed, sharpened with experience, and people's particular strengths and abilities to be noted.

Perception can never extend into the field of motives. These are unknowable. Discerning character is enough. Perception is best not developed conversationally; rather by the crafting and re-crafting of confidential reports. Such discipline in report writing does not come easily to most: it is an art-form. It needs steady refinement, and solid oversight. Acutely significant in the health of the Body, it can engender confidence and fruitfulness. It exercises justice in the detail of Church life. Above all, it allows the best appointments to be made; from curacy to archbishopric.

Judgment is appropriate in the examination of deeds, in gaining understanding of crises and making good decisions, sometimes quickly. In such circumstances, discernment should have no place. It involves dismissing preconception, searching out and examining all obtainable factual evidence: witness-evidence of words heard and read, deeds and activities observed.

Church conflict will often stem from wrongdoing. Wrongdoers can become skilled in deceit, and may have developed this evil art over many years; whether in matters of power, money or sex. The deceiver may be skilled in presenting himself as innocent. Like a ventriloquist, he can make another seem to have caused the trouble. As with paedophiles, he may have groomed the great and the good to achieve a solid reputation in their eyes. For such reasons, immense care is necessary. Where deceit is in the air, *opinion* poses grave danger. It should never be heeded, never sought: hard evidence alone is necessary for judgment.

Two men, each in his way a master of deceit, aroused British media interest during 2014: Kim Philby, the spy, and Jimmy Savile, the entertainer and molester of vulnerable women and children. Kim Philby, whose notorious treachery sent hundreds to their death, offers an illuminating lesson in the ways of deceit. He was a charming and engaging man, conveying effortlessly a picture of high professionalism. He rose to the top of his tree. Yet even when troubling evidence about him emerged, it took years before his superiors and colleagues felt able to take strong action. Jimmy Savile committed an astonishing catalogue of abuse across many decades. Whilst developing a public reputation for his charity work, he ingratiated himself with the people 'who counted'; the 'great and the good' in public life, key elements of the police service, health authorities, charities, and the broadcasting establishment. His proclivity for young women seems to have been common knowledge for years in many areas of public life, but no one had the resolve to take appropriate action. More than 500 reports of abuse emerged subsequently.

Deceit can be a significant theme in misconduct within any profession. The Church needs to be braced for the rare occasions when it may emerge within parish crises. When deceit is around, as is likely in cases of fraud, sexual misconduct and power abuse, the mechanisms of *perception* are inappropriate and risky. It is nigh impossible to uncover truth except by painstaking inquiry and collection of verifiable evidence. Only this can lead to, and enable, *judgment.*

Without such rigour, the guilty may walk away, the innocent be blamed and the surrounding community's distress perpetuated. There may be substantial collateral damage, and community life soiled for years. With a proper collection of evidence, it is likely that every parish crisis is soluble. Indeed, if well-handled under God, the resultant healing can open up a new level of parish life.

In the relational leadership scheme described in the previous chapter, the assigned episcopal leader should invariably be the investigator: it is part of their healing ministry. She or he will need to allocate generous time to hearing and recording eye-witness statements; or to overseeing this process. Its importance far outweighs any council or committee meeting that appears to stand in the way. Ambulance paramedics offer a model of priority-setting that may apply here. It may be painstaking work, but that is what episcopal leaders are there for. Pieces of evidence, taken together, should make the nature of the crisis' origin and its instigator plain. An investigator must distinguish between incompetence or inadequacy, and real culpability. Sometimes a minister will make mistakes that do not mount up to much. A church officer, hoping to get the minister replaced, can for example seize on a frailty. Then, by deploying bullying techniques, turn the mistake into a full-orbed crisis. Clergy deserve protection from such manoeuvring. Well- handled crises strengthen relationships and the episcopal leader's position. King Solomon showed this to be so.[275]

The Church should be wary of turning to mediation except as a last resort. Mediation will be an exercise in futility unless prior investigation has shown there to be no misconduct actual or alleged at the root of the distress.

Knowing the clergy

God's pattern of relationship rests on mutual knowledge between two people. If they do not really know each other, the relationship has yet to start. Pastoral care has no meaning without a pre-existent relationship. A minister can only minister if she or he is in substantial relationship with those in their congregation. *People can only receive pastoral care if their episcopal leader knows them, their family, their strengths and frailties, their pains and aspirations.* The present system in the Church of England – structures, reporting system, and oversight system and geography – together make it nigh impossible for such relationships to form. It is possible that many clergy, getting into some need for pastoral help, would turn to an archdeacon or bishop as a matter of last – rather than first – resort. If they see them as authority-figures with power over their futures, more than pastors and friends, this is bound to be the case. It then means a confident description of clergy, their strengths and needs, is unlikely to be deposited in a clergy file.

Clear knowledge is more likely to be held in fragments, somewhat randomly, across a wide field in the present organisation. If anywhere, it will be held in the heads of those in a close, trust-based relationship with the priest: by confidants, spiritual directors, personal friends, churchwardens, perhaps rural deans, senior colleagues, pastoral counsellors, or those overseeing continuing ministerial education (CME). It cannot readily be captured and collated, although ministerial review procedures seem to be heading in this direction. The main point, nonetheless, is that the person exercising pastoral leadership and oversight of each priest should be the one with the most rounded, informed understanding of them; gained from substantial personal contact and observation.

The necessary tools Jesus used – encouragement, training, warning, rebuke, cajole, laughter and time together – are likely to be deployed with difficulty, if at all, in our present frameworks. Bishops really cannot get to know adequately the majority of their clergy, nor clergy their bishop. Appropriate pastoral care is therefore barely available to clergy in their sacrificial ministry. The last chapter's patterns offer a way of achieving it.

Bureaucracy, relationships and paper records
Where a culture of trust imbues an institution, the reach of bureaucracy is pushed back. This, however, should not mean that paperwork becomes valueless.

Most clergy would, I imagine, place a high value on two primary contributors to their wellbeing; each enhancing their confidence to serve as ministers of the Gospel. Firstly, they deserve reassurance that should they find themselves in crisis embroiled in discord judgment of the highest professional standard will be reached and justice applied, and subject to appropriate oversight. And secondly, they deserve reassurance that their personal files, detailing their qualities, character, achievements and potential, are prepared by master craftsmen – trained for such a task, and subject to appropriate oversight. It seems clear that written perceptions, and written judgments, carefully and thoughtfully crafted, are each essential; for relationships and wellbeing are at stake. They are particularly important in those areas where unaccountable and superficial opinion can creep in to soil God's work: in recommendations for ordination training, or ordination, in reports of those under training, in appraisals and preferment reports of those occupying church posts. When complaints, crises and reported wrongdoing are investigated, they are utterly essential.

- Reports on individuals

The 360° appraisal system, increasingly adopted for clergy, has undoubted value.[276] It should however be seen as second best. It is a 'work-around' in an organisation where bishops have insufficient contact, confident knowledge and mutual trust with those they oversee. This is a matter of inheritance, not blame. Within the relational oversight described in the previous chapter – within a cascaded network of friendship and oversight – episcopal overseers would be able to write clergy reports based on intimate knowledge and observation. They would, apart from exceptional and sensitive cases, share their report with the clergy themselves; having consulted appropriately with two or three other informed and close colleagues. This approach could build up professionalism and confidence; disproportionate to time and effort invested. It is less bureaucratic than other methods. It is fit for an organism. Such a system has the potential to *increase* trust through the entire relational network.

I lived in such a system of pastoral and professional care for thirty-four years. Overall, I found the sum of reports on me erred on the side of generosity, yet they enabled me to hear truths within the safety of an overseen and accountable system. Over time, this approach could give the national Church a far greater competence and confidence in appointments and preferment than today's systems easily allow.

- *Crisis investigation.*

Crises are always unsettling. Discord may erupt in local churches for a range of reasons. They always have the potential to worsen – sometimes disastrously – or to be resolved. This might depend solely on the way it is handled. A crisis may stem from perceived misconduct, a major internal row, bullying, an unaddressed significant deficiency or an unresolved complaint.

Well-handled crises can bring benefit. But if mishandled the reputations of the parish, diocese or even the national church may be affected. Mishandling can damage clerical and church officers' reputations, and affect the church's local ministry, possibly for years. Some damage is certain. For this reason, overseers are unfailingly obliged to resolve every crisis with thorough professionalism.

The overseer's theological view may influence their perspective – whether they believe in original sin or in the progress of man. Those who subscribe to the latter view may be baffled and search for some 'personality clash' to be faced and possibly settled through mediation; hoping for some middle-ground compromise with its implication of shared guilt and apportioned blame. Tom Wright's observation that the original Gnostics 'were not interested in God's Kingdom coming on earth as in heaven, but rather in a non-confrontational heavenly Kingdom'[277] may have some bearing on it.

A crisis ought not to shock. We know we are born to trouble, as the sparks fly upward;[278] with human fallenness being the likely cause, and wrongdoing the consequence. Parish crises will generally be relational at root. Since God's great genius is displayed in making relationships new, crises offer substantial opportunity for relational healing. And discipline, well managed, may result in benefit to the individual that they'll come to acknowledge. This I have seen. Such unwelcome intrusions provide evidence of need and an entry point for help. They should be neither feared nor despised. Relational sinews in a community may become stronger than might otherwise have been possible.

In this section, I draw on my experience across some 46 years. Here are some mistakes that may – all too easily – be made.

- *Failure to fathom the practice of deceit.* Most significant church crises are likely to involve sex, money or power – with a perpetrator well-practised in deceit.
- *Mis-identifying the cause.* The unschooled may intuitively want to identify the 'culprit' at the outset. This very unsafe approach puts cart before horse. Many crises stem from wrong words or wrong deeds. The first priority must therefore be to identify and locate the activities and occasions that catalysed the crisis; in terms of date, time, place and persons present.
- *Preferring opinion to evidence.* The unschooled may seek understanding by asking opinions of significant office-holders or trusted persons in that parish's orbit: an archdeacon, an area dean or lay chair, a trusted 'pillar' in the parish or benefice – perhaps a treasurer, churchwarden or a 'significant' professional in the congregation who has held high office in the secular world. Such opinions are worthless in themselves. They don't constitute evidence unless they testify to actual events. I even heard of a PCC gathered to express its views. This yielded nothing other than bleak evidence of ferociously divided opinion.

Even the pagan Emperor Trajan (98–117 AD), no lover of Christians, did better than this. He sent instructions to his governor Pliny, in the Roman Province of Asia, over handling troublesome Christians. He emphasised the need to *prove* any charge against Christians, giving no weight whatsoever to anonymous charges. This would 'constitute a very bad precedent... out of keeping with this present age.'[279]

St Paul's oversight of the Corinthian church delivered some stiff challenges. He depended decisively on taking hard evidence rather than sifting opinion. 'This is the third time I am coming to you', he wrote. 'Any charge must be sustained by the evidence of two or three witnesses.'[280]

There is no way of gaining dependable evidence except by questioning eyewitnesses to a significant event, painstakingly one by one. Careful written records are here essential; for if manipulation is afoot, such rigour may well protect an innocent person. In addition, within the church community, the minister's position demands that they be the first – not the last – to be interviewed. All witnesses deserve an equal hearing, innocent or guilty though they may prove to be.

- *Attempting to second-guess motives.* The unschooled person may be tempted, when having a 'likely culprit' in their sights, to try to discern motives behind the reported events. Not only are we barred from doing so by our Lord's command not to judge but also, if deceit is involved, it risks yielding the wrong verdict.

- *Confusing frailty with wrongdoing.* Bullies sometimes target ministers with the hope of their removal. Ministers with some professional frailties – felt, or actual – are likely to be particularly vulnerable in such cases. If a minister is endowed with the spiritual fruits of gentleness and humility, he or she may seem an easy target for bullying. Bullying can manipulate a victim to over-react in reprehensible ways. This is how bullying works. Nowhere is carefulness more important. Whilst misconduct may provide grounds for disciplinary process, professional or relational frailties probably do not. Any verifiable frailties should prompt careful reflection on prior circumstances; the possibility of some adverse contribution by those in positions of responsibility. For example, weak decisions taken at Selection Conference, or in the bishop's decision to ordain, or inadequate post-ordination oversight and training, or ill-judged appointing, can all catapult a person into a place where professional inadequacy – even incompetence – becomes likely; and not of his or her fault. Wilful wrongdoing is a different matter altogether.

- *Confusing misconduct with sin.* When an investigation starts to head toward disciplinary options, the character of Church discipline needs to be remembered. If criminal activity is uncovered, the Church has no real option but to bring in the police. This frees the Church leaders to exercise their proper role of regulating Church life for the general good. They are in the business of regulation, not punishment. Regulation hinges on a minister's fitness for office and fitness for a particular appointment. It centres in the licensing process – the licence being the bishop's public declaration to a parish of unfettered confidence in the minister's fitness. The decision-base for licensing is constant, regardless of whether the courts or the Church's disciplinary processes exercise the judgment. Here the bishop is exercising his authority for the work of the gospel, and his ministry for the wellbeing of people and minister.

Disciplinary decisions have little bearing on matters of repentance and forgiveness. Such questions, essential though these be, are for separate handling outside the scope of regulatory decision-making. They are separate fields for attention, with separate vocabularies: one focused on community wellbeing and the other on an individual's healing.

In all cases of wrongdoing, deception can make lies believable. Deceivers can present a false appearance of dependability and stature. As suggested earlier, like ventriloquists, they can make interruptions seem to come from elsewhere; not from themselves. They can manipulate cause and effect; making 'effects' seem like causes, and the causes invisible. Hitler used such techniques on an 'industrial scale', not least in his 1939 invasion of Poland.[281] Robert Mugabe appears to be a master of such deceit today in southern Africa.

The Sadducees and Pharisees instigated crises that beset Jesus' three-year ministry and brought him to eventual trial before the Chief Priests, Herod and Pilate. Their techniques included harassment, threat, menace, false testimony, undermining, and ultimately the gross manipulation of both Pilate and the crowds by the Chief Priests at Jesus' trial. All these things had created and stoked the crisis. Utter injustice and public humiliation resulted. The Sadducees and Pharisees seemed driven by fear, envy and their own insecurities. They tried to second-guess Jesus' motives and misconstrued both his character and his goal. From early in his ministry, and without due process, they resolved he should die.

Their deadly hypocrisy was exposed at his trial and thus was its nature perfectly displayed. The leaven of the scribes and Pharisees, and of Herod, had never been clearer. The crisis-makers became the accusers and prosecutors before Pilate, motivated by fear-fuelled opinions. Opinion became indistinguishable from evidence. Assessments of cause and effect were muddled. The significance and implications of deeds were missed. Presumed motives became 'fact', and were determinative. In this way the prosecutors suppressed truth and validated deceit. Bereft of factual evidence they made the innocent seem guilty. Thus did bad leaven's power and influence throw its worst – its nature chillingly displayed.

Yet, this same leaven of Herod, the scribes and Pharisees may well be abroad in any parish crisis.

The processes outlined above, maybe seeming bureaucratic and burdensome, substantially protect individuals and communities. Words, wisely and carefully deployed, serve to embed love more deeply in the Body's sinews. They strengthen organismal life. In a different context, the literary theorist and critic Terry Eagleton has written,

'In the end, only love (of which faith is a particular form) can achieve the well-nigh impossible goal of seeing a situation as it really is… Clinical, cold-eyed realism of this kind demands all manner of virtues – openness to being wrong, selflessness, humility, generosity of spirit, hard labour, tenacity, a readiness to collaborate, conscientious judgment, and the like …'[282]

IMAGINING THE OUTCOMES

As they stand, all these unseen processes make some sort of impact on clergy morale and wellbeing; for good or ill. Unseen zones allow wrong leaven to exercise its power unnoticed. It's where Caesar's organisational skills can purvey lovelessness, numbing the Body. The leaven of heaven is the antidote: love's power gaining a fuller entry where customs and systems lack relational quality.

If Body-life evolves in the direction outlined in the previous chapter, the unseen processes can work in a quite different way. I served in a warship of over 2,500 men, responding to a captain they trusted. He gained knowledge of his people through friendly engagement with them, buttressed by reports of dependable subordinates. I have seen ships working in testing circumstances, with sailors knowing what to do and getting on with it, with instructions kept to a minimum: all working to a common aim, glad to be in a team.

Relational sinews are the key. They alone allow an organisation to migrate in the direction of organism. The cascading pattern of friendship, oversight and example already portrayed carries a further, incalculable benefit. It will come to foster a rounded professionalism amongst all church ministers. Within such relationships, good practice is readily identified and then carried forward in corporate memory. It provides nurture and training 'on the hoof'; with new understandings and new competences being achieved in the process.

In time a new culture forms, with new professional norms. These would range from communication skills to churchyard management, from doctrine to bereavement counselling, from evangelism to financial oversight, from church-community management to discipling skills, from faculty process to youth-work, and from crisis-handling to liturgical practice. New clergy would be inducted in perceiving and judging, and in the ensuing, critically important, report-writing on which Bodily health depends. Such an approach might even be expected to absorb into healthy church life the present distinctive roles of archdeacons and specialist sector ministers.

All this offers an opening for placing the Kingdom's leaven in the heart of the Church's Body-life. Good leaven has illimitable creative power – bringing growth, health and strength, bearing hope – making attractive bread for the hungry.

CONCLUSION TO PART 3

Having glanced at Kingdom history and refreshed ourselves on the meaning of Kingdom leaven, we looked at some obvious inherited divergences before turning to some generalities of structure, system and custom. The way ministry is developed and then works, and the constraints of parish- and building-based patterns are clearly central to any review of how Kingdom leaven can be streamed into the lostness and fragmentation of 21st century life.

For such reasons, ordination – selection and training processes in particular – have had some mention. This book has attempted to look afresh at some of the principles standing behind them.

Whilst the book has been forming, 'Fresh Expressions' has been developing across the Church: unconventional, enterprising and imaginative. Its emergence and characteristics speak of the workings of Kingdom leaven.

It is significant that in the Fresh Expressions initiatives, Church leaders have estimated that, in 37% of cases, networks were the major or total factor in how people came, *not because it was their parish or local church*. Fruitful outreach is clearly more dependent on networks than church building activities. Their further experience is that 52% of their initiatives are lay led and, what is new, is 40% are people without any official badge or training. They are as likely to be led by women as men.[283]

The initiative of ordained *pioneer ministry training* has sprung from Fresh Expressions; for ordained as well as lay ministers. Various models such as the CMS Pioneer Mission Leadership Training Course are now available. They seem to concentrate less on academy (emphasis on knowledge) and more on practical experience (emphasis on understanding).

In God's grace, such developments may bring us to a new place as Church in the nation: in our humanity, a little hard to imagine. There are wide spaces between local ministry and the places of national and diocesan leadership; spaces of structure, system and custom that form the institution, and to which the book's primary arguments attach. Renewal of the institution assuredly needs Kingdom leaven here, in full measure.

Part 4: Love's Satisfaction

Every follower of Jesus has the vocation to live as Jesus in the world, for other women and men to see. God's love is both the message and the empowerment. It is a godly contagion – a palpable reality.

At the same time, the Church's vocation is to make known the wisdom of God, in its rich variety, to the rulers and authorities in the heavenly places; to the principalities and powers exercising usurped dominion amongst the nations. The institutions, multinational corporations, public bodies – and indeed, governments – become repositories of lovelessness in God's world, unless his love breaks in. We need, as Church – as people and as institution – to embody love, palpably, to a watching world. We have the privilege to model God's quality of institutional life in a way that speaks of heaven, and cannot be contrived. The world stands to be amazed.

Demonstration and Display

12

'*Declare his glory among the nations, his marvellous works among all the peoples.*'

Ps 96.3

'*My speech and my proclamation were not with plausible words of wisdom, but with a demonstration of the Spirit and of power, so that your faith might rest not on human wisdom but on the power of God.*'

1 Cor 2.4,5

'*For I think that God has exhibited us apostles as last of all, as though sentenced to death, because we have become a spectacle to the world, to angels and to mortals.*'

1 Cor 4.9

When people see or hear evidence of God's goodness, his interventions and miracles – over and over again – things happen. People believe. The power of testimony has a long pedigree. It is visible within Old Testament worship patterns. Psalm 107 portrays extraordinary events prompting ordinary people to bring live testimony to the worshipping community. Such was the impact that someone had it embedded in the faith community's worship, where it remains still. Then, Psalm 111 is suggestive of believers sharing personal testimony to encourage the community, stimulate faith and praise.

Sadly, the reverse is also true. The Church community will have scant impact without lively recollection and testimony of God's reality, presence and miracles. Faith will falter and fail. Daniel Everett went to the Amazonian tribes-people, the Piraha, as a Bible translator and wrote a book *Don't Sleep, There are Snakes.*[284] A newspaper review gave this summary,

> 'Everett did not convert the Pirahas to Christianity because they believe only what they see, or hear from a reliable eyewitness, and once they realised he hadn't met Jesus they lost interest. He, however, found their viewpoint so persuasive that he abandoned his faith.'[285]

This may be a prophetic word for our Church, and for me. When experience includes events where we feel and see God's power and glory – Kingdom leaven palpably at work – it triggers a compulsion to testify. It prompts fresh thinking and opens understanding. It will deepen faith, stimulate worship, and inform ministry and lifestyle. Its power upon the onlooker is equivalent to that of example.

Such experience leavens a leader's ministry.

The ministries of Jesus and his apostles depended substantially on God demonstrating his reality – his presence, and displaying his character – his glory.

Then, within a few years, John's gospel burst on the Church with trumpet sound and blazing light: like no other book. He used words to express the inexpressible; to announce the eruption of God's presence and glory in time and place, in human frame. They disclose an unprecedented occurrence, the experience of an immeasurable power; yet in the frame of a humble, seemingly ordinary man, Jesus. They shout out the arrival of a real life: utterly unique. It displayed a light that overwhelms darkness, illuminating the path for everyone.

At the same time John described some 'negatives'; blindness, rejection and hence incoherence. The world that came into being through him did not know him, even when he stood before its gaze. He came to his own people, yet they would not accept him. But to those who did receive him, who believed, he gave power to enjoin in relationship with the creator God, as child with Father.

John suggests the key to understanding – to new relationship and redemption – was more in seeing than listening. People could recognise spiritual reality by *seeing* unusual life in a single person.

The only possible explanation was to ascribe God's character to this demonstrated life. Words were not the main channel for persuasion or interior conviction; albeit necessary for explaining and validating the visual. The 'attention-grabber' was glory, characterised by the suffusion of unconditional love and a visible integrity dominating one man. He had a unique *presence*. The Word had been given through Moses; Jesus brought the greater revelation through becoming a God-filled human being, and living in front of people's eyes. This was how they came to see his glory.

During his Galilean ministry, Jesus fed large numbers miraculously. It begs the question: why were upwards of 10,000 people[286] wandering around a fairly small area? Some had travelled up to 100 miles to reach him; from Jerusalem and today's Lebanon, Syria and Jordan. Those with family commitments, work to be done, and maybe only just scraping a living, do not take such journeying lightly; especially on foot. His appeal was astonishing. So far as the crowd was concerned, this was not rocket science: people were not drawn by argument or theological explanation. They merely saw, heard and were gripped by his humble authority and gentle kindness. They were drawn from that lostness of their daily lives – opaque and wearisome – by an indefinable man. His presence exuded reality; a confident wisdom and hope. Here was someone who demonstrated God's presence, displaying a glory words cannot capture. He was like none other. Whether they realised it or not, Jesus was fulfilling Isaiah's centuries old prophecy:

'The people who walked in darkness have seen a great light; those who lived in a land of deep darkness – on them light has shined.'[287]

As the time neared for his earthly departure, Jesus needed to prepare his disciples. John's final discourse underlined the critical significance of his intimate relationship with the Father, and of theirs with him. To reinforce their faith for the looming challenge, Jesus emphasised what they had *seen*; not his words they had *heard*.[288]

Jesus would return to the same themes in his High Priestly Prayer: of relationship and glory.

As the Last Supper drew to a close – in John's account – Judas Iscariot slipped off into the night. It suggests God's revelation through his Son now entered a new phase: a greater revelation of divine glory.

Jesus here identified his betrayer and prompted his departure.

With the Passover celebration imminent, the moment is pregnant with meaning. Jesus was following the Feast of Unleavened Bread's introductory ritual of searching out the old leaven, to cleanse his gathered community of faith. Judas, who had once exercised Jesus's authority to cast out evil spirits, and to heal every kind of disease and illness, was now fatally tainted.[289] Driven by Herod's and the Pharisees' old leaven – its compass pointing always to killing and death – he had failed to recognise and opt for the promised new Kingdom leaven. As the sacrifice was being readied, he had to go. John relates that 'when Judas had gone out', Jesus said,

> '*Now* the Son of Man has been glorified, and God has been glorified in him. If God has been glorified in him, God will also glorify him in himself and will glorify him at once.'[290]

For God to reveal a fuller glory, Judas – with his resolute old-leaven convictions, and consequent commitment to disunity – had to leave Jesus's company. For the remaining disciples, Jesus completed their cleansing of any persisting patches of Big Four fungal activity: cravings for earthly power or status, Old Temple distractions, appetites for individualism and dogmatism. A thoroughgoing rejection of old leaven was essential throughout the following seven weeks of 'unleavened bread'.

God's time-cycle in the Passion matched the ritual delivered to Moses. It anticipated the world-changing festival of Pentecost when the two *newly leavened* wheat loaves were to be offered to God: loaves to celebrate the Kingdom's new leaven, with its explosive power of love. God's long conquest of the reigning culture of lovelessness was on the cusp of a new phase through the provision of the Spirit's power.

When one considers the range of issues Jesus might have crafted into his 'high priestly prayer' in John 17, his single-minded simplicity and emphases are striking. Unity and Glory were the big issues as the disciples-become-apostles received their final shaping for empowerment with the Christ-leaven of the Kingdom. They represented Jesus's offering of new-wheat loaves to his Father.

Unity and Glory were to be the Kingdom's hallmarks. Ezekiel perceived this with considerable clarity in his chapter 37, with peace, unity, sanctuary and holiness receiving emphasis in the concluding verses.

At his ministry's beginning, Jesus had declared his redemptive purpose for the world he had made.[291] Then at its earthly conclusion he disclosed his purpose for his shortly-to-be born Church:

'I ask not only on behalf of these [his present disciples], but also on behalf of those who will believe in me through their word [us], that they may all be one. As you, Father, are in me and I am in you, may they also be in us, so that the world may believe that you have sent me. The glory that you have given me I have given them, so that they may be one, as we are one. I in them and you in me, that they may become completely one, so that the world may know that you have sent me and have loved them as you have loved me. Father, I desire that those also, whom you have given me, may be with me where I am, to see my glory, which you have given me because you loved me before the foundation of the world.'[292]

This revelation of purpose is almost overwhelming. We are destined for unity and glory, indeed specifically prayed for in these terms. Unity and glory are interdependent: no unity means no glory, and the obstruction of God's main purpose. It gets worse: if there is no unity, the world will not believe that the Father sent Jesus. Such obstruction means that the loveless will continue to be loveless.

Unity is a word well-worn in ecumenical contexts yet under-valued in day to day local-church life. It needs to convey the strength of meaning evident in the life of the Trinity: a holy intimacy, an intuitive mutual understanding, and a heady, joyous inter-dependence. Training or rigorous self-discipline alone cannot bring it. It is a gift from God, providing bystanders with evidence of his reality and presence.[293] In his exposition of John 17, Lesslie Newbigin puts it this way:

'It is a unity which not merely reflects but actually participates in the unity of God – the unity of love and obedience which binds the Son to the Father. .... The unity of believers thus has its invisible source in the work of the Spirit, *but it is a visible reality which challenges "the world"* to recognize that Jesus is not what "flesh and blood" supposes (Mt 16. 17). .... . Moreover, this unity will enable the world to know the love of God not just as *an idea* or *a doctrine* but as a palpable reality experienced in the supernatural love which holds believers together in spite of their human diversities'.[294]

Eugene Petersen describes a comparable solid *reality* in the display of glory:

'[Glory] is evidence of God's substantial, though invisible, presence – the weight and glow of God in contrast to the flimsiness of jerry-built structures that we throw together when trying to construct something satisfactory without going to all the trouble of dealing with God. It conveys a sense of God's foundational solidity as an alternative to a culture built on sand.'

We have to reject, decisively, anything that makes for disunity. We are at war, and disunity loses wars. As this Section progresses, we shall be looking for ways of dealing with those roots of disunity: imbalance, dysfunctionality and disagreement. And each of these ways is to do with restoring or renewing relationship within the Church's sinews.

To our shame, we seldom hear of glory being shown in God's New Temple. Somewhat perversely, numerous church buildings declare their dedication to the glory of God in engraved stone; something God has never stipulated. Yet where is glory visible in his *people*, which he deserves, and for which he prayed?

Unity and Glory have far greater force than words in extending the Kingdom's reach. They enter people's consciousness by a route other than the ears. Indeed, unity and glory bypass the brain to reach heart and understanding, being visible and palpable. This is God's main way of imparting Kingdom leaven. *Demonstration* and *Display* – the *glory* of God's presence demonstrated, and supernatural *unity* displayed – are better than words. They are better than argument. They hit on the head any notion that dogmatism or individualism have any place in Kingdom culture. They specifically declare that Old Temple is dead, and that Jesus – not secular wisdom and power structures – is Lord.

The God we worship covets for us, his Body, the same aura he bestowed on Jesus: so that the world may behold his glory in us, full of grace and truth; and so that the Word may in us become flesh. Isaiah and John are in agreement that people are enlightened, first, by what they see; not by any stream of words we may utter.[295] We get it wrong too easily, confusing what has to be 'caught' and what needs to be 'taught'. Teaching, primarily through example, is God's major way of imparting wisdom and nourishing understanding. Yet it only becomes effective when God in Jesus has become 'real' through the Holy Spirit, and grasped by the individual. Thus are the spores of Kingdom leaven received. They have to be 'caught'.

It seems such demonstration and display is anticipated for every level of Christian community; from the two or three gathered together in his name, to the level of the national or international community – the institution. Moreover, we know that God's vocation for his Church is one of 'display',

'that through the church the wisdom of God in its rich variety might now be made known to the rulers and authorities in the heavenly places.'[296]

At some significant moments in salvation history, demonstration and display preceded God's speech, his words. It happened at the burning bush, on the occasions when Moses had to deliver God's words to Pharaoh, when God gave Moses the Law and on other occasions when he met with him on Mount Sinai. It happened when the Word became flesh at Bethlehem, and then in Jordan before Jesus spoke a word in ministry.

The final discourse and high priestly prayer were vital for the apostles' understanding of where they were heading. It disclosed how they were to purvey the Kingdom leaven into their surrounding culture; how it would supplant the culture of Herod, the scribes and Pharisees, of Caesar, of the rulers of this present age. They seem important for us today, defining where we should be heading.

The time has surely come for us, the Church, to see the need to be re-positioned.

An intended, rich fruitfulness of the apostles' ministry is described (Jn 15.8,16). It seems significant that Jesus's prayer at this point is *not* for the world (Jn 17.9). It implies that making disciples in that needy world is not so much the aim; rather an outcome if relational connections are intact. Thus flows the whole of this prayer. The world they will encounter is so hostile that he prays, not for their physical safety, but for their relational security; safety from the evil one's reach. There is no mention of their coming task: instead, a repeated emphasis on relationship. The 'vertical' relationship brings reflected glory; sensory evidence of God's reality and presence. The 'horizontal' relationships give sensory evidence of the Kingdom's leaven-power of love; showing an out-of-this-world quality. How else can frail, limited human beings – of differing social background, different gifts, personalities and life-experiences – possibly achieve such a profound unity of purpose, humble intimacy and mutual affection? It has to be God-given, especially when surviving persecution's fire.

We ought therefore to be convinced. This is what Kingdom culture should deliver. It will produce this naturally if our institutional and local relational connections are intact. According to this prayer, this was God's highest priority at that point: not mission or evangelism, a priority the Church seems to miss. Paradoxically, this emphasis will not make the Church inward looking, but the reverse. If we become confident in God's leaven-power, he will enable and use our seemingly random connections with the spiritually hungry, the moment we step out of our doors. We see this in Peter and John's catalogue of events and opportunities, described in the early chapters of Acts. They had no governing plan that we know of. They were just approaching the Temple one afternoon for the 3.00pm prayer time. A man accosted them whilst being carried to his customary begging billet. Lame from birth, this was his survival mechanism; he can have known no other. He asked for money. At no point did Peter or John see any great need for initiative. Yet extraordinary events were set in process; like dominoes falling, one setting off the next.

Peter and John then did what they had seen Jesus do. They responded to each development with humility and honesty. In contrast to recent weeks, they showed no fear. They were resting in their Lord's perfect love. They followed the Spirit's prompting, radiating the love and grace invested in them. God did the rest, with remarkable outcomes.

This remarkable healing happened as though Jesus was doing it; which, of course, he was. The man testified. This opened opportunity for public explanation that could hardly be declined. The preaching bore fruit, gave rise to arrest, then to appearance before a council of all the rulers and elders and teachers of religious law plus Annas, Caiaphas and other relatives of the High Priest.

A fresh anointing of the Holy Spirit upon Peter followed, which led to one of the most dramatic New Testament scenes. Peter spoke with authority and clarity. It caused amazement and great puzzlement. On the one hand, they were *ordinary men with no special training in the Scriptures* (hope for us all, here!). On the other hand, the healed man was standing in front of them saying nothing, but declaring everything. Unsurprisingly, there was nothing the council could say. Peter and John spoke at the Spirit's prompting; again, not much call upon their own initiatives. Finally, the council threatened them further and let them go – stumped, not knowing how to punish without triggering a riot – for everyone was praising God for the miraculous healing of a man whose forty-year disability had been removed in a moment.

Peter and John returned to a gathering of believers, and then naturally laid out the whole drama before their Lord in prayer. There was no hint of considering their next move; the initiative was with God. Their building then shook and they received a fresh filling of the Spirit. This meant they went out and preached God's word with boldness.[297]

All these events sprang from Peter and John's split-second openness to a needy man laid out on the ground. With our conventional dependence on planning, careful preparation, initiative, objectives and timetables, we need to look for a different way of doing Kingdom work. Peter and John's unsophisticated, trusting obedience shows us how to do it. We see a pattern of their seeing where Jesus was heading, doing what they could see he was doing, in the same way that Jesus followed his Father's will. The initiative was His.[298]

Was this Peter and John healing story a 'one off'? Was it just part of God's Pentecost 'special-package', or was this way God wants to work as often as we will let him? Surely it's the latter. We seem slow to accept Jesus's yoke principle. We prefer to hang on to the control. We struggle to let go of individualism.

The Revd Regina Stierlen, pastor of two village parishes in the German national church, decided to experiment. She wrote:

'I tried to walk through the village with a few visits on my 'to do' list, yet with time enough to pause for 'small talk' on the way. It was amazing! I met a widower who never goes to church but was very open to share his grief; then a woman who had just been diagnosed with cancer; then another one – who stopped in her car – with an operation next week; and a former member of our choir, here on vacation…

'I am strongly convinced that people have an instinct whether you are willing to talk and listen to them, or whether your desk is waiting and you are in a hurry. And God gives 'kairos' moments of grace…'

She continued:

'There is often a lack of competence with clergy – when we avoid relationships; but maybe there is also the contrary: we 'enjoy' it, if we are so important that people need us, depend on us and rely on us as human beings… In training the young curates who come from years of academic work at University, I find it the most difficult task to help them to build relationships. They are very much afraid of time-consuming visits or of letting parishioners share their more private lives.'[299]

Time is to relationship what oxygen is to the lungs. It belongs to our Lord, and needs to be yielded for him to use, perhaps in surprising ways. Yet I do not see us having a laissez faire 'licence' in God's Kingdom. Paul clearly did some planning as he pursued his apostolic course, as did Jesus in his ministry. Yet, in both cases, the impression given is that it was lightly held, tentative. Such intentions were offered to the Father in the form of ongoing conversation, open to adjustment as the conversation flowed. Primary decision-making rested with the Father, and events would often open up to indicate where he was heading.

In his final discourse, Jesus was not inducting his disciples into a ministry of 'niceness'; to be 'tummy-strokers' in future ministry. Neither was he grooming them for the boardroom table. He was readying them for the tough challenges beyond D-Day, when he was to release the Kingdom's Pentecost power. The immediate task was to secure a foothold on the occupied territory of the powers of darkness. They were not being prepared for peace-time advocacy; but for living in the midst of persecution in the presence and power of Jesus.

This begs two serious questions:

What is the aim of today's shepherds for their flocks? Is it to induct us ever more securely into the structural life of the Church, or is it to equip us – with the resolution of Jesus – to face persecution for our faith, should it come to that? That resolution of Jesus should be hallmarked on the side of every church community.

And what is their governing aspiration? Is it for God's demonstration of unnatural unity, and for his display of unnatural glory? How may shepherds stir such aspirations into ravenous appetites?

'Christ, whose glory fills the skies, Christ, the true, the only light,
  Sun of righteousness, arise, triumph o'er the shades of night;
Dayspring from on high, be near; Daystar, in my heart appear.

… Visit then this soul of mine; pierce the gloom of sin and grief;
  fill me, Radiancy divine, scatter all my unbelief;
more and more thyself display, shining to the perfect day.

Charles Wesley

Tomorrow

13

Jesus was in the business of *regime-change* – not with Caesar's brute force but the greater power of love. He was not an establishment figure – he seemed a revolutionary. He was a prophet, not politician. He prescribed little, but revealed much. He depended less on human logic and reasoning; more on unwrapping and handing on God's wisdom.

Much of first-century religious practice in Judaea was out of step with his Father's purposes, yet some of righteous faith – or openness to it – lived within its fold. We know a little of Nicodemus and Gamaliel, and somewhere in the establishment was Joseph of Arimathaea. Others are likely to have been susceptible to reform. Luke told of some Pharisees who tipped-off Jesus about Herod's plan to kill him. He later reported the conversion of priests, not long after Pentecost.

NT Wright tells us that 'the Pharisees saw themselves as standing firm for the old ways, the traditions of Israel, against paganism from without and assimilation from within.'[300] Why then did Jesus not identify any common ground; had he no appetite for reform? Why had he nothing to say about the Roman occupation, about the scale of crucifixions, about slavery or about stoning for adultery? Why did he offer no analysis of temple corruption with its abuse of power and financial operations? He could have gathered a small number from within the religious system: taught, discipled them and at the right moment launched them from within the religious framework. Empowered by the Holy Spirit, they might then manifest a reformed community; able to go out into the world to make disciples of every nation.

Leaven

We cannot know the answers, except that this was not what his Father handed him through the Spirit. His course instead was to supersede the entire religious and cultural edifice with one New Temple; not governed by human ingenuity, logic and planning, but by God's wisdom through the Spirit. It was not to be powered by the lovelessness of human organisation but by the organic power of the Kingdom, by love.

How do we then look at the present character and trajectory of our Church that, with other Churches, God loves and regards as his Body?

First, we need to have a godly pause over our emphasis on 'going into all the world to make disciples of every nation'

Though it was undoubtedly Jesus's command, he gave it in very particular circumstances. The disciples had spent three years in sacrificial itinerancy, trying to process the meaning of an extraordinary life lived before their eyes; with explicit and implicit authority like nobody else's. God's new message was being delivered. It was counter-intuitive, sparklingly fresh, unique. Their journeying had exposed them to emotional extremes, from deepest delight to abject fear and despair. They had been trained rigorously for an ill-defined future. They were entering a seemingly uncharted programme of events and travels. It would include fruitfulness, persecution, hardship and suffering – we now see – as part of the package. They were promised divine relationship, support and the Comforter's indwelling.

Towards its end, the net closed in and Jesus's anticipated execution drew close. Those few harrowing weeks took them to the limits of psychological endurance. The final days, before disaster struck, involved Jesus's intense preparation – his final cleaning them of old leaven. For them, Passion Week re-enacted the disciplines of Passover and the Feast of Unleavened Bread. When Jesus first called them, old leaven's power had shaped them. He gave them windows to see the new leaven's power. Like the Israelites with Pharaoh's chariots on their heels, Jesus led them into, and through, powerless desolation; a vale of misery, using it for a well.[301] The journey prepared them for Pentecost, with its great commission. Within it their fascination over their own, and their companions', futures needed to be dealt with. All this had first to be done.[302]

So, I dare to suggest, will it be that making disciples of all nations

224

is more an outcome than an aim. The evidence in Acts of Pentecost and afterwards is that, in God's providence, that outcome was inevitable through persistent living in union with Christ: through the emergence of a unity on which Christ's glory could alight, through the empowerment of Kingdom leaven.

The Acts narrative is surprisingly quiet about any dynamic activism in response to the Great Commission. No great initiatives are evident. Peter and John had no obvious appetite for travel into the outside world, though Peter was to trample on parts of the land where Jesus had walked. Without mission-initiative the Jerusalem church – but not the apostles – was scattered throughout Judea and Samaria from the great persecution triggered by Saul. Philip travelled south towards Gaza on the basis of angelic instruction; not initiative. His further travels seemed decisively not at his own behest! After his post-conversion visit to Jerusalem, Paul was sent by the brothers to Tarsus. The post-persecution scattering caused believers to reach Phoenicia, Cyprus and Antioch. Barnabas and Paul were only commissioned and despatched on mission because of the Holy Spirit's direct instruction. They only moved on from Pisidian Antioch to Iconium because they had been expelled, then for the same reason moved on to Lystra, Derbe and the surrounding country. Thereafter their itinerant ministry was to places already visited or as directed or constrained by the Holy Spirit.

All the while communities of believers were mushrooming across the region; substantially because displaced believers were giving evidence to random spectators of a new type of living in unchosen circumstances. There is no sign of strategic planning by the apostles, nor of any act of commissioning in response – or in reference to – the Great Commission. What we see is something else: the aspirations of Jesus's High Priestly Prayer being worked out and fulfilled largely through the apparent randomness of believers' lives.

All this suggests that John 17 is the pivotal revelation of God's intention, with Matthew 28 being more of a *dismissal* than a *command*; a little like the 'Go in peace to love and serve the Lord', in today's liturgy. Yes: they might travel, but on God's terms; and they would make disciples of all nations (or of all 'people-groups' – an ethnic as much as a geographical understanding), teaching them etc ... solely because the Spirit's leaven-power had done its work in drawing people into the Kingdom and into God-connection. Discipling and teaching could then begin.

So, I suggest, will it be for our Church if we follow the same route. We have to clean out every scrap of old leaven. In some way, it has to become habitual. We have to process and appropriate afresh the meaning of Kingdom leaven. We have to offer up – maybe lose – our individual or corporate ambitions, all defined aims other than listening-obedience. We need to return to the point of 'wanting to know Christ and the power of his resurrection and the sharing of his sufferings, by becoming like him in his death.'[303] From there we may expect Pentecost's explosive power of love to generate Kingdom culture, with fuller rein. Then we have to locate where the Spirit is leading, and tag along. There is no other way to fulfil the Great Commission.

Secondly, we need a greater wisdom in imparting love to a loveless world

The Church was born to channel God's love, under Christ's headship and through the Holy Spirit. If, as Church, we aspire to a good future, to leave a good bequest to future Wayfarers, we need God's ongoing refreshment of our corporate understanding and experience of divine love. We have noted how the Father imparted *a deposit of understanding* of the Kingdom to the Son through the Spirit, then the Son to the disciples and these apostles to the early church, all through the same Spirit. This may help us recognise and quantify losses of this thrust through succeeding centuries, and maybe more recent decades. These are losses from which we need to recover. They seemingly result from a weakening of community life, a forgetfulness of example's central role; and most tragically, from any loss of community memory and story-telling of God's interventions, demonstrations and displays. Then, of course, our message is incomplete without an intrinsic truth-telling of God's judgment; love's necessity.

Thirdly, we must attend to institutional health

The Church has consistently proclaimed Kingdom values for the individual, but shown less inclination to apply them to the institution we inherited; in which we live.

Bodily health means God's love flowing out through a number of courses. We already know it needs visibility within individual and family life, for the world's sake. Yet we have been less aware that *it needs a matching visibility in church communities*, and needs an equivalent, compelling visibility at the institutional level. The world acutely needs good models of community life. If we do not *demonstrate and display* a coherence found in Christ, the world has nowhere else to look. Their institutions and organisations need an example of organismic life – of structures and systems supporting people well – nurturing relationship. We need to display a supernatural excellence in relationships, in trust, loyalty and integrity.

To borrow from St Augustine, our lives on this earth are like dust blown in the wind until we glimpse, are then drawn into – relationships of grace that signal unconditional love, acceptance, forgiveness – and impute immeasurable value on the other. When people experience relationships that work, trust is born. When trust forms, we open up to example and word. When we recognise God's works and receive God's words we are on a transforming path; as individuals, as members of families and larger communities. Such is the world of the Spirit of God. Such should be our aspiration for future church.

Fourthly, the time for ecclesiastical fine-tuning and institutional spanner-work has passed

For too long the Church has sought to reform itself in Caesar's way, one new initiative, one new synodical measure after another; one new technique after another imported from the secular world. The sum of this process has not worked. We have produced an edifice that can barely exude the fragrance of Christ, or gain fulsome trust and confidence of member or minister. Worst of all, we have little in our institutional life to arouse the envy of institutions in our lost and confused world. Does anyone envy the way we do things?

This reflection attempts to show what we all knew all along, that our human wisdom is not enough. How then should we, *as institution*, view our vocation to make known to the rulers and authorities in the heavenly places the wisdom of God in its rich variety?[304] If the Principalities and Powers dominate institutional life in the secular world with the loveless power of Caesar, how do we – as the Church – speak to them? The Church has no power. The Principalities and Powers continue their malevolent work through the medium of culture, barely constrained. So, therefore, what appetite do we have to address our institutional lifestyle: to speak to the powers with God's power and authority?

A good number of godly, faithful and effective leaders burn their intellects and energies selflessly in trying to make our existing structures and systems work fruitfully. Yet the evidence suggests this is not enough. Something is missing.

Fifthly, we must now reject rank in the Church, decisively; elevate relationship to our highest priority; and choose to give example its rightful supremacy over word, in teaching and proclamation

Rank has no bearing on anyone's worth or significance. In this sense, it is valueless. It is merely a crude measuring device for estimating someone's suitability for specific responsibilities; nothing more. We need to deal in the language of role, not rank.

Rank is the enemy of relationship: incompatible with an organism. It keeps people apart. It plants lovelessness in the Body, not love.

As I write, the size of personal debt in our nation exceeds some £1,200 billion – some of it unmanageable. Social and economic disaster may stand closer than we think. If so, debt's shadow should fall across the thinking of all having care and oversight of others. Yet we have our 'elephant in the room'. Few within the Church seem to notice the size of *our* institutional deficit – an organic deficit of love, of which rank is a critical part.

The former Times Editor William Rees-Mogg offered this challenge:

'Christianity is a religion of love. The world is starving for love. Therefore the world is open to the Christian message if Christians can make their message heard.'[305]

As part of this, the Church and its members need to recover the use of example: God's preferred teaching method. Such things help the message to be heard.

Sixthly, love is God's power for supplanting wrong culture

Spiritual dilemmas demand spiritual solutions. Jesus knew about having to endure a culture that pressed the wrong way. Introducing a culture of infinitely greater power was his answer. It would supersede the world's enwrapping culture: thought-by-thought, action-by-action, sign-by-sign, word-by-word, person-by-person, moment-by-moment and element-by-element. It is our only option, but its release has to follow a biblical pattern; demonstration and display, beckoning into relationship, and exposure and denunciation of lovelessness.

God gave the world his pattern, initially through the Jews, in the world-changing drama of the exodus. We can see it in the sequence of the incarnation, passion, Easter and Pentecost. The apostles demonstrated it. It hinges upon the regular, systematic identification and removal of old culture, old leaven; and provision of clear evidence of Kingdom leaven.

Seventhly, wrong culture has to be denounced, persistently

The Church cannot *proclaim* in the pattern of Jesus without the contrast of *declamation*. Contrast brings clarity and reinforces message. We must declaim against the *leaven* of Herod, the Pharisees and scribes – exposing the heart of darkness – but only if, as institution, we have been careful to search out that same leaven in our own nooks and crannies.

Like Jesus, we ought to be wary of condemning the *detail of public policy*. The Church has, for example, neither inherent experience nor competence to condemn fracking. We should not expect anyone to bother with our pronouncements on such specialist matters. We add to the public noise, giving the illusion of being *rightly involved* whilst unconsciously adding to the likelihood of our Kingdom talk being ignored. 'The Church talks too much,' Rowan Williams once observed. It is true. A Times leader said as much:

> 'Where religious organisations undermine their prophetic role is when they decide that it is not enough to highlight an injustice and decide to offer certain solutions to problems.'[306]

Eighthly, God intends us – as visible institution – to be more in the business of display than of words

This book attempts to suggest how this may begin to happen. We have to conclude that in Christ's pattern, God really does intend us to be more in the business of *display* than of *words*. But that is not all. As Body – as both national and local institution – our vocation is to declare God's supremacy and righteousness to the principalities and powers. We need to reach the place where fair-minded commentators can say 'There is something about the Church's coherence and relational effectiveness that beckons – that invites enquiry. How do they do it?' We need to arouse curiosity.

Ninthly, a liturgical opportunity – or challenge?

This book is not pressing for perfectionism. It is simply urging a return to a God-ordained discipline we seem to have missed. The accumulation of stuff that inhibits the Body's life, built up over centuries and decades, has yet to be faced with clear-eyed realism and humility. We need to search out old leaven, systematically, year upon year, by conscious and decisive process. Whenever found, we need to destroy it.

This was the approach of Hezekiah and his great grandson Josiah. Each had inherited the throne at a time when Judah had been grossly infected by pagan culture. Each acted with courage and vigour to search out the old leaven and destroy it.[307]

There is a liturgical implication here as well. Do we need to find new ways to reflect the Body more solidly – not just the individual – in its connection to the Head and alignment to his purposes? We conventionally move through the Church's seasons until, in Lent, we reach Maundy Thursday with its profound celebration of the eucharist, charged with remembrance of Jesus's last supper with Passover connotations, through Good Friday, Easter Day, Ascension … then Pentecost.

Two aspects of our practice may need to be rethought.

First, we tend to travel in pilgrimage through the liturgical seasons along one plane rather than two: the personal, rather than the personal *and* the institutional. In our corporate worship and meeting together at communion, the unmistakable emphasis is that we are all thinking, praying, worshipping, repenting and thanking as individuals in the company of fellow-believers. This is all good, but is it sufficient? How may the Church travel the liturgical seasons expressing as Body, in some way, its institutional life and journey to fulfil its Body-vocation?

Secondly, and perhaps as a consequence, the Old Testament 'book-ends' of the Feasts of Unleavened Bread and Pentecost seem inadequately transcribed into our Christian liturgical patterns. That first feast did not start with the preparation of the Passover meal but with the ritualistic cleaning out of old leaven; performed individually by each household across the Israelite community. At the end came that harvest feast of Pentecost, carried forward triumphantly into the New Covenant time with the outpouring of the Spirit. This needs to be celebrated, not just by individuals who have tasted the Spirit's presence – celebrating together – but by the church, as a single Body. I suspect this distinction is worth attention, for this treasure is God's animation for his Body, to advance his purposes in world and cosmos, and fulfil our given vocation. The Jews offered two barley loaves in the temple at Pentecost to reflect the joy of harvest. These were no longer leavened with the old leaven of unrighteousness, no longer unleavened, but now empowered symbolically with the new Kingdom leaven: the leaven of love.

Hezekiah and Josiah offer us a precedent. Once the old leaven had been cleaned out, they were ready to keep the Passover. Each king called the whole nation to Jerusalem for the feast, with evidence of an extraordinary collaborative response.[308]

HOW, THEN, DO WE MOVE FROM WHERE WE ARE TO WHERE WE NEED TO BE?

Back in 1944 Allied armies landed in Normandy, charged with freeing a captive continent from Nazi tyranny; of rule and culture. After months of fighting, and with the dominant Soviet contribution from the east, the allies fulfilled their mission. It is axiomatic that success needed – amongst other things – the right moment, the right point of entry, and the right processes of attack. The attack processes worked because they gave initial priority to hard-edged instruments of naval bombardment, air attack, airborne forces, artillery, armour and infantry. Following close behind were the essential support elements: hospitals, strategic logistics, engineer, signals and headquarters staffs, and infrastructure. These latter elements were not less important than the former, but had a lesser priority on the beach.

We may compare aspects with God's mission-launch of his Kingdom. It was going to recover God's sovereign territory. It would subvert and supplant the unlawful occupation by the *king of this world*: using love's power to vanquish the powers of lovelessness, to set the captives free. Scripture claims that *the right moment* and *right point of entry* were determined in the incarnation and in that 'first' Pentecost, as the Church knows well.[309] What receives less attention are the priorities – the sequence – Jesus gave for introducing his Gospel's elements in hostile territory.

Jesus's final discourse suggests that God's historic methods of *demonstration* and *display* were the necessary precursors. It implies that effectiveness in social action and evangelism depends substantially upon a prior demonstration of God's presence and his love's power; and a display of unity and glory. Such things are his tools of persuasion, not those tools we prefer: of warning, of facts about Jesus, of logic, theological argument and social action. Such demonstration and display reveals a coherence flowing from relationship with the living God and each other. It evinces a palpable integrity, rooted in love.[310] Their attractiveness to the lost – the hungry and thirsty – is immeasurable. These elements of demonstration and display are pre-requisites of the mission elements of going out and making disciples. Trust and an incipient relationship with the hearer has first to be formed. The individual Christian and the institution have both to display these values. If the Church as institution wishes its voice to be heard and testimony believed, it has to take its organisational *display* seriously.

We need to do several things within the institution – each a spiritual exercise.

First, we must pray:

Walter Wink says,

'we need to escape idolatry, not this planet. We do not seek to rid ourselves of subsystems and structures in order to secure an individualistic paradise on earth or an after-life in heaven. We seek, rather, to relate these systems to the One in and through and for whom they exist, and in whom all things hold together (Col 1.16-17).

... Those who pray do so not merely because they believe certain intellectual propositions about prayer's value, but because the struggle to be human in the face of suprahuman Powers requires it. The act of praying is itself one of the indispensable means by which we engage the Powers… It is the interior battlefield where the decisive victory is won before any engagement in the outer world is even possible.

Prayer is the field hospital in which the spiritual diseases that we have contracted from the Powers can be diagnosed and treated.'[311]

Secondly, we need to reshape our imagining:

We have no power to offer the world. The Holy Spirit is the Trinity's agent of power, on whom alone we are to depend. His power is personal, not abstract. We should not understand it as a psychic power, in some way extraordinary. This power is the power of the Kingdom: Kingdom leaven. Coming from the true Lord, it is ordinary; the divine norm. It alone displaces that other leaven. It is God's means of conveying love into the spiritual and physical world.

His power operates like the 'finger of God', with precision upon the place of human need. It is a transformative power; healing and bringing into coherence. He can heal his Body, bringing the members into unity. The health he bestows has a glow, a reflection of his glory. At the corporate and individual levels, his power brings our thinking and understanding into coherence. In physical healing, he brings a person's body back to coherence, for which he formed it. His finger touches unauthorised intrusions – such as cancerous cells – with the heat of his holiness. *Kingdom power is the power of non-coercive divine love.*

Thirdly, we need to develop a habit of institutional review, of our inherited organisational systems and customs:

We need wisdom to see where those leaven lumps of Herod, the scribes and Pharisees still reside. We need to aspire to God's way of looking at the cultural and institutional landscape.

God's way of change is not iconoclastic. He deals through appetite, supplanting unhealthy appetites with godly ones. Thus, if we find we worship buildings too much, pulling them down is decisive but probably wrong. So when we see our appetites with God's eyes, and yield them, we shall see buildings – their furniture and our habits of use – for what they are. Then we shall be open to God's next step.

As things stand, myriad second- and third-order issues entrap our attention inordinately. A glance at General Synod agendas makes this plain enough. We need a willingness to face our proclivity to make wrong attachments; to confront our affection for *old ways*. Our unreformed parochial system with its buildings, boundaries and massive administrative overheads was shaped for a bygone age and culture. Our unreformed theological training system is in inevitable bondage to it, as is our unreformed system of stipendiary ministry. They are inordinately costly and were not, I think, shaped for the evangelisation – or re-evangelisation – of the nation. In too many ways, they frustrate more than facilitate the purveyance of Kingdom leaven. Undoubtedly, many of our leaders have developed a substantial expertise in obtaining some fruitfulness from our unsuitable structures and customs. Yet this should not blind us to the ever-present need for new wineskins to hold God's ever-fresh gift of wine.

As Hugh Rayment-Pickard wrote in the Church Times,

'...the ideas that Jesus outlines to his followers involve no religion at all. Instead he speaks of bringing good news to the poor, healing for the broken-hearted, release to captives, sight to the blind, and freedom to the oppressed. These are phrases that we are unlikely to find in any parish mission-statement. This does not mean that religion has no part to play, but it must be in service to the kingdom.

'If the Church of England is looking for a New Year's resolution, it could consider putting Jesus's big ideas about the Kingdom back at the centre of its mission. *This would require a massive readjustment of priorities away from "cultic" religious activity and towards ethical and political engagement.* But there would, in truth, be nothing very strange about this move. After all, Jesus himself tells us to seek first the Kingdom; the strange thing is that we are not doing more of this already.'[312]

I would suggest that ethical and political engagement – in Jesus's pattern – requires a prior relational discipline. In time, we must audit our institutional structures, systems and processes, measuring their ability to enhance trust and relationship: individual with individual, and individual with the organisational. We need to gauge *relational effectiveness* at each organisational level: national, diocesan, episcopal area, deanery, benefice and parish. Love and trust are defining characteristics. They have to be visible in the church's organisation; its structures, systems and customs. We need to learn how people at each level view their *higher* levels: what generates trust, and what distrust. We need to learn where churches and church-members feel the weight of imposed burdens, and where these are being lifted.

We must resolve to destroy all harmful strands in our complex culture; not leaving a vacuum, but supplanting with love. Love flows. Its regenerative power is remarkable.

Fourthly, we must manifest more confidently God's three-fold pattern of demonstration and display – testimony to what God is doing – of proclamation and declamation, and of wooing into relationship, in our public life:

Elizabeth Welch wrote that,

> 'the leadership challenge for the church at present is to play its part in the raising up of values in the public domain so that a new direction for the whole of our society can emerge and be taken forward.'[313]

But first, the Church needs to give increasing evidence that its culture, its style, its organisation and management methods speak of common purpose, relatedness, harmony and contentment. Or even more, evince the miracle of being held together coherently, through love's power; despite disparities in age, gender, race, profession, ability, wealth and education. The building or rebuilding of trust is a reasonable aspiration for our Church set in a nation whose institutions, laws, culture and language – once rooted in Christian foundations – show signs of an increasing dysfunctionality, the bleakness of lovelessness. As it gathers lateral and generational momentum, only intervention – of either death or love – can arrest its flow.

And love needs demonstration and display: in individuals, communities and institutions that carry Christ's name.

'The logic of Christian experience is very clear,' said the Superior General of the Jesuits, Fr Adolfo Nicolás, upon his election:

'God is love, and so we too love. God is mercy, and so we too show mercy. God is good, and so we desire to be good. If we do not love, we really do not have anything to say… Here is our *raison d'être*. Why do we want to love the poor, to help the lonely, to console the sad, to heal the sick and bring freedom to the oppressed? Simply because this is what God does. Nothing else.'[314]

I am imagining a church structured on cascaded friendship. Trust forms and permeates the Body no other way. Then would the needs for enforcement and discipline recede. The necessary responses to parish or clerical crises would come to be handled at an early stage within the frame of friendship and the understanding this brings – drawing upon an adjusted and enhanced corpus of professional knowledge and competence.

Godly church relationships would foster a greater and natural regard for law and regulation. Authority becomes calm, and a rich resource. Such are the prizes within reach. They are for a single purpose, that we may comprehensively channel God's love, corporately and individually. We shall see the power of example unlatched from its stable; a greater contact, oversight and accountability emerging through un-ranked friendship; and find a greater trust forming. Clergy will gain a greater professional confidence and sense of wellbeing. We shall see a healthy corporate pride develop across the Church.

Let us imagine, then aspire to, and then, under the Lordship of Christ anticipate something like this: *People love being Church. Leaders and led find Church no longer a duty. They love meeting together. Ministers' dominant aim is to prepare and launch disciples into places bound by the wrong leaven. Episcopal leaders' dominant aim is to nurture and strengthen ministers and parishes in this equipping task. Mutual affection becomes palpable, attracting comment and interest. People love looking for where Jesus is at work, and joining in. Jesus's Lordship becomes public knowledge. The New Temple, especially when in the place of suffering, becomes energised by Kingdom leaven. Here God demonstrates his relational unity, releases his power and displays his glory.*[315] *The loan-sharks and lap-dancers will hammer at his doors to get in. The nobodies become somebodies, and maybe, somebodies become nobodies. The unlearned instruct the learned; the once-damaged and derelict heal the healthy; those who have lived on the streets bring comfort to those in palaces; one-time terrorists bring peace to the secure; one-time prisoners free the moral from their bondages; and widows and orphans become royalty. Love reigns, and lovelessness withers.*

The spiritually hungry are not looking for lucid arguments. Certainly, the Church's opinions are unlikely to recruit the lost to the Kingdom. They need the oxygen of the Kingdom. The lost are leavened by their enwrapping culture; through 'the air they breathe.' After his resurrection Jesus commissioned his disciples privately. He breathed on them. Here was surely the wind of the Kingdom, the breath of God, as they received from him the Holy Spirit.[316]

God wishes to reveal himself through both individuals and community. The equipping of individuals is well emphasised by the Church. The time has come for the community's role to receive proper emphasis. God assuredly wishes his Body to manifest a coherence, harmony and ease-within-itself, inexplicable to those floundering in our world's prevailing culture. The highest aim in Jesus's high-priestly prayer was for unity and glory to be manifested. At this final moment, the world's rescue was consequence, not aim – the consequence being 'that the world might know...'[317] God-in-Christ is a specialist in demonstrating the inexplicable. If this is what we covet for his Body, it is on offer.

NT Wright offers these insights:

'For Paul, then, "evangelism" was not just about soul-rescuing, and "mission" was not just about the wider advancement of Christian understanding. Paul's apostolic task was, so to speak, tabernacle-construction, temple-building .... the Messiah is the new temple where heaven and earth meet, reconciled through his sacrifice. Paul's vocation was to announce that this had happened .... and so to extend this temple-shaped mission into the rest of the world.'

He goes on to explain God's intention that every single Christian would be a living example of this. 'But whereas much western understanding has seen the individual as the goal, Paul sees individual Christians as signs pointing to a larger reality.' And 'the larger reality to which this points, the new creation itself, is to be symbolized by *the whole church, united and holy.* The new temple is to be the place to which all nations will come to worship the God of Abraham, Isaac and Jacob.'[318]

God has revealed that profound, attentive obedience is the key to effective demonstration and display; of unity and glory. This is epiphany. Yet it depends on the willingness of each Temple stone to be regarded by the watching world as a mere stone, a non-entity after the pattern of Jesus.[319] We New Temple stones were once embedded in the kingdom of this world, without clear purpose. Rough and seemingly unsuited for anything, we were selected by the master mason. He saw our potential, then shaped us for a specific niche. The stones now fit together, holding firm through wind and storm; across centuries. Yet, for all this, it is the building – not the stones – that commands attention. It lingers in the mind. Christ stands ready to bathe his New Temple stones with his light and warmth, granting a glow not of ourselves. The glory belongs to the Son.

Our Father in heaven,
Reveal who you are.
Set the world right;
Do what's best –
as above, so below.
Keep us alive with three square meals.
Keep us forgiven with you and forgiving others.
Keep us safe from ourselves and the Devil.
You're in charge!
You can do anything you want!
You're ablaze in beauty!
Yes. Yes. Yes.[320]

ANNEX: My song is love unknown

My song is love unknown,
my Saviour's love to me;
love to the loveless shown,
that they might lovely be.
O who am I, that for my sake
my Lord should take frail flesh and die?

He came from his blest throne
salvation to bestow;
but men cared not, and none
the longed-for Christ would know:
but oh, my friend, my friend indeed,
who at my need his life did spend!

Sometimes they strew His way,
and his sweet praises sing;
resounding all the way
hosannas to their King:
then "Crucify!" is all their breath,
and for his death they thirst and cry.

Why, what hath my Lord done?
What makes this rage and spite?
He made the lame to run,
he gave the blind their sight.

Sweet injuries!
yet they at these themselves displease,
and 'gainst him rise.

They rise, and needs will have
my dear Lord made away;
a murderer they save,
the Prince of Life they slay,
yet cheerful he to suffering goes,
that he his foes from thence might free.

In life, no house, no home
my Lord on earth might have;
in death, no friendly tomb
but what a stranger gave.
What may I say? Heav'n was his home
  but mine the tomb wherein he lay.

Here might I stay and sing,
no story so divine;
never was love, dear King!
Never was grief like thine.
This is my friend, in whose sweet praise
  I all my days could gladly spend.

Samuel Crossman 1623–1683
Hymn writer and Anglican priest;
latterly Dean of Bristol Cathedral

Notes

1 Natasha's Dance, a Cultural History of Russia p.xxxiii Penguin 2003. Another good definition is 'a shared set of shared meanings, assumptions and understandings which have developed historically in a given community. Communication and Language – a handbook of Theory and Practice by N Thompson, p.109. Palgrave MacMillan 2003.

2 The number of parish clergy had fallen to 8,872 (in 2007) from 18,196 in 1951 (Christopher Howse's comment on Beeson's Round the Church in Fifty Years, SCM, in his Sacred Mysteries column, Daily Telegraph 8 December 2007)

3 'A survey by the National Churches Trust found that 8 per cent were in a bad state of repair with urgent repairs costing around £80,000 on average to carry out. The total cost of urgent repair work on churches across the UK was estimated by the charity to be around £1 billion.' Report in The Tablet 23 April 2011. In the following month the Tablet reported Quinlan Terry, architect of Brentwood RC Cathedral, expressing concern that the next generation of clergy and church leadership will be left with 'an architectural millstone round their necks'. Tablet 28 May 2011.

4 Dr Trevor Beeson 'still believes that, though the ancient parish system is "on the verge of collapse", the Church of England retains "the capacity to survive a little longer and indeed to expand its influence", but only if bold steps are taken'. There have been no signs of any bold steps in the succeeding half-decade. (Christopher Howse's comment on Beeson's Round the Church in Fifty Years, SCM, in his 'Sacred Mysteries column, Daily Telegraph 8 December 2007).

5 Other signs include clergy distress. Some 20% of parish clergy across the CofE sought counselling in 2009 (according to national conference of bishops' advisors in pastoral care & counselling). In 2006 22% of clergy who were off sick were absent as a result of stress, anxiety or other mental health issues. And in 2006 nearly 25% of the turnover among clergy was because of retirements due to ill-health (according to Rebecca Paveley's report on clergy stress When it gets too much, Church Times 25 April 2008).

6 Article in The Times, Our false oracles have failed. We need a new vision to live by. 30 October 2008

7 Sermon in Monterrey, Mexico reported in the Daily Telegraph 22 Aug 2013

8 Quoted in Tomlin: The Provocative Church p.9 SPCK 2002

9 Sermon on 25 Jan 2013, reported in the CEN 2 Feb 2013

10 Canon Robin Greenwood: Church Times review of Patrick Whitworth's Prepare for Exile: A New Spirituality and Mission for the Church. 6 February 2009

11 Transforming Communities DLT 2002, pp.20,21

12 Bishop Nick Baines' blog, reported in the CEN 9 Sep 2012

13 As summarised in The Tablet's editorial Prophet for our times, 8 Sept 2012

14 Article Stop, look, listen – and die, Church Times 13 January 2012

15 John 17 esp vs.21; Eph 3.10.

16 Creation, Power and Wealth p.76,77. SPCK 2013

17 Moral Combat p.100; quoting also from Richard Pipes' Russia under the Bolshevik Regime 1919–1924

18 Moral Combat p.76,77: 'There are those non-God religions, Nazism and Communism. We are urged from the Continent and from different quarters that we must choose which side we are on. I repudiate both, and will have nothing to do with either.........You leave out God and you substitute the devil. You leave out love and you substitute hate....... Let us keep to our faith and let us go somewhere and stay there where your breath is not frozen on your lips by the secret police. Let us not wander away from broad fields of freedom into those gaunt, grim, dismal, gloomy regions.' Winston Churchill in a prescient speech to the Leeds Chamber of Commerce, 1937

19 Dictionary of Paul and his Letters. p.274. IVP

20 Eph 5.11
21 Summarising John Zizioulas' reasoning, in Power p.25. SPCK 2005
22 Mat 13.33; Lk 13.21
23 Mat 16.6-12; Mk 8.15; Lk 12.1
24 1 Cor 5.7 (REB)
25 Christ lag in Todesbanden für unsre Sünd gegeben
26 End-note 12 in Grove Booklet Leading a Whole-life Discipleshipmaking Church.
27 Ex 20.5,6
28 Jn 1.4,5 (The Message)
29 The New Testament and the People of God p.189 SPCK 1992
30 Amongst his disciples was Joanna, wife of Herod's steward Chuza; and both Nicodemus and Gamaliel were leading Pharisees with at the least some sympathy for him.
31 Mk 7.1; Lk 5.17 (and Jn 1.19,24)
32 Mt 2.16
33 Mt 2.22
34 Lk 23. 6-12
35 Lk.13.31
36 Jn 11.48
37 Jn 9.15-34; 11.45-57
38 Lk.22.1,2
39 Mt. 5.44
40 Acts 3.17
41 Mt 26.42 (NIV)
42 Lk 23.34
43 Mt 26.3,4 (NLT)
44 Jn 4.1
45 Jn 12.42
46 Jn 16.1-4 (ESV)
47 Jn 15.18-25
48 Col 2.8 (NLT)
49 Gal 4.3,9
50 Rom 12.2
51 *Paul and the Faithfulness of God*, Vol II, p.1504. SPCK 2013.
52 From *Afterwards* by U A Fanthorpe. *Consequences*, Peterloo Poets 2000

53 Phil 2.7,8 (NLT)

54 Luke 3.23; 4.1,14,18,21,22,32,36. John 1.32-34 ; 3.34,35.

55 64 Acts 10.38

56 Is 50.4,5

57 Is 50.4,5

58 *The Gulag Archipelago.* Collins/Harvill Press and Fontana 1974

59 Eph 6.12 (NLT)

60 Admiral Collingwood, quoted in Max Adams' *Admiral Collingwood*, pp.48,138,142. Weidenfeld & Nicolson. 2005

61 *Napoleon, His Wives and Women.* Christopher Hibbert. HarperCollins 2002

62 Quoted by Paul Johnson in *Napoleon*, p.119. Phoenix. 2003

63 Johnson, p.192,3

64 Gal 5.17 (NLT)

65 *The Second World War* p.209. Antony Beevor, Weidenfeld & Nicolson 2010

66 1 John 4.7

67 Angela Tilby. *Reflections for Daily Prayer* 2012/2013 p.277 CHP 2012

68 John 3.16

69 See Annex

70 p.214 Penguin 1949

71 From an article *The spread of Europe syndrome* Sunday Times 5 April 2009.

72 *Desocialisation* p.6 Matthew Fforde. Gabriel 2009

73 Times letter from Terence Crolley, 18 April 2015

74 Lk 18.9-14

75 Acts 10.38

76 Reported in the Sunday Times 11 July 2010

77 From GEM (magazine of South Staffordshire & Shropshire Healthcare, NHS Foundation Trust) issue 4, 2009

78 Lately consultant paediatrician in North Staffordshire.

79 *Ceaucescu's Children.* p.14,16 HarperCollins 1998

80 *The Interesting Narrative of the Life of Olaudah Equiano*, p.105. The Modern Library, New York 2004 (Paperback Edition). Originally published 1789.

81 The feeding of the five thousand does not contradict this point. Jesus was not addressing social need – rather the need of the

moment – they were hungry. He saw their presenting need as lostness (Mk 6.34).

82 82 Mt 9.36, Mk 6.34; Lk 9.41,42; Mt 11.16,17 and 12.41, Lk 19.41-44; Mt 17.17-20; Mt 23.37, Lk 13.34; Mk 8.38; Mt 9.37,38, Jn 4.35.
83 Jonah 4.11, see alsoDeut 1.39;
84 Lk 23.34
85 Is 50.4
86 pp 147-149. Collins (Fontana) 1952
87 p.83 in Paul for Everyone – 1 Corinthians. SPCK 2003
88 Col 1.15-20 (*The Message*)
89 Chamber's Thesaurus
90 2 Cor 2.14-17
91 p.101 *The Shack* by Wm Paul Young. Hodder & Stoughton 2008
92 From: *Religion teaches us that we are part of the whole.* Credo 28 March 2009. See website www.chiefrabbiorg (emphasis added)
93 *Looking through the Cross* p.56. Bloomsbury 2013
94 From *Welcome to the Real World:* Godfrey Rust
95 *The Powers That Be* p.39. Doubleday 1998
96 Bishop of Waikato, Archbishop and Primate of the Anglican Church in Aotearoa, New Zealand and Polynesia, writing in *Reflections for Daily Prayer* CHP 2010, p.303.
97 Article *When I was Murdoch's man* The Tablet 23 July 2011
98 Anne-Marie Wilson talking to Terence Handley MacMath 31 Jan 2014
99 Wikipedia entry, quoting *von Moltke, Helmuth James* (1990). Translator: von Oppen, Beata Ruhm. ed. Letters to Freya – 1939–1945. New York: Alfred A. Knopf.'
100 Luke 10.25-37
101 John 4.4-43
102 Eph 2.11-22
103 Angela Tilby. *Reflections for Daily Prayer* 2012/2013 p.278 CHP 2012
104 *The Hubris Syndrome pages* x,xi Politico's Publishing (Methuen) 2007
105 Op cit. p.xii
106 Op cit. pp 2,3
107 Quoted by Max Hastings in *Armageddon* p.24, Macmillan 2004

108 *Orthodoxy* 1908
109 *The Storm of War* p.138,9 2009 Allen Lane (including the quotation from Ian Kershaw's *Hitler, the Germans and the Final Solution* p.90 2008).
110 *Armageddon* pp.197-201
111 Quoted by Archbishop Justin Welby when addressing the House of Lords. Church Times 11 October 2013.
112 On http://leantechnologytransformation.blogspot.co.uk 14 May 2013. Patrick Phillips of Utah Disaster Kleenup (UDK)
113 Article *Don't just be religious – try helping people.* Church Times 3 Jan 2014.
114 Rom 12.2 (NLT)
115 Col 2.8
116 *The Powers that be.* p.4 Galilee Doubleday 1998
117 Quoted by Brian McLaren in *The Secret Message of Jesus,* p.10
118 Exodus 1.12 is of interest; and of course Roman fear was implicit in their extravagant use of crucifixion as a deterrent.
119 The theme of organism vs organisation is explored further in Chapter 10
120 Article *Rebel on the road,* The Tablet 24 Aug 2013
121 Reported in Church Times 17 July 2009
122 From an address to the priests of the Diocese of Dublin in December 2009, published in The Tablet 19/26 Dec 09 and 2 Jan 10
123 *Reflections for Daily Prayer* (CHP) 9 July 2009
124 *Out of Babylon.* pp35,36. Abingdon Press 2010
125 Sir Roy Strong's launch article in Country Life 17 December 2008
126 Gal 2.11-14
127 Acts 17.24,25 (NLT)
128 Acts 7.48 (NLT)
129 Jn 4.23
130 Jn 2.2,3
131 Jn 2.19-21
132 *John for Everyone Pt '* p.26. Also NT Wright's *The Resurrection of the Son of God'.* pp 671,2, and his *Jesus and the Victory of God.* p.426 All books SPCK
133 2 Sam 7.11b-14

134 *Jesus & the Victory of God.* p.432,3

135 Mark 2.21,22.

136 1 Cor 3.16-17; Eph 2.19-21; 1 Pet 2.4-7

137 Tom Wright: *Simply Jesus.* p.213 SPCK 2011

138 *People of the Spirit.* p.211 SPCK 2009

139 Mt 23.3-7 (NLT)

140 Lk 17.32

141 National Association of Decorative & Fine Arts Societies

142 Amos 5.21-24 (NLT)

143 Acts 7.51 (NLT)

144 Jn 4.23 (NLT)

145 *A New Kind of Christianity.* Note 16, p.377. Hodder & Stoughton 2010

146 http://www.cofe.anglican.org/info/funding/ These seemed to be 2004 figures, and exclude cathedral costs and cathedral charitable/mission giving.

147 Jas 1.27

148 Nicholas Henshall *He emptied himself.* The Tablet 18/25 December 2010

149 Reported in The Tablet 10 April 2010

150 *The Responsive Church*, Spencer and Tomlin. P.48. IVP 2005

151 Report *Immigration slows decline.* Church of England Newspaper 13 June 2014

152 *Space in the City* – talks on the Lord's Prayer (privately published).

153 The Tablet, Letters, 25 June 2011

154 *People of the Spirit.* p.211. SPCK 2009

155 Article *One of our very own*, The Tablet 9 Nov 13

156 Book review on consumerism by Fr Jonathan Ewer SSM, *Consumers' rites*, Church Times 3 Jan 2014.

157 Jas 1.27

158 www.businessdictionary.com

159 *A Good Childhood.* by Richard Layard and Judy Dunn, p.6 Penguin 2009

160 1 Cor 12.13; Gal 3.28; Col 3.11;

161 1 Jn 1.7

162 *The Foolishness of God.* p.372. DLT 1970

163 Jn 1.4

164 Brian McLaren *A Generous Orthodoxy.* p.221 Zondervan 2004

165 Brian McLaren *A New Kind of Christianity*. pp.226,7. Hodder & Stoughton 2010

166 *Reflections for Daily Prayer* 2010/2011. p.48. CHP 2010

167 Review headed *Heart of "holy Mouley"*, Church Times 18 March 2011

168 Article *The senses have it*, The Tablet 23 July 2011

169 1 Cor 2, esp vs16.

170 *The Light Has Come: an exposition of the fourth gospel.* p.200 emphasis added. The Handsel Press 1982 (Eerdmans)

171 *Jesus: A Very Short Introduction.* p.79. OUP 2011.

172 Acts 3.14,15

173 Acts 9.2; 8.1; 26.11; 8.3; 9.1; 11.1; 11.19; Gal 1.13

174 Phil 3.5,6 (NLT)

175 Galatians 1.14 (NLT)

176 Lev 20.18 – quoted by Jesus in his summary of the law, Mt 22.39.

177 Phil 3.7-9

178 *Life Together*, pp19,20. Italics added. SCM Press 1954

179 Op Cit p.10 Italics added

180 Brian McLaren *The Secret Message of Jesus*. p.64 W Publishing Group (Nelson) 2006

181 Op cit. Chapter 1

182 *The Powers That Be.* p.83 Doubleday 1998

183 Mt 10.17,18 (NLT)

184 Mk 8.14 (REB)

185 *The Powers That Be* p.200

186 Phil 3.10,11

187 From New York Times 13 Apr 13; quoted by Damaris (damaris.org) in The Reader, Winter 2013

188 Letter to the Corinthian Church

189 *Nightmare of a necrocracy that refuses to die*, Oliver Kamm. The Times 16 Dec 2013 (Emphasis added)

190 Ex 29.45,46

191 Deut 4.20; Lev 20.26

192 Lev 20.23

193 Acts 7.38

194 Comment on Romans 8.1-4. *Paul for Everyone Pt 1.* p135 SPCK 2004

195 1 Pe 2.10

196 Acts 7.39-41
197 Hos 11:3-11
198 2 Sam 7.12,13
199 Ps 103.19; 145.11-13
200 Dan 6:26
201 Is 2:3
202 Jer 29.1-14
203 Gal 4.4
204 2 Tim 3:5 213 Mt 10.16-42
205 Mt 3.2; Mk 1.15
206 Lk 9.22
207 Mt 3.2;Mk 1.15
208 Jn 5.44; 7.18; 9.24; 11.4; 17.22
209 Jn 14.9-11
210 Jn 14.12-14
211 Jn 3.34 (NIV)
212 *The Prodigal God* Hodder 2008
213 2 Cor 4.7-12
214 As an aside, in reading military history and biography covering
the Napoleonic wars to the present day, I perceive an interesting
imbalance. Some authors seemed to fix their verdicts primarily
upon a commander's strategic and tactical skills, facts and statistics,
yet were in varying degrees unreflective of how commanders
gathered commitment to the cause, gained the trust of their
men, and inspired men to fight ferociously and, if necessary,
sacrificially. The human and personal side of leadership is critical.
(Should readers baulk at mention of ferocious engagement, they
may need to reflect on our Lord's resolve to face the ferocity of
the dark forces that propelled him to Calvary). I mention such
topics since we need to engage our understanding on how Jesus
prepared his disciples for the tough battles they were to face. He
did not prepare them by being 'nice'.
215 Mt 5.20
216 Lk 12.1
217 Mt 21.45
218 Mt 15.21-28; also Mt 17.17
219 Heb 5.8
220 Jn 20.21-23

221 Mt 11.29
222 Jn 13. 12-15
223 Mt 10.1-15; Mk 3.13-15; 6.7-11; Lk 9.1-6; 10.1-24.
224 Mt 10.24,25
225 Mt 16.17 (NLT)
226 Mt 11.25 (NLT)
227 Lk 10.22 (NLT)
228 Jn 14.12 (NLT)
229 *The Prodigal God.* by Timothy Keller. Pp 15,16. Hodder 2008
230 Mt 4.23-25
231 Mt 14.21, also Lk 12.1
232 Jn 16.33
229 *The Prodigal God* by Timothy Keller, pp 15, 16 (Hodder 2008)
230 Mt 14. 21 , also Lk 12.1
231 Jn 16.33
232 In the Church of England, 'preferment' means selection and appointment to senior posts as bishop, dean or archdeacon
233 In the Church of England, 'preferment' means selection and appointment to senior posts as bishop, dean or archdeacon.
234 *The Shack.* by Wm Paul Young. 2008 Hodder & Stoughton p.122. Emphasis added.
235 *Paul for Everyone* (1 Corinthians) p.166 SPCK 2003. Italics added.
236 Perhaps we should be wary of the term 'Human Resources'. It has overtones of lovelessness – suggesting people have value because of their potential contribution, not because they are God's creatures.
237 To name some: Caister Retreat, Keswick Convention, Spring Harvest, New Wine, Additional Curates Society, CPAS, Reform, Forward in Faith, CEAC, Modern Churchpeople's Union.
238 *An Interview with Lamorna Trahair: The life of an adventurist.* by Fiona Harding in LTFocus, the quarterly publication of the Leadership Trust. Spring 2009.
239 *A Brief History of Mutiny,* p.284. Richard Woodman. Robinson 2005
240 Jn 10.14,15
241 Private letter 2008
242 Simon Jones' report in Church Times 5 June 2009
243 Source untraced

244 Church Times 19 June 2009

245 Heb 2.10,14-18

246 Quoted by Bp John Pritchard in *Reflections for Daily Prayer* 12 May 2015

247 'Engaged in a journey with God' – Church Times 7 Feb 2014 (emphasis added)

248 From *The Penguin Ronald Searle.* 1960

249 Lk 11.17 (ESV)

250 From an address to the priests of the Diocese of Dublin in December 2009, published in The Tablet 19/26 Dec 09 and 2 Jan 10

251 *Reflections for Daily Prayer* – notes for 30 April 2009. (CHP) (Emphasis added)

252 I refer to the Pioneer Course, available in some colleges and with CMS Oxford.

253 *Oxford Dictionary*

254 For example, Acts 20.25-38

255 For example, in *Transforming Church* Robin Greenwood recounts the outcome of an episcopally-funded psychotherapist, identifying some 11 'sharp issues' – such as isolation and future security anxieties – from within clergy 'support groups. All betray relational distresses and inadequate pastoral understanding and care – signs of an organisation more than an organism. SPCK 2002, p.5

256 1 Tim 1.15; Eph 3.8

257 Article *The three-fold ministry of bishop, priest and deacon is no longer fit for purpose* by Clifford Longley in The Tablet, 28 Sept 2013. Whilst he seems to favour Caesar's other option, of democracy, for his RC Church, his analysis of the problem seems to fit the C of E equally.

258 *Life Together* pp 84,85

259 Gal 2. 1,2,6-10

260 Jn 17.20,21

261 Lk 10.1

262 *Transforming Church* p.8

263 Phil 3.7,8

264 *A Nearly Infallible History of Christianity*,p.429 Hodder & Stoughton 2013

265 The West Malaysian Diocese's *Anglican Messenger* of December 2011.

266 Article *Signs of hope as church swells with new recruits.* The Times, 18 April 2014

267 A letter to the Archbishop of Canterbury before the Lambeth Conference of 1930. She was referring to vigorous maintenance of inadequacy – specifically, in this case, the shallowness of clergy interior life as she saw it.

268 2 Cor 1.8

269 Sheldon Community 2002. 'A manual of accessible, specific, practical, realistic guidelines; for the purpose of reducing clergy stress, sickness and ill health retirements; Providing a benchmark to spread good practice; and addressing issues relating to the person (including family), the roles and tasks of clergy, and the system as a whole (church as organisation).' The Society of Mary and Martha.

270 *Continuing Affirmation and Accountability* by Revd Jonathan Williams. Nov 2008

271 Ex 18.13-26

272 *The Memoirs of Field-Marshal Montgomery* p.85. Collins 1958.

273 High Court Judge and founder of the Marriage Foundation. The Tablet Interview: *Just like wine and cricket,* 30 Nov 2013

274 Jn 2.23-25

275 1 Kings 3.28

276 The 360° appraisal system is a performance appraisal system derived from the secular world. Feedback on an individual is gathered from a number of sources, typically including colleagues and those the individual serves,

277 'Creation, Power and Truth' p.19. SPCK

278 Job 5.7

279 From 'Trajan's Policy towards Christians'. Documents of the Christian Church. OUP 1943

280 2 Cor 13.1

281 See for example Anthony Beevor's 'The Second World War' pp.16-24 Weidenfield & Nicolson 2012

282 Terry Eagleton: Reason, Faith and Revolution – Reflections on the God Debate. Yale University Press 2009 pp.121,122

283 Church Growth Research Project, Report on Strand 3b, Oct 2013. Church Army

284 Profile 2009

285 Sunday Times 9 August 2009

286 Mat 14.21; 15.38 indicate the additional presence of women and children. See also Lk 6.17; 12.1

287 Is 9.2

288 Jn 14.11

289 Mt 10.1,4

290 Jn 13.31,32

291 Lk 4.16-21

292 Jn 17.20-24

293 Jn 13.35

294 *The Light has Come*, pp 234,235. The Handsel Press 1982 (emphases added)

295 Is 9.2; Jn 1.14

296 Eph 3.10 (NRSV)

297 Acts 4.5-31

298 Jn 5.19,20

299 Personal letter

300 *The New Testament and the People of God.* p.187. SPCK 1992

301 Ps 84.6

302 Jn 21.18-22

303 Phil 3.10

304 Eph 3.8-10

305 Times article *Will this be the man to bring us to our knees?* (2002): William Rees-Mogg

306 The Times Leader, *God's Manifesto: Church leaders should not avoid politics but they should be careful about policy.* 22 Aug 2013

307 2 Chr 29 & 34

308 2 Chr 30, & 35 (esp vs 18)

309 Gal 4.4,5

310 It is notable that Jesus used this precise method to reassure the imprisoned John-the-Baptist in Mat 11.4,5

311 *The Powers that be.* p.200.

312 Article *Don't just be religious – try helping people.* Church Times 3 Jan 2014. Emphasis added.

313 The Revd Elizabeth Welch: foreword MODEM Matters, January 2010

314 Quoted by Fr Michael Holman SJ, provincial of the British

Jesuits, in his Tablet article *Lives on the edge*, 6 December 2008
315 1 Pet 4.12-14
316 Jn 20.19-23
317 Jn 17.23
318 *Paul and the Faithfulness of God*, Vol II, pp 1493,4. SPCK 2013
319 Phil 2.7
320 Mat 6.9-13. Scripture taken from THE MESSAGE. Copyright ©
      1993, 1994, 1995, 1996, 2000, 2001, 2002. Used by permission
      of NavPress Publishing Group.